AF408593

THE EINSTEIN STONE

The Einstein Stone

JOHN M. WHITTEN

Merryjohn Publishing

Copyright © 2022 by by JOHN M WHITTEN

All rights reserved. No part of this book may be reproduced in any manner whatsoever without written permission except in the case of brief quotations embodied in critical articles and reviews.

First Printing, 2022

CONTENTS

~ 70 ~

AFTERMATH

332

~ 71 ~

EPILOGUE

335

~ 72 ~

THE END

338

Dedication

This story is dedicated to my Wife Merry, the love of my life. A woman with intelligence and compassion. Thank you for loving me. It also dedicated to my sons Paul and David, grandchildren: Phoenix, Andrew, Alexis, Nickolas, and Neala. Special prayers to son Mark a loving man, husband and father we lost far too soon.

There is another dedication I wish to share. I dedicate this book to real Americans. People who understand that Freedom is not a sanction for ignorance. Real Americans are those who look past color and creed and see human beings, and judge another by their character not their appearance or bank roll. Americans are generous, empathetic, intelligent, hardworking, dedicated, and understand that freedom isn't free. It comes with conditions. Freedom means you are accountable to the next person and they are accountable to you.
Freedom is an agreement among citizens, because there must be a common understanding of what Freedom means. Maturity is realizing inclusion is strength, exclusion is fear.

~ 1 ~

PROLOGUE

"One thing I have learned in a long life: that all our science, measured against reality, is primitive and childlike." Albert Einstein

PROLOGUE

The old sailboat, "Pakalolo," a venerable, Bermuda-rigged, forty-two-foot ketch complained bitterly, as a vicious wind shrieked through the bare rigging. The clings, clangs, of metal on metal sounds created a high-pitched counterpoint to the harsh, merciless scream of the storm.

Pawnee Painter leaning a heavy shoulder against the bulkhead grinned.

"Now comes de fun."

Pakalolo made a creaking, groaning roll, 5 degrees, 10 degrees, Pawnee braced against the bulkhead, worried now about capsizing.

"Hoa," Pawnee called out. "Tangaloa, the Sea God, give me passage today." Zawahiri, God of the Storms, I am but a humble sailor, heading to see my son." He prayed.

Slowly the craft righted itself.

The storm was coming in fast, faster than he believed possible. Pawnee, in his seventy-third year, was surprised by very few things. He thought of himself as a battered, scarred, and toughened old sea turtle living in shark-infested waters all of his life.

He knew one of the main life lessons was that Mother Nature was powerful and unpredictable, deadly to the unprepared.

With a heavy forefinger, he tapped the barometer and worried. Reading a normal 30.1 Hg just a few hours ago, it was now falling below 22.5 Hg. Big storm, moving fast.

Crossing the rolling galley, he checked the date. He did not want to miss his son's birthday, and he had two weeks, a little over.

Pawnee tilted his beer, Dead Man's Ale, a brew straight from Southern Oregon, and drained it. Then, he checked his GPS and compared his maps against his position; so far, so good.

The Hawaiian island of Kauai was only a few weeks distant.

Sailing north up the California coast from his home in Mexico, Pawnee wanted to avoid the North Pacific High, which was sometimes becalmed, not even a light breeze—a sailor's worst nightmare.

He began storing anything loose he could find.

As he worked, he dreamed of home, which only existed in his hopes so far. He longed to sit on the beach with his family, eat Puu puu's, Kailua pig, get drunk, laugh, watch the children swim, learn to love again.

Opening the engine's hatch, Pawnee ducked down into the cramped interior, squeezing into gaps around the motor to check the bilge.

Everywhere he checked the engine compartment was dry and tight. Pawnee was delighted.

Climbing out of the compartment, memories clung like smoke, the sacrifices he'd made, gaining adventure, excitement, thrills, but losing his family.

Pawnee shook his head in regret. Despite all of his military duties, by far, the worst was leaving his small family, his baby son Clay, and staying away from them.

"I make many enemies, me," Pawnee muttered.

A lifetime of military and civilian special operations, war, combat, violence, had created enemies and secrets; secrets gained in dark places where death was easy and staying alive hard.

Pawnee knew secrets that others would kill his family to protect.

So he left and stayed away, fearful even a visit would tell enemies where they were.

"Soon, my son, soon! I come back!" Even if only for a few days, it would have to do. He was old now; his secrets were also ancient, and maybe now would be safe.

Closing the engine room hatch tightly, he thought about his next moves.

The boat shuddered underneath him as if to throw a lion off its back. More things crashed and broke in the galley. Regaining his balance, Pawnee realized it was time, and he had to get topside because that was where trouble would be.

Moving to don his wet weather gear and go topside, his eyes caught a file lying on his table. The file he'd been reviewing for the thousandth time just before the storm hit, the file on the Einstein Stone.

In 1966 while assigned to Special Operations Group 221 (SOG) out of Chu Lai, South Vietnam, he stumbled across hints and rumors and barely legible intelligence documents about an extraordinary stone: The Einstein Stone.

According to archeologists' notes, the dark, blue-green Stone radiated power, an aura of some sort. References repeatedly called this Stone a 'Teaching Stone.' This same phrase, 'Teaching Stone' or 'Learning Stone,' was consistently linked with this Blue-Green Emerald.

The Stone haunted him, and he did not know why. He had no interest in money or jewels, or mysticism. Something about this Stone had caught him.

Clad in heavy rain gear and goggles, he poked his head up out of the companionway and looked around. The sky was black as a boiling cauldron of ink and ashes; the storm winds twisted and screamed, lashing the waves into foam.

He stared at a world gone mad.

Pawnee threw back the hatch and laughed as the pelting rain stung his face and shoulders.

He felt the raw freedom of chaos.

Despite more than a few tenuous moments at the pulpit where he inadvertently hung out over the bow, staring directly into the raging sea, Pawnee made a safe circuit of the topside, keeping a death grip on the safety line.

The storm was growing stronger. The wind was more biting, more ferocious, way beyond anything Pawnee had ever seen.

"This will be one for da record books, yah." He screamed into the wind, his words snatched away immediately by bitter-salt spray of ocean water.

Pawnee looked about him, a tiny boat in a monster hurricane, and considered the situation. Pulling his storm gear tightly around him, he adjusted his goggles and opened a Dead Man Ale.

The only easy day was yesterday.

"To you, son!" He drank his beer, preparing himself for a long journey in a wet boat.

~ 2 ~

THE MISSION

"A human being experiences himself, his thoughts and feelings as something separated from the rest, a kind of optical delusion of consciousness. This delusion is a kind of prison for us, restricting us to our personal desires and to affection for a few persons nearest to us. Our task must be to free ourselves from this prison by widening our circle of compassion to embrace all living creatures and the whole of nature in its beauty." Albert Einstein.

CHAPTER ONE

"Charley, Doc, can I interest you two in a small adventure?" President Bessie May Chowder leaned forward on her desk, eager to meet her guests. "Come in, come in; we are on a time clock, however, so we must act as quickly as possible. Please, gentlemen, have a seat and let's get started. This involves your old friend, Pawnee Painter."

Both Charley Brown Bones and John James Jefferson Betters the IV, known as Doc, looked at each other.

"Pawnee Painter?" Doc muttered.

"You know," Charley turned to his friend. "Vietnam or rather Cambodia?"

Doc nodded. "I thought that was him." He looked at Chowder. "Ma'am, the last time we met, Mr. Pawnee Painter threatened to gut Charles and me from...top to bottom," Doc put it delicately.

"He meant it," Charley added. He recalled that last visit with Painter like looking into an abyss. He and Doc had seen a lot of combat, up close and personal. But sometimes, there was too much combat, too much killing. Soon killing, although necessary, became routine, and emotional numbness set in, the guilt of killing less troublesome.

Charley Brown Bones hoped he wouldn't have to go that far. He saw the hollow look in Pawnee Painter's eyes, like ice-cold caves in which only rage and sadness lived. He had no desire to follow Painter in that journey, and on the spot, Charley made the call that this was his last deployment. Three tours in Vietnam were enough.

"Ma'am, maybe we should explain our last contact with Mr. Painter," Charley hated to dredge up old memories but there was no choice.

***

December 2, 1970, Snoul, Cambodia, four kilometers from the Cambodia/Vietnam border. Michelin Song Be Rubber Plantation.

Sergeant Charley Brown Bones, team leader, and Specialist Five Doc Betters, medic, from Black Squad, Long Range Recon, 11th Armored Cavalry Regiment, US Army, stood in the spacious, open-air master's bedroom of Pedro Guerra Pen, foreman for Song Be Michelin Rubber Plantation in Cambodia.

Like most tropical buildings, the walls were open to the fresh air; colorful gardens could be seen in every direction. A black and white crow-like bird flew in, landing on a chest of drawers. It pecked at a wristwatch sitting in a monkey pod bowl.

Outside, Charley could see manicured rows of tall rubber trees covering the surrounding hills, slender trunks moving gently in the hot and humid jungle air bringing scents of garden jasmine into the room. A sudden motion caught Charley's eye as a small brown monkey slipped into the room; the bird squawked and flew out the other side.

"Ugghh." To their right, lying on the nearly black, polished teakwood floor, Mr. Pen lay gagged and tied, his fearful eyes darted from one American to the other as he struggled to understand what was happening. "Uggghh," He pleaded.

"I'm Captain Painter, #221 SOG," The Special Operations Soldier explained bluntly. "I have a mission here." The heavily camouflaged Green Beret carried a sawed-off shotgun and wore a .357 Colt Python Revolver on his right hip. Two knives were visible, one on his left shoulder, the other on this right leg; he bulged with ammunition clips and grenades.

Sgt Brown, a sturdy six-foot, looked up at the huge man, guessing he was a Hawaiian or Pacific Islander, thought, *this is the largest man I've ever seen. He must be six foot six or seven.* Briefly, Charley wondered what this monster looked like on a surfboard.

"This man is mine," Captain Painter pointed at the now terrified Mr. Pen. "This guy is to be assassinated. We will blame the NVA for his death, and that will be the story. Now you go away. Go back to Vietnam, fight that war. This Cambodia, different war, brah, you go away."

Sgt Bones wasn't going away.

"Captain! We are 11th Armored Cavalry, Long-range recon, US Army," he explained tightly. "We're here to bring this guy back to Quan Loi. What does it matter we are in Cambodia? He is an informer for us, a good guy; we want to reward him, not murder him. The guy helped us." Charley thought he made it clear, simple, no room for discussion.

"Doc, untie Mr. Pen and see that he's okay."

"No." Pawnee shook his head, slowly talking as if explaining this to a distracted six-year-old. "No, we cannot do dat."

"No? What do you mean no?" Charley didn't like the way this was going. "Captain! We have orders to keep him alive, and we will follow our orders. Mr. Pen goes home with us. Check him, Doc...."

"No," Pawnee said simply. He wouldn't explain because this was beyond these ordinary soldiers' duty. "Not tell you again. This over, decided. I take him, you go away, brah."

"Now, look, we're on the same side here; we can work this out..."

Pawnee shrugged. "Chee, you no listen." Pulling his Colt Python, he calmly put a round through Pen's head, killing him instantly. The report of the enormous weapon was sharp and loud. The black and white bird squawked and flew away.

The gunfire still echoed as Charley erupted at Pawnee. He yelled at him, livid. It felt like a betrayal. "You didn't have to kill him!"

"No! Goddamn it!" Doc was right beside Charley, angry at the unnecessary loss of life.

But after a few minutes of arguing with a hardened killer, Charley saw the futility. "Never mind, Doc, never mind. We lose this one." He looked down at the shattered skull of Mr. Pen. "Sorry, man, little too late," he apologized.

Pawnee Painter's last words to Doc and Bones were chilling: "You say nothing about this! My mission was set up to kill and blame NVA. This war, different places, and rules, and no one can change what is, brah. Everybody blames NVA for these killings. You talk story different, and I will gut you from assholes to eyebrows."

When Sgt Bones and Sp 5 Betters returned to Quan Loi Base Camp, they reported: "Mr. Pedro Guerra Pen was gone. He found another way out of Cambodia."

****

"Mr. Bones and Mr. Betters," Chowder's voice interrupted Charley's musing. "I am sure it was a challenging time."

Chowder had missed these two. Two years since they had last met, it seemed like forever ago. She smiled at them, "I think you may find Mr. Painter changed a bit by now."

Bessie May studied these two old friends she first met twenty years ago. Just appointed to the Bench, US Court of Appeals, Ninth Circuit Court, and Bessie May hired Bones and Betters for private investigations. She trusted these two men; they would bring her the truth no matter how grim it may be.

Charley Bones looked older, heavier, moving slower. He gave her a warm smile, but she could read the effort it took. Charley, always in control, appeared hesitant in his movements. He had let his hair grow long had a slightly unkempt appearance since retirement from the Thurston County Sheriff's Department. *Charley looks more Indian these days, braids, his face fuller, darkened from more sun exposure,* she thought. She knew he was not a happy man when he entered the room. Since his divorce from Jade, Charley had become a recluse.

On the other hand, John James Jefferson Betters IV, better known as Doc, dressed in pure white seersucker suits and white Panama hats, always had a white cane with a silver knob clutched in his hand. His mustache and beard were snow white as well. To Bessie May, Doc resembled a Southern Plantation Owner from the 1700s, with decidedly liberal and progressive attitudes.

Bessie May Chowder once told her husband, Freddie, she believed Doc was a man who traveled to his music; sometimes it was a full orchestra and sometimes just a kazoo, but his devotion to the music was profound.

"So let me explain what is going on," Chowder leaned forward and laced her fingers. "A few years back, Pawnee Painter brought my attention to a legendary gem." Chowder explained. "Pawnee had uncovered information from a Mayan archeology dig in which an unknown and undiscovered Mayan Codex was found," Chowder continued, "In addition to a treasure trove of Mayan relics and glyphs, they found this Mayan Codex written exclusively about a Blue-Green Emerald. The Archeologists on site have named this mysterious stone, The Einstein Stone."

"Einstein? The Mayan knew about Einstein?" Charley wondered.

"Ah, no, the Mayan name for this Stone is nearly unpronounceable, so the Anthropologist simplified it. The American scientists named it after Einstein." Chowder told them. "Why, we don't know, but there was a quote associated with this Stone that might explain some of it:

"Time and space are not conditions in which we live, but modes by which we think. Physical concepts are free creations of the human mind, and are not, however it may seem, determined by the external world." Albert Einstein

Doc looked at Charley. "That clears it up for you? Make the external world more real?"

"No." Charley was sure he understood reality when the first bullet zipped past his head in Vietnam. Nothing, before or since, had defined 'real' as that moment; much of life was more dreamlike in comparison to the reality of life and death. But he could not follow Chowder's logic on this.

"But what is a "Codex?" Charley decided he would try another tack.

"Sacred Mayan records of their advances, their knowledge, literally a library of a well educated, scientific civilization, written on the inner bark of the wild fig tree. Hundreds, probably more, were destroyed by Christian zealots until only three, now four, are left. Terrorists for Christianity, I call them. All that knowledge was lost! So you can imagine how valuable this fourth Codex is? This one, however, is very different from the others, and it is devoted to only one topic: The Blue-Green Emerald we have given the name 'Einstein.'"

"They wrote a codex about a gem? This must be some kind of Stone for sure?" Doc was awed.

"This Einstein Stone could be a game-changer for humanity." Chowder continued. "The Codex was badly damaged by water, so, unfortunately, much of it is unrecoverable. This Blue-Green Stone, reportedly an Emerald, was highly respected by the Mayan people because it could influence civilization. It is just scientific guest work, but some anthropologists believe the Mayan people had this mystical Stone for several generations. Then it was lost somehow, and their civilization fell apart."

"What does this thing do?" Charley wondered how much of this was hyperbole.

"In a moment, Charley. Let me explain a little more." Chowder smiled a conspiratorial grin, and her voice lowered. "Because this story gets even more interesting." Chowder thought this next part was intriguing. "This Mayan Codex about a mystical Blue Green Emerald was created around 555 AD, the Sixth century in Belize, Mesoamerica. Then we have a sacred Christian object, carved in 1200 AD Europe, Thirteenth Century, which reveals information about a Blue-Green Emerald called a 'Teaching Stone.'The next recorded history came from Francisco Vasquez de Coronado in 1543 AD, Sixteenth Century. Scraps from his journals report a Mystical Blue-Green Stone being held by indigenous tribes somewhere in the Midwest of North America. In his diary, Coronado called this 'El Profesoro Stone,' the 'Teaching Stone' or what we have re-named 'The Einstein Stone."

Bessie May Chowder chuckled. "It is a strange name, but every reference, no matter the civilization or language, used the same description: 'Teaching Stone.' From 555 AD to the present, every reference has been identical for this Stone. Obviously, these advanced people treasured this as more than a gem. Presumably, this Teaching Stone is a point of knowledge of some kind, perhaps inscribed with some arcane understandings, I don't know," She threw up her hands in gentle frustration. "But it was and is important!"

"Mayans in Belize and crumbling artifacts from medieval England?" Charley looked curious. "Now, North America?"

"They all had the stone thingy in common?" Doc wondered.

"Doc," Chowder smiled. "The 'stone thingy' made quite an impression.

"So, what do you want us to do?" Charley asked. Curious about this, Charley nonetheless felt his spirits sinking. He wanted to please President Chowder. Charley was both awed and honored to be asked to help her but ached with exhaustion. He had been in the game, solving problems, completing missions, for far too long, and more than anything, Charley Brown Bones wanted to sit on the sidelines for the rest of it.

"I want you two to enter the new America. They call themselves the United Christian States of America, as you know. I want you to meet with Pawnee Painter." Chowder handed them a folder. "Here are the particulars: Pawnee has information on an English artifact held by the Homeland Office of Antiquities. This Artifact may have a direct bearing on the location of The Einstein Stone. In fact, from the few details we have uncovered, we have some reason to believe this Stone itself could be somewhere in the Midwest of the country. The Mayan Codex was much damaged; this English antiquity might fill in the gaps."

President Chowder, her face grim, explained. "Gentlemen, I need for you to locate the artifact, and then use it to find The Einstein Stone and bring it back to Cascadia."

"Ma'am," Charley was uncomfortable with this. "We are looking for a gemstone? When Washington State, most of Oregon, and Northern California voted to secede from the old United States, we knew this would be complicated. But a mythical gem? Do you want us to find a rock with all that is going on in the US and here?"

Doc held up his white, silver-tipped walking stick for emphasis. "What my old, doddering friend here is trying to say is the United States has become a religious dictatorship, a one-party state run by oligarchs, going in there uninvited will stir up a hornets' nest. There are checkpoints everywhere, and Homeland Security now runs most of the Government." Doc shook his head sadly. "How utterly sad, they thought individual weapons represented freedom but they represent fear."

"That is because nations are built on cooperation and acceptance and tolerance. Without those gifts everything falls apart." Charley observed. "The Golden rule: 'Do unto others as you would wish done unto you is literally the foundation of all civilization. Otherwise, humans are just too fucking egocentric to share."

"Doc, Charley, have you heard the phrase, 'desperate times call for desperate measures?'" Chowder said.

"Heard of it? Those words on carved on my family crest." Doc replied.

Chowder always enjoyed her time with these two, regardless of circumstances. "Gentlemen, we are in desperate times. We are facing a showdown. The United Christian States has coalesced around a sole religion and a strict Republican philosophy, abandoning a two-party system which then functionally destroyed Democracy. So we on the West Coast seceded to re-establish our Democracy. Unfortunately, the UCS is bigger and meaner than we are, and we do not have the military capability they possess."

Both Doc and Charley nodded.

"We need a miracle gentleman," Bessie May Chowder glumly explained. "We are beset by a constant drumbeat of antagonism from the United States, lawsuits, military threats, economic threats, over and over. Plus, we have rising insurgency here from Washington down to California."

Chowder nodded grimly and cleared her throat. "The Einstein Stone may or may not be the miracle it is claimed to be, but now is the time we must gamble. This tells you just how desperate we are. But, I hear your concerns; this will be the last mission for you two. Okay?"

Doc held up his cane again, "Excuse me, ma'am, I'd appreciate it if ya'll call it 'retirement,' not 'last mission', okay?" Doc muttered. He looked over at Charley. "Right, ole man?" he continued before Charley could respond. "But, ma'am, this sounds like a simple type of journey. Just meet the man and return. Only need one of us." He pointed his walking stick at Charley, who batted it away. "This old coot needs to return to his ranch and stay there, in my professional medical opinion." Doc looked over at his long-time friend. "Charles, ya'll old, go home. Sit on your porch, pet the dog."

"Gentlemen, I realize this Einstein Stone stuff is hazy and maybe even impossible, but there is one further fact you need to hear." She paused for emphasis. "The United Christian States have threatened nuclear retaliation unless we rescind our secession and return to the fold of the UCS. They have promised to hit Seattle, LA, and San Francisco and have given us seventy-two hours to comply, starting today."

"Holy shit!"

"Pawnee Painter," she continued, "believes this mystical Stone is a weapon of sorts that would either protect us or be a counterbalance to nuclear weapons. Maybe a shield even; we just don't know. But Cascadia is on the crosshairs, facing annihilation."

"Seventy-two hours until the UCS bombs us?"

President Bessie May Chowder nodded grimly.

"You are to meet up with Pawnee just outside of Butte, Montana," President Chowder continued. "Your target is the Homeland Security Office, Western Region. You are seeking an artifact about The Einstein Stone." Chowder paused. "You now have about Seventy hours left. Go find Pawnee, get the Artifact, find the Einstein Stone, and bring it all back to me. Sound like a plan?"

Doc looked at Charley. "Well, you ready old dog?"

Charley wanted to say 'no.' He wanted to explain he had spent a lifetime defending his nation, community, and family. As a soldier and as law enforcement, he answered the call of duty. Now, all he wanted, all he could hope for, was going home, playing with his dogs, planting the garden, just watching sunsets and sunrises come and go with no stress, no worry, no fear of disruption.

"Well...?" Doc asked again.

"Sure," Charley answered simply.

"Good luck, gentlemen. Hurry."

~ 3 ~

CHAPTER TWO

"Muh, you have crashed us in the wrong place!" Jee said accusingly. His ears were alert, neck fur raised, tail held rigidly, signaling unease and distrust. "This isn't Indianapolis, Indiana."

"Is so!"

"Is not!"

Slowly, the three alien beings turned in all directions; everywhere they looked were rolling hills, rocky outcroppings, small groves of trees dotted the withered brown, grassy landscape. Pronghorn sheep grazed in the far distance, a small cluster of low square buildings to the East, and silver cylindrical grain silos to the West. Somewhere a prairie dog barked, and the wind made a whistling sound as it gathered up stray tumbleweeds.

"I spy with my little eye: Trees, grass, rocks, hills, a few birds, and some quadrupeds." Jee arched his ears at Muh. "You notice there are no large buildings, traffic, advertising signs, and a million or so people are missing? Muh, I am telling you this is not Indianapolis."

Muh was distressed. *I am the oldest, I am in charge, and I am the leader. But this was not where we are supposed to be.* However, Muh could not admit failure, making him appear weak.

"You are wrong, Jee. These are the outskirts of Indianapolis, Indiana!" Muh declared with conviction. "I have spoken!"

"Nuh-uh!" Jee complained. "Muh, where are we?"

A gust of wind stirred prairie dust, whipping up bits of vegetation, Muh put on sunglasses to shade his eyes. He could taste the dry, dusty air around them, and the scent of sage was heavy.

Pulling out a packet of maps, Muh unfolded them on the hood of their landing craft. The lozenge-shaped space vessel still smoldered from re-entry, the bright yellow paint burned away in spots. The ventral stabilizer fin had a huge dent.

"My, my, looky here," Jee pointed out the damage. "Muh, you shouldn't apply flea bath while flying."

"Did not!"

"Did too!"

Jee kicked a panel of the craft. "Our Mother Craft won't return to this solar system in another two years, numb nuts. You think we can fix this enough to lift off this planet?"

"Yes! Yes! Absolutely!" Muh hated to be questioned by those younger and less experienced than he. It was time he established authority to take control of this situation. "Jee. You seem to be questioning my leadership. This is unacceptable. Your complete and undying devotion is the minimum you owe me. You will show me the honor and respect I am due as an elder of this clan!" Muh demanded.

"Elder? Clan?" Jee gasped with indignation, "Dude, we're freaking triplets! You saw daylight about two minutes before I did, Muh. Two minutes!"

"So, what is your point? That still makes me the Elder."

"May I add something?" A third voice joined the discussion.

"Jee," Muh growled, ignoring the interruption. "Tradition is everything, and the oldest is always given respect and honor. Why, without traditions, we are no better than...than...humans."

"Let's not get nasty here."

"You listen to me, Jee; we are on a mission, a grave and perilous mission among these human creatures. Do you have any idea how irrational these people can be? We must stick to our protocols, stick to our precise orders; we are to bring this 'Gift' to these humans."

"Yeah, well, I don't think these guys deserve a 'gift,' do you?"

"Jee, I am the oldest; therefore, I am the leader. As a leader, I'm telling you to shut the hell up!"

"Nice language." Yaz, the third alien, muttered glumly. This fighting was getting tiresome. *As long as they fight, I don't even exist,* he fretted.

But Yaz wasn't going to give up. "Look, you guys," He moved in front of the other little green aliens, Muh and Jee, so they couldn't possibly ignore him. "We gotta get to Indiana. Where the hell is it?" As the middle child, Yaz felt he was in an excellent position to referee the family discussion. If only they would listen.

"So," Jee utterly ignored Yaz. "You have the maps Muh; where are we, and where do we go next?"

Muh emptied his small pack, laying out his various instruments. Reading the dials and tweaking a knob, Muh announced: "I am ready to calculate." He pointed to the map. "Okay, my readings put us...just about...here!" He placed a tiny green paw on the map. "Anaconda. Yup, Anaconda, Montana, United States. Outskirts of Indianapolis, Indiana. We are right here."

"And Indianapolis is where?"

"There." His paw, with opposable digits, pointed to another section of the map.

"Not here?"

"No, there."

"'There' and 'here' aren't the same thing."

"' There' is just as good as 'here'; it's just farther away!" Muh said, his voice rising defensively.

"Hey, guys!" Yaz called out, waving to get attention. "I'll bet we can grab an Earth vehicle and use it to get there."

"How much farther away is Indianapolis? Jee didn't think Muh had any clue. "Huh? How far? A thousand miles? Two?"

Muh returned to his notes, adding some figures into his handheld computer; he looked up. "Okay, we are here...on this big cement path called I-90. We are headed here...the new 'White House' of The United Christian States...Indianapolis, Indiana."

"Can you read a map, or do you just stare at the pictures?"

"Oh, my," Muh muttered. Quickly he recalibrated the numbers again. It was a lot farther than he realized. "Okay, men," placing a stern and commanding expression on his face to cover his dismay. "Men, although you have landed us off our target, there will be no punishment. I am a wise and forgiving leader, and I will forgive you. Now, I will get us to our target and lead us to victory. We will fulfill our mission!"

"Say, wait a minute," Jee protested. "We didn't do anything wrong. You were driving, dude...."

Yaz squinted his bright eyes against the glare of the Montana summer sun. It was growing hot, and he was tired of standing on burning asphalt listening to idiots argue.

"IIey," Yaz pointcd down thc road. "Let's go over there and see if they have transport, over by those yellow and red buildings."

"Alright," Muh decided it was time for him to take command as the crew was getting uppity. "I have decided on our direction of march. We will march, single file to those building over there." Muh pointed to a cluster of tall, round silver structures opposite the yellow and red buildings. "There, we go there!" he proclaimed and started trotting briskly toward the metal structures. "Okay, march! Single file."

Jee didn't move.

Yaz didn't move.

"I want to go to the buildings over there." Jee pointed to the yellow and red buildings half a mile away, and he began trotting in that direction.

"We cannot." Muh continued on his march. "I have decided we are going another way."

"Nope, that way."

"This way."

"That way."

"Uhhh..." Yaz held up his hand. "Can I say something?"

Muh and Jee were getting farther apart.

Yaz began to panic. He looked toward Muh, then Jee, then Muh, but couldn't decide who to follow.

"Oh, shit, what now?" Yaz dropped his paw. Then he had a thought. "Hey, you guys, I can smell gasoline! That stuff that Earthlings use to power vehicles? Gas, that way!" Yaz hopped up and his tail wagging vigorously

No sooner had Yaz spoken when Muh paused; he sniffed and then sniffed again. "Wait a minute. Suddenly, because I have superior abilities, I can sense gasoline! Yes, I have determined gasoline is coming from...there" Muh turned and pointed to the yellow and red buildings behind him. "Thank Cosmos, I am leading. Otherwise we would have been misled," Muh said sternly.

Yaz held up his paw. "Ah...wait...ah, I, ah...."

Muh saw an excellent opportunity to teach Jee some lessons. "Leaders must be flexible and adjust to the urgent demands of command," Muh said sternly. "Although you were ignorant of your destination, I forgive you, Jee, for trying to mislead our mission. As Commander, I alone knew the right path. Therefore, I give you permission, Jee, to take point under my watchful guidance and lead this clan to those yellow and red buildings. Begin now!"

Jee ground his teeth. He took a step toward Muh, teeth bared, he growled.

"Remember, Jee," Muh said hurriedly. "We gave a solemn oath to the Galactic Confederacy to complete this mission. All three of us." Muh said pointedly.

"Sure," Jee snapped back. "No problem. No worries."

"Really?" Somehow Muh doubted that, and he decided it was a problem he should worry about.

"March!" Muh commanded. "Single file, Jee, proceed as ordered."

"Sure, boss," Jee snarled.

Trudging along in the hot Montana summer sun, the three little green aliens were widely spaced to reduce further conflicts.

All I need to do is prove my worth to them, Yaz thought, *they will accept me, listen to me, and love me.*

"I believe," Yaz spoke loudly and clearly so his brothers ahead could hear, enunciating his words. "We should investigate the small square yellow and red buildings before us and then use this square vehicle to take us to Indianapolis, Indiana."

Jee and Muh continued padding silently.

"Do you hear me?" Yaz tried again.

Silence.

"Hey!" Yaz repeated.

Silence.

"Hey! Hey! Hey!"

Silence.

Suddenly Jee said, "Muh look," He held his paw up to stop the march. "What is that?" Jee pointed to a small square vehicle beside a small square yellow and red building.

Muh nodded. "I don't know. I will find out." He consulted his handheld Quantum Computer.

"That's a 1954 Studebaker Hawk!" Yaz shouted each word clearly and distinctly. "I know it from my study of Earth mating customs, and that back seat is famous for fornication."

"So, what is it?" Jee asked Muh.

"Quiet, I'm looking, I'm looking."

"A 54 Studebaker! Hawk!" Yaz yelled. "A 54 Studebaker! Hawk!"

"It's ah...." Muh ran his claw down a list. "Oh, yes, right here. A 1954 Studebaker Hawk, that's what it is."

"But, I said that!" Yaz protested.

"Did you hear anything, Jee? A kind of curious squeaking?"

"Okay, real funny, you guys," Yaz responded irritably. "Will that get us to Indiana?" Yaz asked loudly.

"Will that get us to Indiana?" Jee asked.

"You know, Jee, that's a good question," Muh muttered. "I have no idea...glad you brought it up, though."

"Hey, it was my idea!" Yaz shouted.

Muh and Jee stood together, checking the map.

"Muh, Jee?" Yaz wondered if he'd become invisible. "Must I remind you two that I was chosen as the mission morale officer?"

"What was that? You fart Jee?" Muh asked, looking vaguely around.

"Nope, it wasn't me. Maybe indigenous swamp gas." Jee added.

Yaz burned with resentment.

One more time, Yaz said to himself. "Say, why don't we take this 1954 Studebaker Hawk to Indianapolis?"

Silence.

"Hey, I have an idea," Jee said. "Let's take the Studebaker Hawk to Indianapolis!"

"Great idea, Jee!" Muh said, hoping to mollify the arrogant little prick. Muh couldn't allow Jee to get an edge.

"I will drive!" Commanded Muh.

Opening the door, Muh applied the computer to the ignition, and the elderly vehicle started right up, settling into a gentle rumble.

Tammy Faye burst forth in a furious song from the radio speakers.

"I love that old gospel singing... I'll fly away is my favorite song...I just love that old-time religion...."

"Don't you assholes dare sing along!" Muh ordered as his narrow green paw stamped on the accelerator. Immediately he regretted their choosing to disguise themselves as earth creatures. *Maybe if we'd chosen different body shapes, a monkey maybe, but here we are Beagles,* Muh thought. *The last thing I need is to make this more difficult.*

In the back seat, Yaz, feeling disgruntled as usual, opened the backpacks belonging to his brothers and dumped out the contents.

He sorted through maps, dry roasted Yuhn meat for snacks, an 'Archie' comic book, assorted jackets, hats, spats, garters, and widgets.

Curious, Yaz pulled an ugly six-pound lump of irregularly formed Stone, a very intense teal-like color, from Muh's backpack.

Well, what is this? He's seen this thing before. But where?

"Hey Muh, hey Jee, what is this?"

Twenty minutes later, Yaz gave up asking his brothers what this strange rock was.

He'd been answered with silence he had come to expect.

As he gazed into the object, Yaz suddenly heard the distant sounds of chanting, smelled ripe corn, flashes of people and scenes flickered before him. "Wow." Yaz stared down at the odd rock. "Where have I seen you before?"

~ 4 ~

CHAPTER THREE

"A house divided against itself cannot stand."

Lincoln's words, an ironic prediction, haunted Bessie May Chowder piloting the Sikorsky S-92 Helicopter, three thousand feet above the I-5 corridor as they traveled south across Oregon. It was Fall, and mixed into the deep, dark green of the evergreens were sparkling hardwoods in bright yellows and oranges and tans of the Umpqua Forest. Bessie May loved the Fall.

She reached out to the control panel to set the Autopilot (AP), then Altitude, Speed, and Navigation hold, watching the G1000 Multifunction Display (MFD) screen to ensure the aircraft under the AP remained stable.

Chowder turned to her co-pilot, LTC Juwanda Nickels.

"Juwanda?" she spoke into her mike to blur the rotor noise.

LTC Nickels replied. "Copilot has controls."

Chowder acknowledged.

Relaxing from the yoke, sitting back in the seat she scanned the skies for both weather and other aircraft. Thick, dark clouds gathered ominously on the Western horizon. A seasoned pilot, she was very comfortable in the air, but she did not like the look of that storm to the North of them.

"Juwanda, look!" President Chowder pointed at the G1000 PDF display. One corner was showing a blaze of swirling reds and yellows. "That is one hell of a storm over Portland."

Juwanda replied immediately, "Yes, ma'am. Those are massive thunderstorms...hold...." She listened to her headphones a moment turned a knob on the control panel. "Listen for yourself, ma'am."

Chowder replaced her headphones and immediately heard the voice of Charley Parsons, the rotund, histrionic, hyper-friendly weatherman out of Portland, Oregon. Charley wasn't jovial today.

"People! If you are listening, get to high ground immediately. No matter how safe you think you are, get higher. Get much higher! The storm now hitting this area is dumping so much water the flooding is uncontrollable...storm of the century...a river of rain bringing more moisture in one day than all year...run!"

"Portland is going to need all the help we can give." Turning to her Chief of Staff in the rear seat, "Bernard, get Red Cross and FEMA on the line, tell them to get down there." Bernard Tallman Howard, her Chief of Staff, quickly put in a call.

"Tell Governor Dagostino we give the authorization to mobilize the State Guard."

"Yes, Madam President. He is going to need it. Right now, his Republican State Representatives are attempting an end-run."

"Trying to castrate him, huh?" Chowder grimaced at the despicable politics that has stayed with them like a diseased leech. "Tell Governor Dagostino that we have Sedition laws the old United States had but refused to enforce." Chowder said with grim determination. "Cascadia will not allow anyone to subvert our Democratic elections. Tell him that I will personally see that charges are brought against any politician, any citizen, of any stripe who actively works to subvert this nation. Tell him I will back him fully to silence this poison. Any attempt by a political party to stop or hinder citizen voting will never be tolerated in Cascadia."

"Yes, ma'am, your mission to Santa Rosa today will certainly prove that," Bernard replied reassuringly.

President Chowder studied her Chief of Staff and praised the day she hired him. Bernard Howard, nicknamed 'Bunny,' a short, round man with protruding front teeth, was bullied and beaten in his youth. Tainted with the name 'Bunny', Bernard nevertheless went on to earn two Master's Degrees from Harvard and, in a show of defiance, kept the nickname.

Bessie May Chowder admired people with the strength to find roses amid ruins.

So much to do, so many things happening at once.

Cascadian President Bessie May Chowder felt as if she were juggling hand grenades while riding a unicycle. Now, flying to this meeting in Santa Rosa, California, she hoped the hand grenades were not live.

Looking down on the forests of Southern Oregon passing below, she thought of the White Christian Nation, a militant separatist group demanding their state within the new nation of Cascadia. These people were dangerous, unpredictable, growing in number, and they had the direct and illicit support of the United Christian States. As President, she had to step in and resolve this festering situation before a bloody civil war erupted. Looking down at the serene rivers and prairies of Southern Oregon, she knew that fair land was already lost to militant white separatists.

But most important was her meeting with a woman named Bahrain. A meeting that would mark the beginning of a new world or just the end of this one. *The world is changing because we are forcing it to,* she mused. Like women around the globe, Chowder was tired of waiting for men to give her equal rights. She and her sisters were going to take them one way or the other.

The disasters facing President Bessie May Chowder were like Dante's seven levels of hell with sublevels of endless paperwork between.

She opened a thick vanilla folder, the summary of her daily brief: Proposed legislation, food shortages, political infighting, climate problems, international relations, economy; the list seemed endless.

She held up a new trade agreement with Canada, shipping California walnuts to Vancouver.

Freddy loved walnuts.

The thought appeared in her mind, and instantly tears welled up. Frederick Bellamy Chowder was the most handsome, dynamic, and wonderful man she had ever met. God, she loved that man.

She remembered Fred sipping a dry martini in his favorite chair. They were relaxing with drinks after the election hoopla was done and they had won; she turned to him, "My God, the opportunities we now have," she squeezed his hand. "A Social Democracy! Where the people control the government. Where government works for the people, not a subsidiary of the rich and powerful. Oh, Freddy, imagine a country of accountability, fairness, justice, equality, opportunity, all of the things that were sabotaged in the old US we will establish here, in Cascadia."

And she remembered Freddie's reply, "My love, a Social Democracy is a lovely young girl, with promise, and hope, and dreams living in a world of thugs who are egomaniacal fiends with not a whit of care for human life. What we have is special and powerful but fragile because, within our borders, we will struggle against two major forces of resistance: Apathy and Ignorance. We can reduce ignorance with proper education, but apathy only responds to self-interest. We must make Cascadia a place people want to be."

My Freddie, gone now, eighteen months ago. His demise from thyroid cancer was swift and horrid. She shuddered at the loss, the tears just behind her eyes.

~ 5 ~

CHAPTER FOUR

"The true value of a human being can be found in the degree to which he has attained liberation from the self."
Albert Einstein

"Do you know that I am directly responsible for the lives of millions of humans? Millions!"

Price Wayne, the personal assistant to Mr. Barcelona, remained stoic; rants are always rhetorical.

"I am one of the most important humans to ever live!" Barcelona continued boldly. "Everything I say, everything I do is of significance to everyone."

Barcelona settled deeper into his lounge chair at the stern of his 891-foot mega yacht, sipped his Mai Tai, and glanced over at the gorgeous lunch being set out for his pleasure: Wagyu beef from his farms in Japan, Chinese Cabbage from Taiwan, and a sparkling wine from Peru.

The Adriatic sun was just setting in a kaleidoscope of warm pastel shades, and he felt good, on top of the world good, looking forward to a peaceful evening, some cards, cognac, and then plentiful sleep. He briefly considered a massage and sauna, maybe a movie in his full-size theater, bowling was out, a light chop makes a four-ten split impossible. Maybe read Ayn Rand, his favorite. He was bummed out his miniature submarine, tendered on his shadow yacht, was having engine problems. He could go horseback riding. His stable master assured him the riding path around the massive yacht was once again suitable. Maybe a moonlight helicopter flight!

"Of course, you are keeping a record of all my brilliance?" Barcelona asked.

Wayne replied quickly, "Most certainly, sir, every word, saved for posterity." Wayne continued buffing his nails. Stabbing the arrogant asshole with a nail file was tempting but suicidal. "You know I learn so much from you, master," He said.

"But you're not recording anything!"

Wayne tapped his temple. "Memory, sir."

Barcelona lifted a skeptical eyebrow. He was raised with the knowledge that lesser humans simply did not have the intelligence to understand complex issues. Naturally, there were superior and inferior humans, and the losers must realize this natural state of being and accept it. But, stubbornly, perhaps futilely, he continued his attempts to educate them. Deep in his heart, Barcelona believed that all humans, even rabble like Price Wayne, could learn and even understand their place in the natural order of life. His frustration boiled at their stubbornness. Barcelona knew that some of the lesser class was quite capable of extraordinary actions if they just followed orders.

"Bing, bing," a soft chime, then another. "Bing, bing."

Price Wayne handed Barcelona the tiny phone. "Bahrain on the line, my sovereign, and absolute Lord and Master," Wayne regularly buttered up Barcelona, sort of like taking micro doses of Ex-Lax, to keep the system flowing smoothly.

"Yes? Hello?" Barcelona spoke softly. "Is this you, dear Bahrain?"

"Barcelona, my dear, dear wonderful Barcelona! How are you, my love?"

Bahrain's voice sounded like a wood chipper on idle.

"Geez, why don't you take a throat lozenge or something? You gotta voice that would kill a crow," Barcelona complained.

"Yes, I know, I will certainly check into that. Thank you for that wonderful suggestion," Bahrain said readily. "My dear Barcelona, I have concerns I must share with you," Bahrain continued, "You know how I value your every opinion! Well, I need you now." she croaked. "You are so much like an uncle to me, a favored uncle."

Barcelona sighed. Once again, he was called upon to be responsible and the leader. *A great man's work is never truly appreciated in his time; another reason to make the little people understand my goals.* "Why, my dear, how utterly charming of you. Yes, in my heart, you are my niece." He replied smoothly.

Barcelona scratched his nuts, looking out longingly to the clear, cerulean waters of the Greek Archipelagos; he longed to float without a care in the world in these calming waters. He longed to be free of the burden of command, free of the weight of the world on his shoulders, free of constant pressures of command. Then His stomach gurgled; he farted, belched, and shifted uncomfortably.

Pillows were quickly dispatched by staff standing by for just such a delicate situation. Fans were turned on to whisk away the odor. Barcelona was soon comforted by soft surroundings, a nubile young girl stroked his forehead, and the sunshade adjusted over him. A single bead of sweat was enough to send his staff scrambling to prevent any further discomfort.

"Go ahead, dear, you know you can always count on me. I, too, think of you like family, my dear." *Not my family, you understand,* Barcelona thought.

"These climate-changing storms are getting troublesome." The wood chipper moved from idle into low. "I lost another foot of my island this month! The ocean is quite literally at my front doorstep. Qatar has reported that despite spending a billion dollars, they haven't been able to stop the rising seas. Towns and cities up and down the coastlines of the Middle East, all the way to Ad-Dahirah, have flooded. The coastline is now miles inland, and seawater is making freshwater brackish! My side of this planet is in trouble. Barcelona, what are we doing about it!" The chipper throttled up to full speed. "This is costing me money!" Bahrain complained. She hoped she wasn't overplaying this. First, butter the asshole up, and then slip the knife between the ribs. Bahrain had a simple but elegant business plan. Her friend Chowder would hate the implied violence of it.

"Ok, ok, Bahrain, slow down, breathe," Barcelona replied soothingly. He hated raised voices, as they represent a break in civilized behavior. As the personal savior of civilization, he took such things seriously.

"Now, calm down. I know things are a little bit difficult now. But we can ride it out! It doesn't matter what is going on with the climate, dear; we live on luxury yachts the size of aircraft carriers. We come and go as we please, wherever we want, free and unfettered by silly things like nationality or laws. My dear, climate change is an important part of our planning, not a disaster for us, not at all."

A horn sounded.

Barcelona saw his shadow yacht coming in closer to transfer food and provisions. The shadow ship was returning from Athens carrying boxes of delectable foods, wines, and items of luxury exclusive to the lovely Greek islands: Sweet and elegant Bougatsa, delicious dolmadakia, the finest Ellinikos coffee.

Barcelona's network of supply yachts stationed on every continent stood ready to provision him no matter where he chose to travel. He couldn't remember the last time his main yacht touched a port. He looked around for Price Wayne, wondering if his second shadow yacht, the diminutive 357 footer, "The Capitalist," had reached port in Sicily yet. Barcelona was fond of their olives. He hoped they wouldn't forget some cheese as well.

Rising to better look at the incoming boat, he wondered if the new replacement Masseuse was on board. It had been so unfortunate. Barcelona hated losing an employee. But her insubordination was intolerable, and an example had to be set. Given that they were at sea, the solution had been quite simple. He wanted to make a ceremony of it, but Price Wayne persuaded him to hold off. The staff was becoming fractious enough as it was, demanding they be returned to their homes after six years at sea. A ceremonial keel-hauling might push them over the edge.

"Pardon me, Barcelona, but are you listening?" Bahrain inquired. Whenever Barcelona went quiet, either he was no longer on the line, or he was plotting violence. She knew Barcelona better than he thought. "There is a heat dome over Utah!" She continued. "Utah has 114 degrees! For over two weeks, Barcelona!" Bahrain wailed. "I have ranches there, and my cattle are roasting in the fields as we speak! Barbeque Beef on the hoof."

"Calm yourself. There will be inconveniences, my dear. But we are wealthy. Like all of us, you have ranches worldwide: Argentina, Zimbabwe, Thailand, Vietnam, even Barstow, California. Hell, I own half the cattle ranches in Wyoming myself. We diversify our food supply and help the struggling indigenous peasants out. What are you worried about?"

He sat upon his sun-bed and slipped his feet into slippers made of endangered Snow Leopard fur, admiring the crystal white sand covering the sloping deck leading to the sparkling ocean waters. The small cabanas and sun chairs scattered around the transom were surrounded by large potted palms strategically placed, making it appear as a small, exclusive Beach Club on his yacht. An extension protruded from the transom creating a shallow wading pool of sea-water, so he could dip without drowning. His movements caused a sudden flurry of activity among the staff as they tried to determine what their Lord and Master needed or wanted; to be on time with the tea was to be late.

"Do you see now we have little to fret?" He said. The scent of the ocean strengthened with the wind, a two-knot breeze that ruffled the overhead umbrella. The warm tropical sun coated his skin with comfort.

Barcelona sighed with impatience. In response, a crewman rushed over to sprits him with lotion. He lifted his face so the fine mist could cool him. "Everything is just fine."

Suddenly his face flushed, immediately three staff members leaped to his side, measuring BP, spritzing him with more lavender-scented rose oil, and waving a palm frond to cool his fevered brow.

"I am distressed." He nearly shouted but held himself back. His position in life forbade rage. With his power, uncontrolled anger would be dangerous and unprofitable. "Sure, you are new to the Forty but aren't you familiar with how this world works? Wealth is our bubble. Don't you understand this climate change means nothing to us personally? It's just business. Our factories will keep pouring out the ozone killing chemicals, CO2, we will accelerate our drilling and fracking, more oil, more gasoline, why the hell not? Our profits are astronomical. Most importantly, it will not negatively impact you and me in any way whatsoever."

"Oh yeah? My island is losing twenty feet of ground a year, I told you, and I'm taking this personally too," her gravelly voice croaked frustration.

She waited for his reply. It was important.

If Bahrain was going to climb the hierarchy of the group of Mega-billionaires labeled The Forty, she needed to remove a few rungs. She couldn't touch Barcelona yet, but she would someday. Besides, this bullshit about the ultra-wealthy being untouched by climate change is ludicrous. *Rich assholes blinded by the glare of their gold.* Her communications with Bessie May were intensifying, the network of powerful women expanding exponentially as the sordid world of Patriarchy collapsed.

"Barcelona? I know you are brilliant, and I am but a novice, but I think you are underestimating the impact of this climate disaster."

Barcelona didn't know what to say. She didn't seem to understand. Until Bahrain, 'The Forty' always consisted of men, Alpha Males, who fought and clawed their way to becoming billionaires. *Cream rises to the top. Billionaires are men who create the future while others follow. Men who dominate and men who rule.* He was proud of his brilliance.

Barcelona thought; *Why am I wasting time? Bahrain, a weakling girl who just inherited her chair? Her father, the original Bahrain dies, and she gets handed the position? This is not right!* The fact that women and Negroes were inferior intellectually was proven scientifically. Barcelona was amazed the rest of the world couldn't see this obvious proven fact.

"I probably am overstating this," Barcelona continued. "But as you must know, we, The Forty, are the forty richest men...people, on the planet. Through our various holdings, corporations, banks, stocks and bonds, and Boards of Directorships, we control nearly 58% of the world economy. 70% of the World's financial affairs go through our hands: Banks, gas and oil, vehicles, consumer products, even the military-industrial complex bow to our wishes. No entity on earth can touch us. We are like Gods of the Greek Pantheon who sit above the fray of human concerns."

Bahrain listened carefully, seeking nuances, inflections, word choices that would tell her Barcelona's true thoughts. If women were ever to achieve equality, she owed it to the Sisterhood to know where and when to castrate the male empire. She would bring this recording to her meeting with Bessie May in Santa Rose in a day or so. Bahrain didn't know their plan yet, but she admired Chowder and knew she had something up her sleeve. The world was in for a change, and Bahrain couldn't wait.

"Barcelona, don't we have a duty to humanity?" Bahrain's voice rumbled like a '32 Ford Roadster with burned-out glass packs. "My dear, it is likely that a billion people may perish! Don't you think there might be a different way?"

"For Christ's sake! Yes, many will perish, so what? That is the point!" Barcelona's temper was wearing thin, and he was tired of talking to someone who wasn't listening.

I am so tired of talking to women. They are always yammering about life, precious life. Bullshit. They think their ovaries gave them some kind of special place in the world! Barcelona knew from bitter first-hand experience women were treacherous. Twice he'd been physically attacked, both times by women. Barcelona personally believed women were pissed because of their inferiority to men. He would anonymously send the YouTube science report to Bahrain the next time he had the chance.

"I will say this once." He said through gritted teeth. "I and every member of the Forty, including you, are the most humanistic, the most compassionate, the most loyal, and the most responsible of all humans on this planet, maybe in history. But we bear a terrible burden! Our lives are dedicated to saving the human species! So what if we have a few expensive baubles here and there? We have earned it! We are the only hope for the entire human race and maybe for life itself!" He realized he was coming dangerously close to shouting. Quickly, he imaged piles and piles of money to calm himself. He breathed easier.

"My God, woman, don't you get this by now?" He said softly, calmly, rationally. "The Forty are caretakers of Earth. We are the people responsible for all life on this planet! We have been gifted, chosen to be the Masters of Earth, and we are beyond the realm of mere mortal humans."

"Oh?" Bahrain loved it when she could get him riled up but was impressed at how quickly he regained control. Upset people make mistakes; reveal things she might want to know. She had to get Barcelona off balance. "I'm sorry, I don't mean to be dense," She gave her voice rising irritation, a rougher quality. "Isn't killing people to save them an oxymoron?" She held her breath, waiting for the reply.

Barcelona sighed. *Bahrain is female. She doesn't understand. Poor thing can't understand.* This part was the toughest to explain, so he rarely tried. But, since Bahrain was technically a Forty, he was obliged. The fact that she had just challenged him would not be forgotten.

"Humans, on average, are quite stupid and need strict guidance." He began. "Because of liberals and their sick, twisted belief in equality, ordinary humans as been given the notion they deserve a better life." *Bah! People and sheep are the same,* Barcelona snorted. "Humans are eating and screwing themselves out of living space," he continued, "and the population has exploded way beyond the carrying capacity of this Earth. We, the Forty, are working night and day to lower the numbers, establishing the necessary controls, working our fingers to the bones trying to eliminate as many people as possible so that we can save them!"

"So," Bahrain said, clearly and distinctly so the recording could be sent out around the world. *Proof of the evil.* "Barcelona, you are saying global warming, rising ocean levels, deadly storms, erratic seasons, failed agriculture, max forced migrations of billions of humans, and extinction of the majority of creatures, including humans, are your goals? This is all being manipulated by The Forty?" She said with wonder. "Really? Isn't all this a little drastic?" She poked at him, trying for another rise in temper.

"Drastic times call for drastic measures," Barcelona replied smugly. "But now you understand. The Forty exists to save humanity," he told her patiently, "just not all of it."

Cold Blooded bastard, Bahrain thought. She had to disengage before she vomited on the phone.

"Well, my dear sweet uncle, I must run. Please stay well. I want to thank you for your words of wisdom. You are such a brilliant man. I so admire you." Bahrain choked back vomit. "May I call you in a day or so? I have some little thing to discuss with you." Bahrain waited a moment then said. "We must discuss an ancient Mayan treasure, a Blue-Green Stones said to radiate power: The Einstein Stone." She abruptly hung up the phone. Just as she and Chowder had arranged. Drop the reference to see how he reacts.

Bahrain wasn't sure about this 'Einstein Stone' thing, but she agreed with Chowder that humanity only has a short time to get its collective shit together, so even a Mayan myth might be helpful.

Barcelona listened to the dial tone with shock and awe, frozen. No one had hung up on him before, not ever, not once. He was kind of impressed. Barcelona didn't know whether to kill her or adopt her.

"A Blue-Green Emerald," Barcelona said softly to himself, "My oh my." She hadn't mentioned the word 'emerald,' but Barcelona had his sources.

Price Wayne paused as he set out another lunch for Barcelona. *The Einstein Stone?* He wondered if his contact, Clay Painter, would pay for this tidbit.

~ 6 ~

CHAPTER FIVE

"Madam President, Ma'am."

"Yes, Bunny." She shook her head to dispel her thoughts. Grief seemed to linger longer each year as more people she loved passed away. *Growing old means saying goodbyes to those we love.* Bessie May hated this. *Why is life so damn painful? What is the point of so much sorrow?"* It seemed her entire life had been framed by these two questions.

"Ma'am, Senator Imahuffin's..." Bernard interrupted her thoughts.

"Imahuffin? What has that fool done now?"

"When the United States reformed itself under one-party leadership, they changed the name to The United Christian States of America to better inform the world they are a Christian nation founded on Christian principles..."

"But, they aren't. America wasn't founded on Christianity, quite the opposite, it was..."

"Yes, ma'am," Bunny replied, "but this change of name has galvanized Senator Imahuffin into a near frenzy. He leads a coalition to force Cascadia to return to the US, and he is demanding to be part of negotiations between Cascadia and the United Christian States today."

"Yea, which side does he want to sit on?"

Bernard chuckled.

"Damn it, Bunny, we can't have that jackass involved. The balkanization of the United States is a brutal and chaotic affair." She said with frustration. The conference on International Cooperation between Cascadia and the UCS, postponed many times, was now on the agenda again, she was relieved to note.

"This summit meeting cannot happen soon enough," Bernard said as he set up a call to the Santa Rosa delegates waiting for them. "Seventy-two hours? That's all?"

"The deadline from the UCS is just that: seventy-two hours. We have that long to comply with a lengthy list of demands. We do it, or they launch. Now that Washington State, Oregon, and California have legally seceded, we can go our own way from the old US, but the interrelationships of our citizens bind us. We have to resolve issues between our nations quickly. Imahuffin is a time bomb waiting to wreck everything."

"So the UCS Delegates will arrive in time? Are you sure it is all arranged?" Chowder checked her watch and realized they were down to sixty-five hours now.

Bernard felt so frustrated. He had spent so much time stalling and misdirecting an increasingly hostile Senator Imahuffin he had no idea when the UCS delegation was arriving. "I will find out immediately."

****

"Ma'am?" The copilot was alerted by a monitor on the instrument panel.

"Bing, bing, bing, bing..." the alert bell sounded.

"Juwanda?"

"Just a tickle, but I picked up a tracking radar hit just a moment ago. Someone was painting us with a mobile missile." She reached out and pointed at the MFD. A small light in the upper right hand was flashing yellow. "Just a hint, there and gone. No clear threat."

"Ah, yes, keep me informed." Southern Oregon. a hotbed of insurrectionists, people still loyal to the UCS. But if someone painted their aircraft with missile launch radar, even for a few seconds, this was a clear and present danger.

It was not the first time Bessie May Chowder had been targeted for death, and she wondered if, this time, it had anything to do with The Einstein Stone.

"Weeeeeeeeeeeee!" Suddenly, an alarm blared.

Juwanda, in a calm voice, said. "Ma'am, we have missile lock-on...missile lock...."

Quickly, Chowder swung back to the controls, but a fast glance at the radar showed a bright red object closing on their location.

"Chaff!" She ordered. Taking the controls, she pulled the heavy copter into an evasive maneuver, knowing she had no chance of succeeding. As a pilot with over 10,000 hours in various aircraft, Chowder knew they were in trouble, and their only real hope was that the missile was a misfire.

"Mayday, Mayday, this is CP-56, declaring an immediate emergency. Anyone, Mayday, location...."

As Juwanda called in the emergency call, Chowder maneuvered the helicopter evasively, hoping the chaff would decoy the incoming missile.

Although it did not strike the helicopter directly, the explosion blew the aircraft sharply to the right, red warning lights appeared across the dash, and a calm mechanical voice said, "pull up, pull up."

~ 7 ~

CHAPTER SIX

He listened to the dial tone for a moment to make sure *evil libtards and queers* weren't listening in and then dialed.

The Right Reverend 'Jumper Jim' Imahuffin, revered state senator for Medford, Oregon, USA, held the phone closer to his ear. This was an important phone call, and he didn't want to screw it up.

The legend of Jumper Jim Imahuffin was born one hot July morning in Grants Pass, Oregon. High school dropout Jim Imahuffin, recently matriculated from Salvation Sally's Internet Ministerial College, reported for duty as a Suicide Hot Line Volunteer. His first call was from a distraught man standing on the main bridge overlooking the Rogue River.

The man, crying and sobbing, told Imahuffin about his having a tough month at work. He had money problems, halitosis, and excessive perspiration. The man wailed about his inability to find a companion.

Imahuffin politely listened for almost three minutes, then seeing another phone call blink on his panel, he decided to move things along a little. *Other people need my help too, and this guy talks too much.* Imahuffin figured the more suicide hotline calls he handled, the better it would look for his Re-election for State Senator.

"You know," Imahuffin told the distraught, suicidal man. "I have other people I need to save, so we need to move this along. What you've told me is not so bad. Life has its up and downs, and maybe you're just going through a bad patch." Imahuffin explained, looking over at his open copy of 'Suicide Prevention Handbooks for Beginners, Vol. 3.'

"Maybe you should just relax...listen to music...play pool...drink milk."

"I'm also gay and have AIDS."

"You are what with what? Kill yourself! Fucking jump to your death. The world doesn't need or want you!" Imahuffin shrieked into the phone.

The man jumped.

Fortunately for Imahuffin, the jumper was a Bi-sexual named Frank 'Fannie' Smit.

His response wasn't just a personal choice. Staunchly Conservative Eastern Oregon had pockets of citizens who viewed bisexuals with the same level of respect as a pedophile dog thief. Historically, they treated such conditions by tying the pervert to a pickup truck and then scraping them down a gravel road until they rethought their life choices. Imahuffin believed this was a 'personal choice' type of issue the people should decide themselves, and Government should never meddle in citizens desire to enforce their own local standards on people they don't like.

Imahuffin created the term 'Jumper Jim' added it to his campaign, and his constituents saw it as nothing but an honor. He parlayed Mr. Smit's demise into two terms as a State Senator in the Capital of Oregon, Salem in the old U.S. of A and continued when Washington State became part of Cascadia.

Unfortunately, the breakup of America was traumatic for Imahuffin, who found himself, very much against his will, behind enemy socialist lines. His political seat in Salem transferred from one nation to another like day-old bread, and Imahuffin followed hungrily. Despite his hatred of Liberals, he had his voter base to consider and become a reluctant Cascadian.

"Come on, come on!" Imahuffin shouted into the phone. "I haven't got all day."

His call into The United Christian States Homeland Security, Western Division, Butte, Montana, was going slowly, winding its way through various secretaries, sycophants, and stooges. All of whom were beneath his contempt.

"Who are you holding for?" A bored voice answered.

Imahuffin's eyes bulged from their sockets in a fury. "What? What? What are you saying? I have been holding for an hour! You are the seventh person I have spoken with! I am Senator Jim Imahuffin! I demand to speak with the Director, Peter Paul God-Kock, immediately! Immediately!"

"Sure," came the reply. "I'll get right on that."

Silence.

Ten more minutes went by.

He knew screaming wouldn't help, so Imahuffin settled into his favorite pastime while waiting: Self-flagellation. Pulling off the heavy hair shirt he habitually wore; he pulled out a much-worn cat o nine tails and began to flail away at his back and shoulders, already covered in welts and bruises.

Imahuffin took comfort that Jesus would love this bloodshed.

Each blow produced a grunt from Imahuffin followed by muttered words of self-praise for his piety.

"Yes," a guttural mumble emerged from the phone.

"Brother God-Kock!" Imahuffin responded with enthusiasm, dropping the whip.

Taking a deep breath, he settled himself. Imahuffin wanted to convey confidence and strength when speaking with the Homeland Security Chief for Western, UCS.

"Imahuffin?" Peter Paul God-Kock sighed. He vowed to fire the asshole that routed this call to him. "What do you want?"

"Brother God-Kock!" Imahuffin repeated. "This is Senator Jim Imahuffin! I have news of great importance!"

"Imahuffin, you're a fucking Senator from Cascadia, another fucking country! We have nothing to talk about."

God-Kock stared out the window just a pigeon landed on the sill. The pigeon looked peaked and moved slowly. One wing drooped lower than the other; its tail had blank spaces missing the feathers. Suddenly it shit a bright yellow poop and dropped dead on the window sill.

Staring at the newly created corpse, God-Kock sighed. That's the third one this week, and I've got to get out of here.

"Sir, your honor, sir," Imahuffin began unctuously as per usual, "we are Christians and share a duty to bring Jesus Christ back to our world. I am calling to you as one devout Christian to another."

Jesus Christ! God-Kock thought. *The 'Jesus Card'! These guys always pull the 'Jesus Card'.* God-Kock yearned to announce his own personal 'Godhood' to mere mortals but knew he needed just the right stage for this kind of announcement. His self-elevation to God-hood started with a name change, from his family name of Kock to God-Kock. *So Far, So good.*

"Just tell me why you're calling and then go away." God-Kock challenged.

Today was a busy day. As Homeland Security Director for the Western U.S., P.P. God-Kock scheduled a drone strike against a group of disabled Veterans who illegally occupied a local V.A. outpatient clinic demanding medical marijuana.

God-Kock ordered SWAT to use C.S. gas and a nerve agent to set an example to others who wished to question authority. Peacekeeping was part of the job he took seriously.

"Brother God-Kock...I have news...." Imahuffin hoped Peter Paul was in a good mood. "The nation of Cascadia is on the brink of a Christian revolution!" he announced. "Jesus Christ himself has chosen us; he has sent us on a holy mission to preserve the motherland!"

Peter Paul sighed. He snorted. "What has this to do with me?"

"Well, sir, Jesus is coming back, and we have to get this world ready for him."

"Funny, the Muslims divided into two sects over that very question. The Shiites believe he's here; the Sunnis believe he is on the way. They have been killing each other for centuries over that question.

Imahuffin's sphincter contracted into a knot.

Muslims.

"If one person in a village worships a false God, then everyone in the village must be destroyed. Deuteronomy 13:7-12." Imahuffin muttered darkly. "King James Version, of course."

He hated them with a vengeance. Imahuffin hated their languages, customs, and Holy Book. He hated their ugly men, hairy women, dirty children, and most of all. He hated their refusal to accept Jesus Christ as their Lord and Savior.

As far as the Jews went, they were expendable for the greater glory of Jesus Christ. The way Imhauffin saw it; the Kike's were going to be the shock troops launched in waves against the rag heads. While the sand niggers were busy killing the Hebe's, Christians would come in and shove nuclear missiles up their asses.

It was a perfect plan for the Rapture.

Jesus will return to Earth to greet the victorious Christians, all except the Presbyterians, of course, who would surely suffer as Satan's servants because they don't take Jesus seriously.

Only the Faithful would be whisked away to sit at his right hand for all eternity.

Imahuffin couldn't wait to meet Jesus.

Lately, he'd been working on his grip strength as Imahuffin was sure Jesus would have a robust and masculine handshake.

"Brother God-Kock," Imahuffin assured him. "My son, we have our people in place. Within a fortnight, we will launch our campaign to retake Cascadia for the United States."

Peter Paul God-Kock nodded. "We've given those Goddamned liberals seventy-two hours to return to America, or we nuke them!"

"Praise Jesus!"

God-Kock stared at the phone. *Praise Jesus? What about me?* God-Kock was puzzled that Jesus constantly got the attention, but he didn't. He noted to have Homeland Security Information Office, FOX broadcasting, and produce a documentary on his ascension to Godhood. He'd already asked the Homeland Department of Christian Values to declare his New York Office building, Kock Towers, as a World Heritage site, similar to Mecca or Jerusalem.

"I have learned of a secret mission," Imahuffin continued shakily. "Very secret. Very. President Chowder is sending a team into the U.S. on a top-secret mission."

"And...?" Peter Paul couldn't believe he was wasting his time listening to this shit. *What has any of this to do with me?*

"And, Brother God-Kock, my son, President Bessie May Chowder, maybe after some top-secret item...something of incredible value...."

"And...?" This time, Peter Paul's voice got a little rougher.

"And...sir...I think an invasion of our beloved homeland is imminent, sir."

"Do you realize I am omnipotent and infallible?"

"What?"

P.P. God-Kock realized his divinity was beyond the understanding of a mere mortal. Checking the mirrors strategically placed around his office, he admired the orange hue of his makeup, recognizing his incredible masculinity and presence. All that time at the golf course was paying off.

"Sir, I am trying to tell you about a mysterious Jewell. It is called," Imahuffin paused for dramatic effect, "The Einstein Stone," he whispered furiously.

"Why are you whispering? And what the fuck is an Einstein Stone? That's not right. I think you've been slugging too much sacramental wine, dude." Peter Paul heaved a heavy sigh.

Imahuffin realized his message had met a dead end.

"Okay, okay," God-Kock said into the phone, hoping to soothe Imahuffin enough to shut him up. "I tell you what. We'll keep our eyes peeled for suspicious liberals and lock all our precious jewelry up. Anything else?"

"Brother..." Imahuffin added quickly. "Do you think you could send me...oh...say a small tactical nuke or two? Just for display purposes in recruiting, of course."

Peter Paul God-Kock smiled. "Why, of course, dear friend, you can expect delivery in about...seventy hours or so."

~ 8 ~

CHAPTER SEVEN

"Everything is energy, and that is all there is to it. Match the frequency of the reality you want, and you cannot help but get that reality. It can be no other way. This is not philosophy. This is physics." Albert Einstein

"Just for the sake of curiosity," Doc muttered. "Do ya'll know where we're going, or do ya'll make it up as you go along?"

"And there it is!" Charley turned onto a narrow gravel road that disappeared up a hill. The road sign said: 'Road Narrows, No county maintenance.'

"This is Sheep Slaughter Rd. We stay on this, cross the border Oregon into Idaho, and are in the United Christian States."

"Guess I will have to take ya'll's word for that," Doc looked out at the utterly black night. No moon, no street lights, just dark. "Course, if there is a lot of sheep slaughtering going on, that might slow things a bit, but ah am not going to get involved! Let those sheep defend themselves, ah gots places to go and reasons to go there."

The crossing was as Charley had hoped, quiet, discreet, and without gunfire.

"So, what's wrong with you, old man?"

"Stop it. I'm only a year older than you."

"Yes, sir, Charles, but it was a very troublesome year for you."

"Ha, ha."

"Ya'll can't fool me, Charles. I stopped you from bleeding to death in a nasty rice paddy. I know you, son. So tell me, what is wrong with you?"

"Nothing is wrong, Doc. I am just tired. Since we met in boot camp, we have marched and fought and lived, and I am tired. We have been at war and peace, and now I want to go home and sit. Doc," Charley turned to his friend. "I am fed up with it all, Doc, just so burned out. I want to be left alone. I think the majority of humans are idiots and the rest are delusional."

"Charles, ya'll have a far too high opinion of humanity, but we'll get back to that. Tell me."

Charley knew his friend well. Doc was doing his best to take care of his blood brother. Charley wanted to go home, but his life's many mistakes and fumbles had taught him a simple fact: Obligation. *A person is only as good as their actions. Once obligated, a person is responsible for finishing the task, no matter what they feel or want.* Charley figured that sometimes self-worth was found in the deed, not the doer.

So Charley gave Doc a song and dance about just being physically tired. He was okay, rested now, and no need to worry. *Everything was just fine, and the last thing he needed was to trigger Doc's compassionate response.*

"Naw, you just lazy," Doc told Charley. He knew his friend was lying but also knew Charley would confide in him eventually, and he always did. "In my medical opinion, y'all just need adrenaline. Yup, y'all need something to stir your blood, get you moving again. This is a perfect adventure, secretly traveling in a country where the citizens each believe they are more entitled than the other guy and everyone is armed to the teeth." Doc cringed at the level of violence that erupted once the U.S. became a totalitarian state. However, what was most curious to him was that the Conservatives always feared the Liberal Government would come for their guns. But in reality, it was the Conservative Government who went for the conservative guns because a dictatorship cannot allow their captive citizens weapons.

"You're medical opinion? Doc, l am not your patient, and you aren't a Doctor. You are an old, beat-up combat medic from long ago. Yes, you have a Silver Star and three Purple Hearts, but, man, that was forty-four years ago! You grow medical marijuana now, dude."

Doc's face flushed with anger. "What part of the phrase 'medical marijuana' didn't you understand? I run a clinic, Charles, a clinic for suffering people. I have patients! I treat conditions! I have an aura!"

"Doc," Charley replied, "you are a Medical Doctor as an ice cream vendor is to a five-star restaurant."

"That seems to be a little harsh, Charles," Doc sniffed.

"Harsh? Dude, you have the bedside manner of Attila the Hun."

"Charles," Doc sighed. He hated to explain this but realized his friend did not understand his perspective. "My medical skills were developed under the most hazardous of conditions; gunfire, mortars, grenades, rockets, booby traps, even knives. Every moment I was terrified for my life. You do understand? So terror, dude, conditioned me. I get in, I get the sucker stabilized, and I get us the hell out of there. No time for small talk, no time for pleasantry. My medical training and my traumas are the same."

Charley had seen his friend up to his elbows in blood and gore as deadly fire rained all around him. Doc was the bravest man Charley ever knew, so he figured he had earned his rough bark.

Twelve miles inside the border, Charley pulled over at a small Laundromat called "Grubs and Suds," an automated beer/Laundromat combination beloved by bachelors around the world.

"Luck, Idaho, pop. 231," Doc read the sign. "We are in Luck! Let's get drunk and steal clothing. Of course, all they would have is cheap beer and coveralls."

"Very funny, Doc." Charley knew they needed to get in disguise before going much farther. "But you are half right. We need transport and new duds,"

Doc pointed to an Amazon Prime Delivery Van sitting outside the Gas Station/KFC/Hardee's/Long John Silver store. "Ever see a combination like that?"

"Looks like they sell whiskey too. Nothing better than a full-service gas station."

The Amazon Prime Van driver emerged from his truck, struggling with several heavy packages, and disappeared into the station.

"Why looky there," Doc chuckled. "You know, Charles, when the lawman puts out an APB, an All Points Bulletin, for a stolen Amazon Truck? Out of hundreds of identical vans, which particular truck are they going to stop?"

"Good idea, Doc," Charley said as he parked their stolen 2005 Chevy. "Let's go."

Running across the parking lot, Charley reached the idling Amazon Prime Van and pulled open the sliding door. Grinning at Doc, he dropped into the driver's seat, buckled up, released the brake, and in moments were silently rolling down a dark street. The early sun was breaking the horizon, lightening the gloom to a morning haze in the East.

"Wow, would you look at that?"Charley pointed to the sky. Doc muttered. "I have never seen that before."

"Me either, Doc. I didn't know the sky was supposed to glow like a neon sign."

"Aurora Borealis in Utah?"

"No, Doc, I've seen the Aurora, and that isn't it. I am seventy-three years old, Doc, and I have never seen the sky do that."

"Whoa," Doc shivered. "The temperature just took a fucking nose dive, dude."

Charley switched on the heater. "It is only September, and it shouldn't get this cold this fast."

"Wow! Man that chills my very soul!"

"More than cold, Doc, we better find shelter and fast," Charley looked at the sky, and something triggered in his memory- something horrible. The smell of ozone was intense.

"Doc, we need to get to that next town and right now! We need to get inside!"

"Okay, by me." Doc quickly scanned the high desert topography. "Let's get moving, and do not stop. We're just a few miles outside of Beatty, Montana! But we can't stay long. We have to meet up with Pawnee soon!"

The stars seemed to winkle, disappearing and reappearing as the glow of the sky waxed and waned.

"Man, the temperature is dropping fast." Even with the heater going full blast, Doc could see his breath.

"What I have heard," Charley said as he accelerated down the deserted night road. "We have an unstable atmosphere thanks to global climate shifts; because of this, the boundaries between the layers of Earth's atmosphere had begun to leak." Ahead, in the far distance, Charley could see the lights of a small town, a four-store downtown surrounded by citizens' housing.

"Remember your high school science, Doc?"

"Ah am a certified Phlebotomist, sir!"

"You stick people with needles."

"Nevertheless, I am trained."

"Trained? Doc, you practice by throwing darts at a barroom target."

"That is a rumor, sir, just a rumor!"

"Okay, sure," Charley did not want to get sidetracked by one of Doc's long and endless monologues. "Listen, the atmosphere is divided into layers. The ground level is called the Troposphere, then going up to Stratosphere, Mesosphere, Thermosphere, and the very top, Exosphere. Does this sound familiar?"

"Sir," Doc declared. "Why I recall one time when I was teaching science at the Junior College level and I..."

"Doc, you took that same basic science class so many times they finally made you the teacher. Relax, Doc, I'll get to the point. The difference in temperature between atmospheric layers is what's important. Here on the ground, it's September we have 50-60 degrees. Up in the Mesosphere, it can be -90 degrees, and the Exosphere is outer space. Doc, I am trying to explain that outer space penetrates our protective atmosphere right down to the ground. In ten minutes, we could go from 65 degrees F. to -90 F. Do you have any idea the damage that will do?"

"Charles, there is a gas station in Beatty, pull in there."

"We don't need gas. Didn't you hear what I said?"

"Yes, sir, Charles, I heard, and I understand'.

But that there filling' station is also a Restaurant an' they have a walk-in cooler I'll bet, a cooler that will isolate us from the cold, ironically. Gone be a chilly night in the neighborhood."

"A cooler to save us from the cold. Doc, you're a genius!"

"I know, I have been telling you that for over fifty years, and you're just now figuring it out?"

$$\sim 9 \sim$$

CHAPTER EIGHT

"We aren't lost! We're going east!" Muh pointed forward. "Straight ahead!"

"Just because the last sign you saw had 'East' in the title doesn't mean we're headed East, you know," Jee muttered darkly.

"You're kind of suspicious. You know that?" Muh told Jee. "Untrusting."

"Yeah, well, you tell us lots of things, half of which aren't true, and the other half are bald-faced lies. Do you know what they have in common? You!"

"Hey, I resent that!"

"Muh, you wouldn't know the truth if it buggered you."

"I would too!"

Muh peered through the steering wheel anxiously, trying his best to remember if East was the East he thought it was. *Or is south really more north-like?* Muh would never admit he was awful at directions. He had the authority to maintain. If he realized he didn't know things, his brothers would start to doubt. Once they suspected, they would no longer follow him. Even if it meant leading them off into the wilderness to die of thirst, authority and custom must be maintained.

Muh stared forlornly at the maze of control knobs, switches, buttons, and gauges in front of him. A small light to the far right of the panel was glowing red, and it was in the shape of a small thermometer.

"Are we there yet?" Yaz asked from the backseat. "Muh, how much longer?"

Muh worriedly studied the gauges. Now the little red thermometer light was fiercely flashing, and he wondered if that was a little bad or a big bad. He reasoned that if it were a big 'bad' light, it would be closer to the center not moved way over to the side. He decided to ignore it for now.

As they rolled down the highway, Yaz studied the sky, peering at the rough, roiled clouds, the peculiar color, and the smell. The smell is what alerted him. Yaz began digging around in his backpack and pulled out a small, silver instrument. Turning it on, he began studying the dial intently.

"We'll be there any moment," Muh announced while speeding across the vast Montana prairies at a bone-rattling eighty-two miles per hour. He hoped that was true.

"Any moment, my ass," Jee leered at Muh. "Look out there, nothing but nothing, miles of sand, dirt, and rocks, covered by mountains of sand, dirt, and rocks!"

Muh feverishly studied the control board because another red light was blinking. This one was shaped like a little engine. Muh wondered if that was telling him the motor was just fine—maybe the red color was cheerful and optimistic. "Hard to say...." Muh muttered.

The speedometer pinged ninety-two miles per hour, which was a pretty big deal for a hotwired 1954 Studebaker Hawk with 400,000 plus miles. Jee was impressed.

"Hey, have you guys seen the sky lately?" Yaz was looking up in fascination. "I don't even know what the names for those colors are."

Suddenly, the front end started to shake. Then it began to wobble.

"Is this supposed to shake like this?" Jee asked.

"Of course, it is," Muh quickly assured him. "This is perfectly normal." Muh reminded himself that leaders never doubt, and leaders always lead with absolute authority and conviction, no matter what.

"Stop worrying. I am in control. Everything is just perfect," Muh told Jee over the thumping, rattling, grinding, whining, and screeching noises coming from the venerable old Studebaker.

"Okay?" Jee didn't buy that for a minute.

Suddenly the entire interior of the vehicle filled with a bright red glow.

Muh stared at the dashboard, but that wasn't causing the light.

"What the...?" Muh quickly glanced out the rearview mirror.

"What the hell is that?"

A flashing red and blue set of lights was parked on their back bumper.

"This is normal too?" thought Jee as he stared out the back window.

"It's a police drone!" Yaz was fascinated.

Now blue and white lights were added to the red-blue as the interior of the Studebaker lit up like a stage set for Saturday Night Fever; lights were flickering, flashing, strobes added a sirocco beat to the drum of commands.

"RrrrrrrRrrrrrrRrrrrrr! RrrrrrrRrrrrrRrrrr Pull Over! Pull Over! Pull Over!"

Oooh, Muh thought. *This could be a big bad."*

"RrrrrrrrrrrrrRrrrrrrrrrrrRrrrrrrrrr...Homeland Security Highway Patrol. Pullover!"

The UCS Homeland Security Highway Patrol drone was now insistently inches off their rear window.

"Pull over! Pull Over! Pullover!"

"You know," Yaz said, peering out the back window. "I think that thing has Gatling guns and.....two air-to-ground missiles...one says... 'Protect,' the other, 'Serve'.'"

"Ah, boys," Muh muttered. "We might have another complication."

Although the flashing blue, red, and white lights blinded him, Jee looked down at all the red lights across the dashboard. Then looking back at the military-style drone parked on their back bumper, he said, "You think?"

"Muh," Yaz staring at the twin air-to-ground missiles, said, "I think this thing is locked and loaded."

"I can outrun him!" Squeaked Muh as he jammed his tiny paw down on the accelerator of the 1954 Studebaker Hawk.

Suddenly, thick black smoke began to seep from under the dash.

"Uh-oh." Muh smelled an odor of hot boiling oil.

"1954 Studebaker Hawk," the drone commanded. "Pull over immediately. Pullover, pull over, pull over, pull over, pull over...!"

Muh, determined to succeed and show his leadership skills, pushed the old car brutally.

Smoking, gasping, sputtering, valves chattering, the Studebaker blazed down the crumbling interstate highway with a tiny Montana State Patrol Drone flashing red, blue, and white lights now suction-cupped to their rear window.

Yaz stared in fascination at the weaponry six inches from his nose.

"Pull over, pull over, pull, over...!"

"RrrrrrRrrrrRrrrrr!"

"Look out!" Jee pointed ahead.

Muh had to turn abruptly into the left lane to avoid an Amazon Prime van slow poking along in the right road.

$\sim$ 10 $\sim$

CHAPTER NINE

Pawnee slammed the venerable Pontiac Firebird around the tight corner and floored it. The old street rod responded well. Pawnee glanced in the rearview mirror in time to see the following Homeland Security Dodge Durango slide around the corner behind him.

To his dismay, the world was wired; not only were all commercial security cameras linked, but now Google Ring, installed on millions of homes, was also part of the law enforcement observation network. Whole neighborhoods and every intersection were a maze of spy cameras. Once they started looking, there was no place to hide.

Worse, two weeks of sneaking and peaking in the United Christian States of America had produced nothing. He was sure the authorities in Butte had some mysterious artifact, but where? Sneaking into the Artifacts Division of Homeland Security had proved difficult and fruitless; there was an Artifact, it was from England, but that was all he knew.

Glancing in the rearview mirror, the Durango had gained ground. He cursed. He had been careless, not paying attention to details; something he had spent his entire life learning to avoid had plagued him on this mission. *Getting old, me.* Pawnee sighed. Lately, his focus wasn't good, his ability to concentrate even less. It was September 6, and he had two days to meet up with the guys Chowder was sending to help him. Pawnee felt stupid and he had nothing.

Pawnee felt weary to the bone. Wake up! He needed to get his ass in gear and get the job done. This was a mission. He had never failed a mission; from HALO parachute jumps in Vietnam to the caves of Afghanistan, he did not fail.

Back tires screeching in protest, blue smoke rolling behind him, Pawnee whipped into a U-turn, turning back toward Butte, an unexpected move that would throw off any roadblock Homeland had already placed to stop him.

Momentarily flustered by his move, the Dodge Durango slowed, giving him more separation. Right now, he needed time; time to plan his next few moves.

"Oh shit!" Pawnee had to swerve hard into the left passing lane to avoid a slow-moving Amazon Prime delivery van.

****

A 1954 Studebaker Hawk roared by the Amazon Prime van so fast the vehicle rocked heavily in the wake.

"Wow," Charley exclaimed, "that dude was hauling ass."

Just moments later, a bright red Pontiac Firebird closely followed by a black Dodge Durango screamed by, causing the van to swerve violently again.

"What is going on?"

They had just crested a small but very steep hill when Charley and Doc saw the whole thing occur right in front of them.

~ 11 ~

CHAPTER TEN

The 1954 Studebaker Hawk was pushed to the limit.

"Rrrrr...Rrrrr...Pullover, pull over!"

Muh knew the situation was grim. Red lights blazed across the dash, but still, he needed a little more. Muh reassured himself: The color red in some cultures is considered good news. Observing the string of red lights on the dash, he hoped this was true.

Glancing down at his maps spread on his lap, he had drawn a red crayon path to Mission Success: Interstate Highway 15 to Butte, Montana, then I-90 and I-94 across the nation to the Great Lakes and then dropping down South on I-65 straight into Indianapolis. "This would be a lot simpler if it weren't so complicated," Muh muttered. "Why do they have so many numbers?" He could feel his authority melting away the longer it took to get to Indianapolis.

"Rrrrrrrr....Rrrrrrr...Pull over, pull over!"

They were roaring past a prominent billboard advertising 'Dixie Dolly Dachshunds Pet Farm, 2 miles. Ahead' and had just crested a small but very steep hill when the 1954 Studebaker Hawk gave up the ghost.

The venerable old vehicle coughed a piston rod straight through the engine block, followed by a volcanic explosion of viscous oil and dense steam so fierce it shattered metal and blew off the right front tire.

The 1954 Studebaker Hawk dropped to the pavement like a downward dog at the yoga studio, flashing yellow sparks erupted, thick, viscous, steam billowed, and the black, tarry pavement curled and churned up as they slid to a grinding twisting stop.

Muh hung from the steering wheel, exhausted from the struggle to control the crashing vehicle.

"Rrrrrrrr...Grrrr...Stay in the vehicle, do not attempt to escape..." The Drone recording changed.

****

The swarthy, fat UCS Homeland Security agent driving the Dodge Durango was grinning like a shark. Pawnee didn't need to look in the rearview mirror again to know the enemy was hot on his ass.

Just cresting a small but steep hill at 96 MPH, Pawnee stared in shocked dismay. Right in front of him was a broken-down 1954 Studebaker Hawk, lying dead in the road, pouring smoke and oil into the air.

A collision was inevitable and awesome.

"Oh geez, hold on, me!" Pawnee braced himself and glanced in the rearview mirror. He saw the horrified look on the Homeland Security agent probably matched his own.

Pawnee tried to make himself small as the first collision with the Studebaker jarred his teeth, then he rebounded from that collision just in time to set up for the arrival of the oncoming Durango. Like bumper cars at ninety miles per hour, bits and pieces of metal, rubber, glass, and plastic exploded outward as the cars crashed together again.

The UCS Homeland Security Dodge Durango met the rear end of Pawnee's Pontiac Firebird with a thunderous fiery crash.

The three vehicles, like pool balls, ricocheted off each other, each spinning or rolling in different directions.

The Studebaker rammed straight down the road like a drag racer accelerating along the track, trailing engine pieces, bits of metal, and glass.

The Pontiac, squashed now front and back, spun off to the right and crashed into a deep ditch.

The Durango, filled with Homeland Security Agents, did not fare as well. Siren stilling moaning, the light bar blazing red and blue and white reflections off the cliff face as they went over the steep embankment dropping straight into the north fork of Little Sheep Creek.

Crawling out of the destroyed Firebird, Pawnee flopped into the ditch beside the rutted, paved highway and huffed air for a moment. Glad to be alive, but terrified he had lost body parts.

Gradually, he worked up the courage to run his hands along his huge body, checking for damage. It didn't seem to be any; his hands didn't come away wet with blood, and he could feel everything.

"Huuuugggggghhh!" He rolled over and pushed himself to a kneeling position.

"What happened here?" he muttered. "Firebird, she is toast." He looked over at the smoldering car. He kind of liked that car. It seemed to run pretty well for a stolen car, and Pawnee was sorry to see it wind up totaled.

He felt dizzy disoriented. The stench of burned rubber made him slightly nauseous. But his mind screamed danger. Getting shakily to his feet, he glanced around for the cause of his alarm. There were three cars involved. All badly mangled, an Amazon Prime Van was pulling to the side of the road.

He took a deep breath, no immediate threats. "Calm yourself, me," He muttered.

Looking straight across the road from him, Pawnee saw two trails of heavy skid marks leading directly through a metal traffic barrier. The earth was torn up and ended suddenly in a steep drop-off. He went over and looked down, 400 feet or so. The Dodge Durango lay upside down, deep in the middle of a flowing river.

Pawnee had no idea if there were survivors down there. Curious about the people in the car he initially hit, Pawnee looked back across the road. Whatever that car used to be, it wasn't any longer, and he had no idea what kind of car it was.

Just then, Pawnee was slammed by the arrival of help.

****

"Pull over, Charles, we have work to do!" Doc shouted, already free from his seat belt. Doc was ready to be shot out of a cannon, so eager to reach the survivors.

One crash survivor, a large man in a bright yellow and purple Hawaiian shirt, was standing, wobbly, beside a destroyed Pontiac Firebird.

Charley pulled over just as the large man crossed the two-lane highway, following a rutted and churned-up trail of grass and soil, leading to an abrupt drop-off.

The man in the Hawaiian shirt was peering over the edge, presumably at the vehicle that went over.

"I'm coming!" Doc was out of the car like a shot, racing across the road in pursuit of his medical emergency. Doc was struck by how many times he had done this, rushing to the scene of some tragedy. The feelings of adrenaline, preparing himself for whatever blood and gore and hysteria he would find, mentally reviewing emergency first aid practices to keep the patient alive until more advanced help arrived.

Charley watched Doc respond and admired his friend. He wished he had such enthusiasm for something. Anything. He knew Doc was driven by more vital forces than compassion, more fundamental, even primal. Doc told him once, in a spirit of drunken camaraderie, that he was drawn to these situations because he needed to be needed. It filled an ugly emptiness and temporarily silenced that voice of self-hate that shouted in the void.

Charley reminded him that a man with three Purple Hearts and a Silver Star shouldn't concern himself with self-image. The medals do it for him.

They never talked of it again, but Charley Bones wondered what had happened to his friend in childhood that ruined his self-respect.

Doc was one of the finest people Charley had ever known, but he was also the most self-hating person he had ever known as well.

Pawnee backed away from the edge and was just turning to go to the wrecked Studebaker when a bearded nut job in a white seersucker suit assaulted him.

"Where are you hurt?" the skinny man with long white hair and beard demanded, prodding and poking. "Can you describe the pain? Where is the blood? What year is it? Do you know the time?" Quickly Doc was working through his assessment protocols.

"Chee, back away, you," Pawnee pushed the man away. He had no idea who the man was and, besides the man, looked huhu...crazy.

Doc, driven by traumatic forces only he could know, continued to seek a pulse, check pupils for a head injury, and palpate limbs for breaks because he wasn't going to back off regardless of protest. Doc knew damaged people needed him, and he would not allow anything, including the victim themselves, to interfere with his care.

Pawnee batted his hands away. "You keep your hands to yourself, or I gone bust you one, Brah!"

But Doc was set on being Doc.

Charley crossed the highway in time to see the large man in the Hawaiian shirt lift Doc into the air and fling him six feet away, as easy as dumping a wastebasket.

"Doc! Doc!" Charley yelled, hurrying across the road. He pulled his Browning 9mm. "Drop your hands and step back!" Bones had his weapon out, trained on the big man. "Get back, now!"

The man didn't raise his hands, but he did give Charley his full attention.

"Doc! Doc? You okay?" Charley shook his friend, "you alive, partner?'

"I'm okay. I'm okay. I'm okay." Doc was seeing double, and his ears rang.

"Sure you are." Bones kept the large man in view but worried Doc didn't look very good.

"What is your story, 'hula boy'?" Bones asked the man. "You like throwing people around?"

Pawnee realized he was not being attacked and regretted his quick defenses.

He raised his hands. "No worry, no harm." He looked down at Doc, now ignoring Charley. "Chee, brah, sorry, didn't know you were trying to help."

Doc was sitting up, wavering, still a little woozy from hitting the pavement.

"I'm okay, I'm okay," Doc kept saying.

"Your eyes are crossed, dude," Charley told him. "Just like normal."

Pawnee studied the two, reasonably sure he knew them. His eidetic memory had kept him alive his entire life, so recognition of faces was crucial. His head still swam from the accident, but he realized fortune had smiled on him again, as it had so many times. He thought it funny that fortune should send him the very people he was looking for: Bones and Betters.

Suddenly an icy wind caused them all to shiver, as the temperature dropped ten degrees in just seconds. Everybody went silent, hunkered within to withstand the fierce and numbing cold. A bitter wind arose to bring the scent of dust and sage to them.

"Charles," Doc held up an arm, and Charley helped him up. "We got to get to Beatty before this shit turns ugly."

"Whoooo, that is chill, brah!" Pawnee said, and he could see his breath. "What is it, September?"

"We've got a real bad weather situation brewing. We need to get under cover of some kind, I think," Charley said through gritted teeth. "Anybody alive in that vehicle?" He said, pointing to the steaming Studebaker.

The large man shrugged."No know, brah."

"We need to check that last vehicle and get out of the cold, fast!"

"Makes sense to me!" Doc looked at the large man. "My name's John James Jefferson Betters the Fourth; y'all can call me Doc." They shook hands, and Doc hurried off to the third vehicle.

The large man nodded.

Charley and the man shook hands as Doc hurried off to the last vehicle.

"Charley Bones," Bones said.

"Good to meet you," The man replied but said nothing further.

"Your name is...?"

~ 12 ~

CHAPTER ELEVEN

"Reality is merely an illusion, albeit a very persistent one." Albert Einstein

"Charles! Charles! Ya'll get your ass over here now, right now!"

The 1954 Studebaker Hawk laid in the middle of the road like a run-over turtle.

Charley hurried over to the battered old car, the rear end crushed, every window shattered, oil-water pooled around the front of the vehicle, and a thin stream of anti-freeze scented steam arose from the engine.

There was no movement inside the car.

Doc staring into the vehicle interior intently pointed inside. "I think y'all need to see this first hand."

"Are they all right? Are they hurt very badly?"

"Now, that's a little hard to say."

"What the hell kind of answer is that, Doc? Are these people okay or not?"

"Now that's a little hard to say too."

Charley Bones ignored Doc and looked inside the front of the vehicle.

"Holy shit." He said softly. "What the fuck have we got here? Green Beagles?"

Muh's head was spinning as he looked at the humans gathering around them. He was seeing multiples of everything and was overwhelmed by the crowd.

"Arrgggh," Muh said, trying to explain their presence.

"One, two, three. Three miniature dogs with opposable thumbs on their paws? Wearing backpacks? Dark glasses? You see them too?"

Doc nodded.

Pawnee came to the vehicle and stared inside.

"Chee boy, dis is one for the record. Aliens puppies?" Pawnee was genuinely impressed. "Aliens?" he said again. This was very unique through his nearly seventy years of adventure and discovery.

Muh reached over and jostled Jee. "Hey, wake up, wake up, you have a problem."

"Problem?" Jee muttered, trying to keep his stomach from falling out. "What do you mean, 'I' have a problem'?"

"You have failed to protect your mission commander who is about to be captured by savages. Go on, show them your teeth! Growl at them."

"Maybe capture and torture would be an improvement," Jee muttered.

"Now what?" Charley watched as Doc slowly opened the door and leaned in.

Doc wasn't sure what first aid to apply to extraterrestrials, but he took it as a good sign that none seemed to be leaking fluids of any kind. That was a good start, and he would have to trust whatever veterinary medicine he could recall from his Army training.

Two of the three seemed conscious and were making growly noises at each other. A third one suddenly sat up in the back seat, calmly studying the humans, ears perked up.

Now what? Doc asked himself.

The arrival of another sudden cold snap decided him. Doc shivered intensely, then picked up the nearest little green alien and turned to Charley. "Let's get them to the car and warm them up."

"Hey, get your fucking hands off me!" Doc's alien-dog blurted out in English. Muh was appalled he was being maltreated.

Doc stopped and looked down. "Ya'll mouthy little character ain't ya? You speak English?"

"Of course I do, better than you! Now unhand me, you fiend!"

"Doc, maybe we should think about this a bit. They might bite, and we have no idea what kind of extraterrestrial rabies they could have. Mange, maybe even fleas...?" Charley was also reasonably uncomfortable with the idea of bringing unknown extraterrestrial aliens to their Amazon Prime Van, as this was their only means of escape and safety. "Ah, I don't know, Doc; maybe we shouldn't bring them to our truck just yet; they could be dangerous, diseased even."

"Hey, we've had our shots!" Muh fired back, insulted. "We are VIA! Very Important Aliens!"

"You are very important to whom?"

"Come on, Charles," fussed Doc, "It is getting colder, dude, grab one! they don't seem to be aggressive, kind of soft and furry. "

"Get your hands off me!" Shrieked Jee as Charley picked him up. "I'll sue your fat ass in Galactic Courts for maltreating an alien!" He wriggled in Charley's arm, trying to escape.

"Pawnee, grab that one before he gets away."

"Damn, you got cold hands!" Jee snapped at the human. "I am a VIA! I have rights!"

Jee was growling, Muh was whining, Yaz sat quiet and watchful as the large human in the bright shirt reached out and nabbed him.

"What now?" Charley asked Doc. "We have a mission, you know. Alien dog sitting isn't part of it. But we can't throw them out and drive off, Doc. I doubt humans have a good reputation in the cosmos, to begin with, and abandoning three green alien beagles to starve in the wilderness probably would be a negative."

"Well, does Beatty, Montana have an ER set up for extraterrestrials? Are there homeless shelters in place for transient aliens? Or are we headed for the Humane Society?" Doc retorted. "We have us a delicate situation."

"You will take us directly to Indianapolis, Indiana...please," Muh ordered. He added the 'please' to see if it made any difference.

Scrambling back into the Amazon Prime Van, they closed the doors, started it up, and turned the heater to 'high.' Charley looked back at the three green Beagles. "We haven't got much time before more cops show up, but before we travel, we need to get something clear. Who or what are you?" This was the last thing Charley wanted to see, another distraction from their mission. Finding Pawnee Painter was an absolute miracle to begin with, but what do they do with alien beagles?

Muh looked at Jee.

"We are aliens. Take us to your leaders!" Muh had heard this was the more traditional greeting for alien-human interaction.

"Where are you from?"

"Not from around here," Jee added helpfully.

"No shit? Why don't you clarify that a little? Charley looked them over, varying shades of green but looking like Beagles, smelling of sage, peanut butter, and old socks.

"I have never met an alien, let alone an alien canine," Doc told them. "What are ya'll doing on our planet? Do you fetch?"

"We are on a sacred mission for humanity."

"Sure you are," Charley told them. "Just how do three broke-dick dogs driving a rundown Studebaker into Butte, Montana save humanity?" He wondered if maybe they planned some kind of bizarre ad campaign for the underprivileged.

"We are on a mission." Muh declared proudly. "The Galactic High Council for this segment of the Cosmos has ordained we be here. We bear a great gift for humanity. We are traveling to Indianapolis, Indiana, to meet with the President of the United Christian States. We understand he is the head of the Christians, and we will give him this great gift. Next, we have to go to the Middle East and visit Sheik Mohallah Muhammad, a prime cleric in Mecca.

"Then off to Israel to jawbone with good old Isaac Perez Shimon, the Prime Minister of the Jews!" Jee added.

"Wow," Yaz muttered. "I had no idea we even had an itinerary." This explained all the vaccinations.

"What 'great gift'?" Doc asked.

Muh looked at Jee.

"We can't say."

"You can't or won't."

"Our mission is good, compassionate...necessary."

"Ya'll be going to speak with the leaders of the three great desert religions that dominate this planet. Why is that?"

"To help them, of course."

"Help them how?"

"Help them understand their irrelevance."

"Damn," Charley grinned. "I gotta hear this! Can we come along?"

~ 13 ~

CHAPTER TWELVE

"Quiet, dear, quiet," Bernard hushed her. His little President was cut and bruised, but she was alive, for that he was fearfully grateful. "Another patrol is due," he reminded her.

"Juwanda." Chowder said with bitter tears.

Although the missile didn't strike directly, the near-miss did enough damage. Both Chowder and Juwanda flew the helicopter in violent defensive maneuvers hoping to shake the missile. But they lost lift and control, so the helicopter, too close to the ground to recover, crashed.

The crash cost Juwanda her life.

Chowder could barely move her head; neck and back were still stiff and sore.

"We are somewhere in Southern Oregon, the Rogue River Forest area. I have no idea where we are. I think we need to head that way, North." she said to Bernard, hoping it was North. The forest surrounding them mainly was Ponderosa Pine. The air smelled of pine tar and dust.

Bernard shivered. As her chief of staff, it was his duty to know her enemies. Bernard felt humiliated, and in shock, he had let her down. If they were indeed down in Southern Oregon, it had to be the White Christian Militia, and they owned this area of Oregon.

Chowder walked carefully, quietly. She knew they were being hunted, the shoot down was deliberate, and the Republicans had sent teams into the forest looking for survivors. Coming around the curve in the trail, she saw a sign fixed to a tree, carved from a slab of wood, said: Dimmer Trail 2 mi/Neala Pond 4.5.

"We should stick with the Neala trail," she told him. Bessie May was distraught, and they were both in rough shape. Bernard had a limp he was trying to hide from her.

Bernard followed his President, his misery mounting. The sting of his betrayal seemed to grow more intense. Informing Senator Imahuffin of The Einstein Stone mission was a mistake. He saw it now. But at the time, it sort of made sense. He didn't think the mission was a big deal at all, and including the Conservatives in something like this should have given them the feeling of being part of the government rather than just critics of it. All Bernard wanted was for everyone to get along. Bernard had no idea how to tell his beloved President that he had made a horrid mistake.

But the worst part: Did telling Imahuffin have anything to do with being attacked and shot down?

Bernard was sick with fear he had caused this situation.

The trail paralleled a large river that tumbled down through a rocky canyon. The scrub oak and Ponderosa Pines percentage would identify this as the Rogue Forest and not the wetter, cooler Umpqua farther north, so they were east of Medford, Oregon.

"Hush," Bernard whispered sharply. He crouched and looked around furtively.

A small bird chittered angrily at their presence.

Bessie May was alerted to movement in the tree line to her right.

A small group of soldiers appeared and spotted them immediately. They paused for a moment, and then their Sergeant motioned them forward.

"They've seen us!" Bernard cried aloud. "You are saved, Madam President, oh at last!"

Immensely relieved he could now get his President to safety, Bernard jumped up, waving his arms and calling for their attention.

"No!" Chowder tried to pull him back into the underbrush. "No, Bernard, we don't know who they are!"

"Look!" Bernard said, standing and pointing then waving at the soldiers. "They're in uniform. Probably the National Guard."

"For God's sake, Bernard," Chowder hissed at him. "You don't know who they are!

But Bernard only waved the soldiers on more vigorously. He had failed her. Failed his President to protect her, but he would not disappoint her now. Bernard was determined to get his President to safety.

"Come on, Bessie May, it's okay."

Reluctantly, she came out of the brush, stepped onto the trail, and walked toward Bernard.

Chowder saw the Sergeant ahead stop abruptly and point at her.

"Bernard!" She had a bad feeling.

Bernard turned back toward her with a smile of relief when the soldiers opened fire, sending rounds through Bernard's skull, killing him instantly.

~ 14 ~

CHAPTER THIRTEEN

"HANDS UP! DO NOT MOVE! YOU ARE UNDER ARREST!"

A Drone with a twelve-foot wingspan bristling with armaments drifted over them.

"UNITED CHRISTIAN STATES OF AMERICA HOMELAND SECU-RITY DRONE A34C H" stenciled on one side. "JESUS LOVES the US" stenciled on the other.

SPOT. Strategic Police Operations/ Traffic had spotted them.

"Stop! This is the Homeland Security Montana State Highway Patrol. You are ordered to stand; still, hands in sight, do not move!"

SPOT hovered over them menacingly.

Nobody moved.

This pissed Pilot Major Maria Prince off. *Come on, do something, and give me an excuse to roast your asses.* Prince had a short temper and a nasty drug habit, meaning her view of reality was complicated by violence, delusions, and hallucinations.

All six of the strange detainees stood motionless.

"No move," Pawnee whispered. He hated an enemy he could not look in the face, and Pawnee swore long ago that he wanted to look in the eyes of the person who finally killed him.

Okay, fine, cop killers! Have it your way. Major Prince had just seen the video of the upside-down Dodge Durango and the dead agents inside. Like every cop anywhere in the world, Prince bristled at fellow cops dying of anything but old age. No one killed cops on her beat and got away with it.

SPOT fired a warning shot; a laser bolt exploded when it hit the earth leaving a raw wound.

"HAND UPS, DO NOT MOVE, HANDS UP, DO NOT MOVE," Prince commanded over their PA system.

She sighted the Gatling guns on the three...whatever's. Prince blinked and rubbed her eyes. *Three humans and what? Little green...poodles, overgrown rats, what?*

The three humans had their hands up high, waiting for the next move while the green dogs sat quietly, tongues lolling, ears erect, also waiting. Their vestigial autonomic response signaling 'danger' created raspberry scents filling the air.

Maj. Prince quickly turned SPOT's camera filters on as she realized this was no ordinary crime scene.

SPOT's onboard AI computer surveyed the scene, searching millions of algorithms for an appropriate response. What was called for in this case? Traffic? Law enforcement? Animal Control officer? Immigrations? NASA? Pest Eradication?

SPOT'S Terabytes whirred, and the synapses of Major Prince fired, but no answers.

What to do, what to do? Maj. Prince had a problem. Not for the first time, Prince wished she did just a little bit less crystal meth. Staring at the three odd-shaped beagles, she was unsure whether they were real or drug-induced hallucinations. Invasion or delirium?

So, Major Prince fell back on her orders and instincts, reaching for the triggers to blast these cop-killing dirt bags to dust.

~ 15 ~

CHAPTER FOURTEEN

"Everything is determined, every beginning and ending, by forces over which we have no control. It is determined for the insect, as well as for the star. Human beings, vegetables, or cosmic dust, we all dance to a mysterious tune, intoned in the distance by an invisible piper."
Albert Einstein

"Sir, your morning brunch of hummingbird tongues and squirrel testicles is ready," came the unctuous voice of Price Wayne as he laid out the lunch repast.

Barcelona lazily rolled over to survey his brunch.

"It had better be the Ruby Red Throat ones!" Barcelona told him. "I can't stand those Purple Throated Caribs! They taste like bitter almonds!"

"I know, sir."

"Oh...and Price," Barcelona looked up at his servant. Price was white. White hair, white skin, white nails, only his eyes had color: one blue, one brown. "Geez," Barcelona grumbled, trying to shield himself. "Price, you are so goddamned white the sun bounces off you like a mirror. Grow melanin!"

"Yes, sir, I shall certainly try, sir."

"Now, put in a call to what's his name, the new Chief of the Joint Chiefs, General Fig, and have a tactical strike plan drawn up to take out Bahrain's location, okay. Nothing nuclear...let's just use F-16's and air-to-ship killer missiles...use the Gatling cannons on survivors."

"Excellent, sir," Price replied and backed out of Barcelona's presence. "I will have your Air Commander complete this and put it on your desk within the hour. Anything else, sir?"

"Yes, where are we in the seventy-two-hour countdown to hit Cascadia?"

"Missiles are ready, sir anytime, sir. It appears wise of you to arm one of your yachts with ship-to-ship missiles. How very thorough, sir."

"I know for a fact Bahrain," Grumbled Barcelona, "is part of some nonsense to instigate Matriarchal ideas into our well-ordered Patriarchy." Barcelona laughed. "As if fucking women could think! Fucking broads, they go crazy once a month; I can't trust them! You know, I wouldn't doubt that bitch is in league with Bessie May Chowder. That little orphan nigger is a bigger pain in my ass than anything I can recall."

Price Wayne wondered if he'd studied harder in school, he might not be standing here, playing second fiddle to an idiot. But then, it was his choice, this or enlisting in the military. So he chose comfortable, well-paying employment over killing people for the US Army. Wayne wondered if he'd made a mistake.

"Price," Barcelona was feeling in a magnanimous mood now that the race was on for the Einstein Stone. "What would I do without you? To reward you, I believe I will allow you and your wife to have another child...do so immediately before I change my mind."

Price's face blanched.

Seeing the reaction, Barcelona felt pleased his servant was so grateful. He waved his fingers airily. "Thanks and gratitude are not necessary, Price. I am a magnanimous ruler."

Barcelona prided himself on the proper care and maintenance of lesser beings. He knew they responded to praise and rewards— like white mice were given food pellets to push a metal bar or an electric shock when they didn't. Humans were no more complicated than that.

Price replied, his jaws tight, "Yes, sir, thank you so much, sir. My wife will be very pleased, as the last two died of scurvy...so again, thank you, sir!" Price was amazed his voice was so calm and pleasant, while acid boiled his stomach lining.

Barcelona sighed, *so much responsibility, so many important decisions.* He decided to nap a little after lunch.

"Go!" Barcelona ordered. "Oh, and Price, name the new child after me, there, that's a good man."
****

His mind a maelstrom of rage, revenge, and resolution, Price Wayne wanted to howl in outrage; he wanted to hit something as he stomped down the deck, returning to the galley deep in the bowels of the Yacht.

"Go on, add it," he told the master chef, Wing Top, brusquely. The odors of sizzling onion and garlic filled the galley as he watched the Chef sauté the food.

"The warfarin rat poison seemed to go well with Ruby Hummingbirds," Wing Top told him as he opened the bright yellow and red box. "Although, I think it lends a slightly bitter taste with Spotted Owl. It just all depends on the bird, you know, like cooking pigeon...or bald eagles...similar really when you think about it. Now, they like to have a toxin that is...."

"Never mind the cooking lessons, just do it, okay?" Price wanted Barcelona to die in agony, just like his first two children. When Price learned the newly formed UCS of A, Council of Clerics ruled Health Care was an individual responsibility, not a burden to taxpayers, he joined the rebellion. In the words of the Chief Cleric, Council of Clerics, UCS, "A sick citizen is no responsibility of mine. America is a nation of strong, resilient people who stand on their own two feet. We will not tolerate communist socialized medicine in a free nation!"

When the UCS citizens became ill, they had four choices: expensive insurance, pay cash, stay sick, or die.

At that point Price Wayne put out confidential communications to Cascadia, promising them he would turn rat if they just got him out of here.

But the worm turns. Price had learned that twenty-three of The Forty were well on the way to never-never land, one well-cooked, gourmet delicacy at a time by their 'trusted servants.' Fuck you! Price thought savagely as he placed the second course of poison for the day on his serving tray. Despite all your fucking riches, you still need people to feed and dress you. So no oligarch is safe from our revenge.

Satisfied the incremental poison would do its job, Price Wayne returned to his office, where he found a slip of paper:

OFFICE OF BARCELONA

TO: Price Wayne

"Mr. Wayne, effective immediately, you have been appointed the Personal Food Taster for his great imperial majesty Barcelona. Your duties will include tasting all food, drinks, and medicines before anything touching our Master. You are now responsible for guarding against assassination by poison, and you must report to the kitchen immediately.

Price Wayne held his face in his hands, trying to decide if murder was more rational than suicide.

~ 16 ~

CHAPTER FIFTEEN

President Bessie May Chowder looked up from the floor. She struggled briefly against her rope bonds. "Imahuffin? Well, well, well. The rats come out in the light."

"I am Senator Reverend Imahuffin," the man said, glaring down his long patrician nose. He then slung a 'Black Light Jesus, on-a-Rope' crucifix around his neck add to the six others hanging there. "I am a Senator and a man of the cloth, madam President, and you owe me, bless you, the honor of that...er...honorific."

"Imahuffin, you're a moron. That's the only honorific you deserve," she told him evenly. *Guy has six crucifixes around his freaken neck. He'll fall on his face literally if adds any more.* Bessie May wondered if she could get her hands on just one of those. *Bye bye Imahuffin.*

Imahuffin adjusted his thick glasses and widened his stance in what he assumed was a commanding, self-righteous position. "You are a liberal....a progressive liberal!" Speaking as if he were chasing a stray dog from his overturned garbage. "Do you not see yourself for the sinner you truly are? Mark the words in Mark 16:16, 'He that doesn't believe will go to hell!' The very words of Jesus," Imahuffin concluded.

"Imahuffin, let me go now." She told him calmly.

As a former Federal Court Judge in the old US for nearly fifteen years Chowder was a stickler for the law. But more importantly, she believed in justice, even though she also realized justice and law weren't always the same.

"Let. Me. Go."

"Senator! Senator Imahuffin!" A man appeared dressed in Black camouflage, a fully armored vest, gas mask, and so much combat gear hanging off him he looked like an Afghan Christmas Tree. His patches were a red triangle with a scorpion curled in the center.

"You dare interrupt me?" Imahuffin whirled on the intruder like a wild animal defending its kill. His crucifixes swinging with such enthusiasm he nearly fell over.

"His majesty, Oligarch Barcelona wants this prisoner." The soldier told him calmly. "You will surrender her immediately."

"What? How the hell did he even know we have her? We just shot her down a couple of hours ago!"

"I called and told him."

"What? But you're my hand-picked Chief of Security! You work for me!"

The solder wanted to explain to Imahuffin that nobody worked for him. Everyone in Imahuffin's staff was employed by Barcelona, and nobody told Imahuffin.

The soldier said nothing.

"But she is my prisoner. Mine, mine, mine. He can't have her! She's mine, mine, mine."

"Not any longer, sir."

Imahuffin spirits deflated like a flat tire in a Death Valley summer. He had so hoped to torture Bessie May Chowder.

"Okay fine," Imahuffin wasn't going to lose his moment in the sun. "Okay, fine, but I'm coming along. Nothing will stop me from delivering this prize hostage into the hands of Oligarch Barcelona. This is a delicate and valuable prize, and I am far too important not to continue providing my expert knowledge and expertise to this matter. I will be advising Barcelona and will be at his side throughout the interrogation. I have spoken."

"No. You are not." The armored man replied simply. He unholstered his sidearm and chambered a round. "I have orders to shoot you in the head if you even attempt to board the bus to the airport. Feel me, pal?"

Imahuffin, shocked into silence, nodded dismally.

"And, listen, just for full openness here, should you go near the plane out of here...well, you don't want to know what I'll do to you at that point."

"But...I'm...a Senator...A Reverend...I....Jesus loves me...."

"We shall be leaving in about 15 minutes, sir," he turned to leave and then turned back. "Not you!"

****

"You're not serious?"

"Only Jesus can lead us out of our bondage.'He that follows the Lord will live forever, Corinthians 2:34" Imahuffin bent down until he was eye to eye with President Chowdcr. He waggled a finger at her as if admonishing a child. "Before you leave, you should know something. There are going to be changes here. Big changes. Humanity is facing a crossroads. Jesus is coming back and he is pissed. You have failed to honor and worship him, and for this, he will scourge the earth. Jesus doesn't take well to being ignored."

"After being crucified, I would guess he's a little edgy."

Imahuffin didn't appreciate levity at Jesus' expense. "Well, he's going to take charge! Get things straightened out. Jesus is going to make you Liberals bend the knee and worship him or else!"

"Imahuffin, are you delusional? Listen to me closely; I have studied modern religions and what I have witnessed is a complete reversal of purpose. You are nothing but a hypocrite claiming Jesus supports your bullshit? Nonsense!"

"Huh?"

"Many modern-day Muslims, Jews, and Christians no longer believe in their scriptures." Bessie May was appalled. As a lifelong Christian, she believed in a loving God. The Jesus of today was a God she did not recognize; intolerant, bigoted, racist, misogynistic, and favoring rich over poor. "You don't believe in Jesus Christ. You just want justification for your ego-centric greed! Jesus and Muhammad were avatars that taught peace and love. Now you claim they stand for murder and hate."

"That is a liberal lie!" Imahuffin stormed indignantly. "Jesus' love is based on strength, toughness, and freedom! Oh and obedience. Lots of obedience! If you do what HE tells you, you will be rich and prosperous."

"What the hell are you babbling about?" Bessie May returned his attack. "I am a lifelong Christian," she said firmly. "MY Jesus loves you for who you are, not how rich you are."

Imahuffin was taken aback. He hadn't considered that a Liberal could be accepted as a Christian. *Blasphemy!*

The Right Reverend Jumpin' Jim Imahuffin wasn't going to tolerate that.

"Jesus, my Lord, Jesus, has made it very clear, you cannot be a Christian." He wanted to stop this nonsense immediately. Now he had the chance. Jesus knows the white race is superior, other...err...people are tolerated." Imahuffin dropped to his knees, imploring Chowder to see the truth. "I can help you; I can help you find the real Jesus. You see your...err...Liberal Jesus is just...well gone. Poof! Replaced with a real he-man, a man's man..."

He could feel the energy coming from his gut, somewhere around his appendix, energy that gave him righteousness that quickened his soul, an energy propelling more proselytizing. Suddenly, he got a strong whiff of mint julep, which always told him he was in the presence of the divine.

Imahuffin drew in a deep breath and began.

As she listened to Imahuffin's rant and rave, a bound Bessie May Chowder could see her reflection in his watery eyes. She stared at him in wonder. *Usually, people this insane can't even buckle a belt.*

At that moment, the soldier in black returned, bent down and picked President Bessie May Chowder off the floor. "Sir!" The black soldier said to Imahuffin. "She is leaving now. Say your goodbyes like a nice kidnapper."

Imahuffin struggled to sit up. His hair was wildly disarrayed, shirt torn, like the loser of a bar fight. "Okay, okay," struggling to his feet, multiple crucifixes swaying with each trudging step, Imahuffin trailed after them. "One last word: coup d'état."

Chowder stared at him over the black soldier's shoulder.

Imahuffin giggled. "Yes, Coup d'état. You are looking at the new President of Cascadia. Well, I will be after the new Cascadia council of clerics is announced."

"You couldn't pull off a coup d'état at a nursing home, Imahuffin. Who is pulling your strings?"

But Imahuffin, suddenly beset by a 3D mesmerizing daydream of power, as a vibrant, full-color hallucination overwhelmed him. He slowed, fell behind, and then like flashbulb popping in his mind came the thought: Pope Imahuffin the First; the Papacy of Imahuffin. A vision morphed into his brain of a giant Einstein Stone around the neck of King Pope Imahuffin, proudly addressing his loyal and devout subjects.

As the holy hallucinations intensified, Imahuffin let out a slight squeal and dropped to his knees, rocking and sobbing, praying, nodding, fingering each crucifix one after another, fervently calling for Jesus to anoint him Pope of Earth. "Jesus loves me this I know, 'cause the Bible tells me so..." Imahuffin's scratchy singing voice followed Chowder out of the building like a petulant annoying beggar seeking an audience.

~ 17 ~

CHAPTER SIXTEEN

"Energy cannot be created or destroyed; it can only be changed from one form to another." Albert Einstein

As she was stuffed aboard the private jet for a flight out of Cascadia, Bessie May Chowder cast her eyes around. She would see this land again, no doubt. Kidnapping the President was a desperate act. Chowder had no idea what awaited her, but she wasn't finished yet. But most importantly, *what does this do to the seventy-two-hour clock? Is this part of the scheme?* She had no idea what was going on.

"Okay," She muttered to herself as the plane got airborne. "Okay, I've been in tough places before." Looking back on a lifetime of challenges, she knew adversity: Bessie May Chowder, poor, Black, raised in the desperate slums of Detroit until she was 8 and her parents murdered for the methamphetamines they sold. The Holy Name Orphanage, a place of discarded children and disgruntled adults, became home until she was old enough to leave on her own. In 8th Grade at the orphanage, Sister Mary Olive secretly slid her a book, a simple, child's book really, addressing fear. She remembered a quote:

"It is normal to have butterflies in your stomach. So make them fly in formation." Sister Mary Olive was censored and beaten for giving this book to her, but she would show them no fear.

It was openly believed dark skin and sinning were synonymous in those days. Chowder was small, defenseless, and a natural victim. But Sister Mary Olive, a Haitian, gave her hope. She was a solitary rock in the middle of the fast-flowing river, a rock she, a tiny Black orphan, could cling to for only a short while, to gathering her breath, figure out where she could find safety next.

"This thing isn't done yet," Bessie May Chowder muttered. "In forty minutes, I will be in Butte, Montana, and face to face with idiocy." But her words underlie her fear. Bessie May was scared and exhausted and feeling overwhelmed. Suddenly the measures of her loss flooded her: Husband Fred passed less than a year ago, now Bernard and Juwanda. *So much death; always death,* Bessie May mourned. She wondered why human existence needed the heart-breaking reality of death. She asked if that was the purpose for our existence; experience. *We are visitors to this planet in human form, where we live, experience corporal existence, then pass back beyond the veil to our real homes.*

The aircraft took a sudden drop in altitude, and Chowder bounced hard against the metal floor.

She had to get word to Bahrain somehow. She would miss the meeting in Santa Rosa, but they had planned on more meetings anyway. What they were doing was vital. The world was riven with anger, revenge, violence, and a hierarchy of power. *The rage and misogyny of Patriarchy. We have to stop this,* She thought roughly. *We have to! We have to back off the toxins of masculinity and muscle and focus more on cooperation and compassion. If humanity is to grow mature, we have to do this. We have to return to matriarchal ways of being in the world. We must seek equality egalitarianism, rather than a hierarchy of who has the most giant missile. Civilization must be based on sharing, helping each other, reducing the primitive parts of human nature for the more mature.*

One of the pilots turned to face her. "We have crossed into UCS land now, and you will be meeting Oligarch Barcelona in about an hour."

"Barcelona? Where the hell is he?"

Just then, the aircraft hit turbulence and was bounced around the sky, losing and gaining a thousand feet of altitude in seconds.

Bessie May rolled behind a set of passenger seats as the plane banked and yawed suddenly.

"Oh my God, look at that!" The pilot cried out.

"Holy shit!" the Copilot quickly on his radio, reporting what was going on in the sky around them. Bessie May could see the sky streaked with vibrant shades of blues and purples from her half-hidden position, and the clouds were highlighted in gold and the setting sun in silver.

But it was the shape of the clouds that was most terrifying. Raging, boiling, and now morphing from colorful purples into rolls of malevolent gray that stretched from horizon to horizon. Lightening touched and stabbed and illuminated the sky in flashes of brilliant power. Towering Tornado funnels were forming and dissolving all around them.

"Whatever is going on out there, this ain't normal." The Co-pilot shouted into the microphone. "We'd better set this bird down soon!"

She had no idea what was going on outside the aircraft. All President Bessie May Chowder could think of was; With her a prisoner, Cascadia could not hope to meet the UCS demands. *Will they hit us with nuclear weapons anyway?*

~ 18 ~

CHAPTER SEVENTEEN

"I am happy because I want nothing from anyone. I do not care about money. Decorations, titles or distinctions mean nothing to me. I do not crave praise. I claim credit for nothing. A happy man is too satisfied with the present to dwell too much on the future." Albert Einstein

Peter Paul God-Kock wondered why the world hated him. After all, he reasoned, he didn't make the world the predatory jungle of dog-eat-dog it was. Every man, woman, and child was either born into wealth or not. Humans either were smiled upon by God or made to suffer. It was the natural order of life. God blessed those he favored with money.

The son of a multi-billionaire, he knew he was blessed, knew he was always right and was always around twelve people. The more he thought about these facts, the more he realized who he was: God. He had the money, the lawyers, and the desire, so within a short time, Peter Paul Kock changed his name to Peter Paul God-Kock, announcing his elevated status.

He sighed. Great men are seldom recognized in their time, and he was gravely disappointed not one of his five wives and eight or nine or ten mistresses could see it. God-Kock had developed a business model based on defrauding investors and cheating tenets in his slum apartments. He never paid his bills or met obligations, so his lawyers were constantly in court seeking to defend him from thousands of angry victims on his march to billionaire status. Peter Paul God-Kock believed he lived a blessed and God-approved life, only fools paid full price.

P.P. God-Kock looked out the windows of his office; raw dirt was the only thing that seemed to grow here. "They can't do this to God... It's not fair..." God-Kock murmured.

Butte, Montana was a coal mining town that proudly wore that label, but like a 53-year-old stripper, winner of a beauty contest at 18, still strutting her stuff, the reality was a wolf to self-delusional sheep.

Peter Paul stared at bare, naked hills of sandy rocks, tufts of withered vegetation struggling to survive, a few stunted trees that resembled a Salvador Dali painting. The town of crumbling red brick buildings and dilapidated houses spoke of a glorious past and a forgotten future.

Coal dust filtered into everything; people wore face masks year-round and took pride in their sugar bowls that resembled fresh churned pepper. Asthma was epidemic, so the school choir learned to coordinate inhalers to avoid losing their rhythm.

God-Kock looked at a forty-foot, ten-foot-high, and ten-foot-wide slag of coal that lay like a dinosaur turd in the middle of the city children's park.

A large sign announced the slag of coal: "The Butter Mine Memorial to honor the town of Butte, Montana."

Surrounding the coal seam was a small sand and rock park, home to rusting and decaying playground equipment too rickety and dangerous for tender children. A small fountain spat mud that smelled like tar and was allegedly medicinal.

God-Kock noticed that wild animals, even birds, wouldn't go near the place.

"Fuck I gotta get out of here!" God-Kock threw himself back into his chair. "Who knew sick people had the energy to get so angry?" he muttered.

As the former CEO of Kock Pharmaceuticals, LLC. Peter Paul God-Kock decided to raise the retail price of Epinephrine, a drug that saves the lives of millions of people suffering anaphylactic shock, by 1200%.

The backlash hue and cry was so fierce Kock Pharmaceuticals Board of Directors was forced to step in or lose serious market share. They told Peter Paul Kock to back off the 1,200% and increase the medicine by only 800%.

The sick were jubilant in forcing the big bad drug company to back down while Kock Pharmaceuticals LLC went on to set a company record for profits. It was a Win-Win situation.

But Peter Paul God-Kock received the brunt of the blame and was vilified from one side of the country to the other. Relations were so bad his family had him banished to Butte, Montana, as Western Director, Homeland Security.

God-Kock sighed at the injustice of it all. Opening a manila file, he started to read the report but quit after just a few minutes when he realized it was filled with words he didn't understand or care about. He figured it was something about an artifact from England.

"Oh ick!" It was a bone.

Once stored in the Homeland Security Museum of Antiquities and now in his vault, the artifact was the shin bone of St. Catherine. The old bone was carved with intricate symbols, but God-Koch considered this scientific language as unworthy of his precious time. However, he had nothing better to do. He forced himself to spend the next hour reading the three paragraphs in their entirety over and over, trying to figure out the story.

In 1556 AD, A village called Push, Northumbria, England, was widely known for a rock wall that bore the startling likeness of Jesus Christ. When the light was just right, and at a specific time of day, out of the composition of stone, mortar, bits of rock, and moss, a visage of Jesus appears. That year Barbarian Invaders invaded, murdered townsfolk, burning the town to the ground. However, on the way to their next slaughter, they stopped to urinate on the precious sacred Wall of Push.

Catherine of Ale, a fifty-five-year-old maiden seamstress and devout believer, was so inflamed by this desecration; she gave her life defending the image. A hundred years later, she was sanctified by Pope Paul the V.

Peter Paul God-Kock pondered that; sacrificing your life for a piss stain on a wall. Then millions honor you for this sacrifice.

There is a lesson here. I just know it.

~ 19 ~

CHAPTER EIGHTEEN

Jail cells are the same everywhere: it doesn't matter which community, nation, civilization, or even planet.

Muh, Yaz and Jee sat forlornly on the stone floor of their cell, heads down, ears drooping, tail still.

"Your fault."

"Is not."

"Is too."

Muh snorted. "I told you guys, it was an unavoidable accident...."

"Which part, huh?" Yaz muttered. "The unavoidable was avoidable if you hadn't avoided the flying lessons. And the accident part? An accident is when somebody makes a mistake, and you, sir, are an error!"

Muh was hard-pressed to argue at the moment. Instead, he asked, "Who are you again?"

As usual, that shut Yaz up.

Looking up at the bars that held them in the tiny room, Muh had a momentary pang of discontent. But he shook it off, determined to recapture his power and dignity and leadership.

"You bums are just jealous. Everyone can see I am the brightest, smartest, most handsome, and certainly most talented of anyone here."

Jee scoffed. "Nonsense! We are brothers! Got that, Muh? Identical brothers. You look the same as me, and I look the same as you! The only thing different about you, Muh is that you're an asshole."

"You know, you shouldn't swear... it's bad for the liver," Muh replied delicately.

"Something else is bad for the liver...is being bitten! Your fuck up costs us the time we don't have," Jee said threateningly. Oh, the plans he had. Jee was going to finish this last assignment, and then he was gone, out of here, off to pursue his fortune.

"Wait a minute!" Yaz squeaked. "All is not lost. I can drive!"

Jee and Muh began to circle, eyeing each other, looking for an opening.

Muh felt he was exempt from blame. He saw himself as an idea guy, the visionary leader who guides the rest. If mistakes are made, it has nothing to do with him because he only gives orders, which are just words, and therefore Muh isn't responsible for doing any-thing but talking.

"We have to be in Indianapolis within a week." Jee continued to circle Muh, looking for an opening. "With your leadership, we won't be there in months."

"You peasant," Muh scoffed. "Of course, I will succeed! I am the leader! All leaders are winners. You loser!"

Yaz held up a paw. "Shouldn't we just focus on getting out of here first?"

Muh and Jee continued to circle each other warily, cautiously.

"I think we should get out here first, yes?" Jee muttered.

"That is an excellent suggestion, number two!" Muh had learned that subordinates love being stroked, and it was an excellent way to control them. "I think that as a capital idea."

"But...but...I said..." Yaz tried to protest, but neither Muh nor Jee paid the slightest attention.

*****

"So," Bones whispered at Doc. "I wonder why the Drone opened fire and then stopped so suddenly?"

"Y'all worry about shit that didn't happen?" Doc replied, "Charles, you got your hands full with shit that did happen, don't go begging for imaginary shit to add to it."

Charley Brown Bones had no answer for that. So shut up. He would wait until he had something clever to say.

The dungeon was bleak and desolate. The only light was a small torch, which grudgingly threw out small flashes of illumination, defeating the stygian darkness only in flickering seconds. A dripping sound echoed down the dank hallway, rat's claws scrabbled incessantly against the stone.

"You know, I didn't think they still had dungeons these days." Doc looked around them. "This one looks well used. I guess Montana was a leader in persecution, not just prosecution."

Charley Bones remained silent, determined not to talk to Doc ever again in this or any other lifetime. Doc's effervescence of optimism was killing him. If he remained quiet, Doc would stop talking, sooner or later.

"But then," Doc continued, oblivious of Charley's strategy. "You can never keep up with the fashion trends among the rich and powerful. This Western Director of Homeland Security must be a guy who knows his history. You can't turn a country like America back from the twenty-first century to the sixteenth without having a lot of respect for chaos...and chains."

"Are you done?" He couldn't help it. "Don't you ever shut up? As you have gotten older, you have gotten garrulous?"

"What?"

"Garrulous...you talk too much.

"Thank God, Ah thought you were referring to a venereal disease...gonorrhea...garrulous..."

Charley regretted opening his mouth.

"Hey, I'm just trying to be observant. You know, use my time wisely. Learn about my surroundings... think... evaluate... ruminate...educate."

"We're fucking chained to a rock wall, you idiot!" Charley screamed as loudly as he could, his chains rattling harmoniously. "In a fucking dungeon. We are probably going to be tortured and put to death. What is fucking wrong with you?"

"Charles, you always see things so pessimistically."

"You know, it occurs to me that you're a 'glass-half-full kind of guy."

Doc thought about that for a moment. "You know, really, I'm kind of a 'what glass?' sort of guy."

"Bullshit."

"Charles, envy is not a pretty sight."

"Doc, let me explain. In truth, my optimism tends to dim the minute I am confronted by human nature. Human avarice is contrary to the survival of the species. And yet there it is! Doesn't matter what race, color, or creed. Greed is killing our species and nearly every other species to boot. Humankind is a virus, nothing but a damn virus! We infect ourselves and everything around us."

"But Charles, what you don't understand is that everybody out there is just trying to do the best they can. Trying to be caring, loving, respectful, and honest and they just need the opportunity to express these loving feelings."

"Geez, Doc," Bones sighed, not knowing whether Doc was just playing with him or not. "You make Pollyanna seem like a nihilist."

****

"...I lub a little gel across de sea..." Pawnee Painter lay back on the hard metal bench, smiling, tapping his foot, and softly singing a tune," She's a Badian beauty, and she sez to me...Oh, Johnny...Oh, was you ebber down in Mobile Bay...where dey screws de cotton on a summer day?...did you ebber see de ole Plantation Boss...and de long-tailed filly and de big black hoss?..."

He loved old songs, and slave shanties were particularly pleasing to Pawnee. Freedom to Pawnee was life itself. The only time he lost it, busted for running weed and cocaine out of Honduras, and jailed for close to three years, was a time of deep, bitter depression and reflection.

Pawnee would never spend another minute inside a cage and he almost felt pity for anyone who would attempt to put him there.

In singing the plantation slave shanties, Pawnee felt a kinship to the slaves of America. Not in identifying with their captivity but in realizing the incredible significance of their freedom.

Pawnee laughed, and he had suddenly recalled those last moments with the SPOT Drone.

Those wild few moments when SPOT opened fire stirred in his memory. "Chee that was a close one." The Drone's Gatling gun burped just once, and a hundred rounds peppered the roadway with deadly steel. Then the Drone went silent.

The reason became apparent immediately. The Drone didn't want to hit the five incoming helicopters bristling with guns, missiles, and armed Homeland Security Special Ops troops.

Pawnee was very impressed with the vigor Homeland Security conducted their profession.

Nowhere to run, no way to fight, the three humans and three little green beagles were under arrest.

However, being under arrest and held in captivity were two things Pawnee no longer allowed. Instead, he permitted himself to be put in a cell because it gave him access inside Homeland Security. Perfect.

Four hours inside this cage, waiting for the opportunity to slip out, Pawnee spent thinking of his son. Clay Park Painter.

Finally clear, Pawnee left the cell and began checking out the guards and their circuits, breaking into the offices, rifling through the secret documents within Homeland Security. He unlocked safes, broke locks, poked here and there, and suddenly, it was right in front of him:

He found a Homeland Security Department of Antiquities report, a detailed study of an artifact from Northumbria England; A relic of St. Catherine of Push. The artifact he sought was being held in a unique safe inside Peter Paul God-Kock's private office. But before Pawnee could break into God-Kocks' office, people started arriving for work, and he had to return to his cell. He wanted to get a look inside that safe. He could not figure out what this sacred object had in common with The Einstein Stone.

Pawnee would get Doc and Bones to help him, but he had no idea how to use three alien dogs; somehow, they would be an advantage.

Settling back in his temporary cage, Pawnee felt weariness suck energy from his muscles. His body felt tired, and he felt like an orphan from his beloved islands. Feeling the warm caress of the Trade Winds, the gentle movements of the sea, he longed to hear the cadence of his people, eat the food fresh from the ocean and land, and hear the laughter and songs of his ancient ancestors.

He longed to see his son again, and the time they had at home on Kauai was far too short.

"The storm," Pawnee muttered out loud. He smiled with satisfaction at survival. Surviving the storm and seeing his son was marvelous, rewarding, and heartbreaking all at the same time. It had been a perilous crossing, very close to disaster, but it brought him home.

Clay, his beloved son Clay, was strong, intelligent, and a grown man when they finally hugged on the Hanalei beach, North Shore of Kauai.

A tear slid silently from his eye. He missed Clay with a ferocity that surprised him. At that moment, the agony of his choices in life rose in bitter realization. A ghost haunting from his past. What might have been?

Lt. Clay Park Painter, Cascadian Special Forces, assigned to JBLM, Joint Base Louis McCord, Lakewood, Washington, a giant military base outside of Tacoma, Washington, was deeply involved in the resistance movement to free America from the Republican Oligarchs.

Clay often went on clandestine missions inside the UCS; from one of these, Clay Painter had learned of the artifact and its connection to the Einstein Stone.

Even now, Lt. Clay Painter was undercover, somewhere in the UCS.

"Chee, we meet again, soon, my son," Pawnee whispered his promise to the stone walls and steel bars of his cell.

~ 20 ~

CHAPTER NINETEEN

"Ey, Anyone here ordered pineapple pizza?" Pawnee whispered. "Pawnee?"

"Chee you buggahs ready to leave now?"

"Sure, seems like a good time."

Pawnee slipped in and relieved them of their chains. Charley wearily wiped his face and felt his arms. They ached with a deep fire; he felt old, battered, and used up. He honestly didn't know how much more he could handle. "Doc," He said, "As soon as we get out of here, I'm heading back to Cascadia."

"Charles, I do believe it is too late for that. You are here, we are here, and the mission is here, so here we are!"

"Fucking optimists always piss me off." Charley Bones thought of home. The cabin on forty acres, the small pond stocked with bluegill and perch. He'd build his cabin out of fence posts, eight-foot posts, eight inches around. Charley learned of a semi-load of unclaimed fence posts and bought the entire thing for $1200. It took him two years to build a two story cabin using just those fence posts. But the isolation and the hard work were good for him. Each morning, he would get in his rowboat and go out into the small lake by his house and catch breakfast; bluegill dusted and fried beside scrambled eggs and coffee was Charley's idea of heaven. He wanted to be there, right now, right this instant, so bad he could barely breathe.

Sadness shot through him, like an electric shock of loss. He missed his home, his dogs, his land, the peace and quiet of the small forest surrounding his home. Although he owed his life to Bessie May Chowder, Charley didn't know how many times he could answer the call to arms.

"Pawnee," Charley said. "I don't know why you're here, but I am glad you are. Thank you again. Now can we get out of here?"

Pawnee placed a finger to his lips. "Shhh, be still, you." Carefully, he opened the cell door and peered out. As he figured it would be at 2:00 AM, the place was deserted. He motioned. "Cool head, now the main thing, because we are going to cockaroach out here," he whispered as he went left down the hall. "We don't want to be caught now, brah; we are close to getting the artifact."

"Where to?" Charley asked.

"We are going to the safe of Homeland Security boss, a Mr. Kock, I believe. We will find the artifact, brah. Then it will tell us where Einstein Stone is, and we go get that. Then we go home."

"Charles," Doc observed. "I believe Pawnee has figured this all out. It's simple; we just get the shit and go home. No muss, no fuss, and no worries."

In his experience, Charley Bones had never known a single operation to go as planned. Not one. Far too many variables and un-predictable human interference, and no combat plan ever survives first contact.

They had only gone for ten minutes when Pawnee held up a hand. "Shhhh, stop."

Charley and Doc tried to look around Pawnee and see what was holding up their escape.

Three green beagles were standing in the middle of the hallway, looking utterly lost, turning this way and that.

"HO chee, where you little ones come from?"

"Well," Muh explained. "We were not satisfied with our accommodations, so we left, but now...?"

"Now we have to find something." Jee added. "but it's secret, so go away." He flicked his claws dismissively.

"Don't bother us now; we have important work to do."

"No, they can help us!" Yaz spoke up. "We need to find something! A gem...kind of. It is called The Einstein Stone, could you help us?"

~ 21 ~

CHAPTER TWENTY

"So, where do you suppose your Einstein Stone is right now?" Charley asked. Pointing at the solid brick ten-story building surrounded by guards, concertina wire, and armored cars across the street from them, Charley said, "Homeland Security Headquarters, God-Kock's office?"

"Ya'll say you brought the Einstein Stone here? To Earth?" Doc asked the aliens. They were hunkered down in shrubbery across the road from the HQ.

"Einstein Stone? Who? Us? No!" Muh denied everything. "Never heard of it!"

"What he means," Jee interrupted. "Maybe we know something about this here, mystical rock; what's it worth to you?" Eyes bright, ears perked, waiting for a reward.

"The Blue-Green Emerald?" Yaz spoke up. "We brought it...sort of..."

"Okay, Blue Emeral' Chee, yo buggahs wastin' our time. Where is Blue Emeral'? Where is Einstein Stone?"

"Ask him," Muh pointed at Jee. "He's the expert on humanity, he'd know." Somehow, Muh had to regain his position of authority, and he felt the best way to elevate was to lower somebody else. "He's responsible!" Pointing at Jee. "He did it. He lost it, or he knows who has it."

"What? Did what?" Jee turned on Muh with heat. "Say, what is this? You trying to throw me under the bus?"

"Dear Brother, I wouldn't dream of such a thing."

"Would too."

"Would not."

"My best guess is God-Kock's safe," Yaz spoke up softly, timidly. Pointing to the top floor.

Pawnee just nodded as he observed the Homeland Security HQ. Next door to HQ was a rusted and broken children's playground, swing sets tilted severely, a teeter-totter split in half, broken glass, condoms, and litter completed the picture. The place was barren of both children and play, and he wondered what kind of sadist would allow a child anywhere near that ominous play park.

"Looks like a dinosaur turd," Doc observed of the gigantic vein of coal lying next to the playground.

Everyone nodded.

****

"It's 5 AM why some many guards here?" Charley wondered.

"Charles, unemployment is low, but in the UCS, there is a maximum wage standard, ya'll," Doc told him.

"Maximum wage?"

"Yes, sir, man can be worked eighty hours, but by law, you're only allowed to pay him for forty. That is the maximum the employer needs to pay. Makes it easy for the business owner to keep profits high. Every job has a contract that commits the worker to a specified number of year's service that is unbreakable for any reason, even death."

"What?"

"Yeah, once the West Coast and the New England States seceded, America became a one-party state ruled by Republicans. Workers are obligated to their corporate masters even after death. The bodies are either used as landfill or boiled down for a cheap but nutritious paste so the American poor can supplement their meager diets."

"That is horrible."

Pawnee shrugged. "This world she is 'hammerjab' to the max...crazier and crazier each year. It never changes; Pawnee had seen the same situation over and over; greed rules. One group gets rich and beats up everybody else. He'd seen it play out with large groups or small families or nations. Human avarice is the most destructive force on this planet; it destroys whole civilizations and may even poison the world.

Muh had been waiting patiently for the humans to straighten this problem out. Still, here they were, hiding in bushes without the mystical stone, nowhere near Indianapolis, Indiana.

"What are you guys stalling for?" Muh pointed at the building. "Sic' 'em."

"Fuck off you...pet!" Charley snarled at the little green alien. He was tired, it was late, and he'd been chained to fucking wall. Charley was in no mood for friendly banter.

"Y'all calm, Charles," Doc intervened. "Let's not attack our ET Brothers, okay?"

"Doc, you haven't seen attack yet."

Muh moved behind Jee.

"How do we get in there?" Charley pointed at the HQ.

Pawnee was about to speak up with his plan when Yaz beat him to it.

"I know how to get in there." Yaz held up his hand. "Me, me, me, I know, I know."

Muh looked out from behind Jee and said, "Liar!"

"Friendless fucking waif!" Jee added.

"Okay, Yaz, let's have it," Pawnee said softly. "I am curious as to what the little guy would come up with." Pawnee was also irritated at Muh and Jee for being idiots.

Yaz had studied the situation. He noticed an Ice Cream Delivery truck, a shipment of hula hoops, and Girl Scout Troop #89 were bivouacked for a weekday campout in the shitty little playground next to the HQ. Quickly a plan formed, and he could tell they would all mesh beautifully into a functional but noisy distraction.

He told them his plan.

Charley thought the idea was ridiculous. "That's fucking crazy! No way." He looked over at Doc.

Doc looked pale even in the moonlight. "No way. That is nuts!" He agreed.

They both looked at Pawnee for support.

"Chee, dat sounds good."

As they slunk into position, Yaz felt on top of the world and couldn't help beaming with pride. A special mission and he was going along. At last, recognition, approval, *I'm going to be somebody.* He dreamed of being one of the team.

So Charley Bones and Doc Betters watched Yaz and Pawnee pull off the heist. Muh muttered bitterly for two hours nonstop. The guards were now a case study in chaos. Either running after small packs of pre-teen girls, driven insane by smo'res and boredom, or chasing rolling hula hoops, the guards were suddenly very busy doing everything but guarding.

Yaz's plan of transmitting a message to every girls' phone telling her to urgently assemble at the building next door to greet Justin Beiber, Fetty Wap, and Mary J. Bilge who are in town for a concert.

The screaming of teenage females was deafening.

Muh felt like he was lying at the bottom of a well. It was all falling apart. First Jee, demanding to be the leader, and now Yaz speaking up, making himself known! That was just too much. Muh chittered vengeance over and over in a growly mutter.

"So, ah, Muh, you seem a little tense," Jee was delighted in Muh's misery. "Here, let me massage those shoulders, relax you!"

"Get away from me! Don't touch me!" Muh barked fiercely.

"Would you fucking guys shut up? We're trying to do something criminal here, and we don't want people to know. Okay?" Charley snarled at the squabbling ETs.

"He started it."

"Did not."

~ 22 ~

CHAPTER TWENTY-ONE

"Concerning matter, we have been all wrong. What we have called matter is energy, whose vibration has been so lowered as to be perceptible to the senses. Matter is spirit reduced to point of visibility. There is no matter." Albert Einstein

"Extraterrestrials? Like...aliens? Little green men?" Peter Paul God-Koch looked up from the Lego's model of St Peters Basilica in Rome with a sour frown.

"No sir, not quite." Myers, The Butler, displayed a handheld computer, "As you can see, they are green, they are alien, but after that...."

"They're green Beagles."

"We have decided to call the ETs...er....' Kocks' as an honor, sir!"

"Cocks? You want to name these new aliens after your dicks?" Peter Paul God-Kock was astonished.

"Oh, no, no sir, no sir, we named them after you. KOCK."

"I know how to spell my Goddamned name," God-Kock snarled at Myers, The Butler.

"Well, well, well. The Universe has finally found me." God-Kock said with surprise and admiration, flopping back in his chair, a beatific smile across his face.

"Sir?"

"I knew it was only a matter of time before the Universe recognized me. Do you know why I spend so much time on the Golf Course? It is so the Celestial Universe can see me! Out in the open, waiting to be recognized. Why do you think I did that series of television shows? 'The Boss' was the most popular show in the entire history of television. Everybody knew it was pure genius.

"Sir?"

"I am God. Did you know that? I'll be you did. The Cosmos has found me, and now I can begin my true mission...."

"Sir?"

"These extraterrestrial cosmic emissaries are here to welcome and reward me."

"Sir!" Myers, the Butler, was becoming alarmed. God-Kock's grip on reality was tenuous at best, which could spin him off into outer space.

"I, Peter Paul God-Kock," God-Kock climbed onto the top of his massive desk, arms now outstretched. He prayed to the heavens. "I am the new Jesus. I am God reborn, and now the Universe is coming to me, in recognition of my greatness, my sanctity, by God Hood! At long last, I can reveal my true purpose. I am the perfection of humanity!"

"Yes, sir, we know, sir." Myers, The Butler, needed to keep the conversation moving, not allow his employer to be trapped by his own La Brea Tarpit of Crazy.

Myer, the Butler, his official name, had been employed by the rich and powerful for so long he was surprised by nothing. The wealthy were no different from the poor, still infested with psychopathology, but they had the money and opportunity to publicly wallow in it.

Still, his willing servitude did have its rewards. Twenty years of manservant duties produced opportunities for wealth as he became a financial leech sucking up to Wall Street tips, backdoor business deals, and insider trading so common among the rich. Myers the Butler, after so many years of investing, raiding safes and jewelry boxes, now owned his estate, his servants, a Harvard Education for the kids, a 32 ft yacht, and a specific, bitter hatred of humanity.

"I am the Savior humankind has always anticipated." God-Kock was so happy he skipped across the top of the enormous desk. "The Cosmos has sent emissaries to beg for my help! Bring these fine foreign aliens brought to me immediately. In style! Get a stretch limo, red carpet, get somebody playing the piano...flowers...maybe leashes, and dog treats too."

Myers, The Butler, waited to see any further revelations. He'd noticed that P.P. God-Kock seemed to prefer his perspective over reality. The idea that the Universe sent three beagles to Earth to honor Peter Paul God-Kock seemed a little farfetched.

"Could there be any better days than today!" God-Kock was beside himself with joy. "Wow! Wow! First, I get recognized by a Galactic Honor Guard, then I get to capture three Cascadia invaders to torture, we are set to nuke those fucking Liberals off the face of the Earth! Wowoie Zowie!"

"Sir, your greatest Excellency, your supreme highness, there is one further bit of news." Myers, The Butler, observed to see how God-Kock was reacting.

God-Kock was humming with serotonin.

That's good. Still, Myers, The Butler, proceeded with caution. Though this news could go either way: excellent news, Myers The Butler would be rewarded or very bad, and Myers must endure the self-indulgent whining of an oligarch, with the added possibility of a firing squad.

"A large and mysterious jewel has been delivered by these three...little green...Galactic Honor Guards." Myers, the Butler, paused, waiting to see how God-Kock was reacting. So far, so good.

"They have an Einstein Stone."

The blood drained from Peter Paul God-Kock's face.

Myers the Butler was out the door in a heartbeat well ahead of whatever gonzo reaction gripped God-Kock.

~ 23 ~

CHAPTER TWENTY-TWO

Imahuffin was a lost man.

When President of Cascadia Bessie May Chowder flew off in handcuffs as the prisoner of Oligarch Barcelona, Imahuffin's life disappeared as well: faithful followers, senatorial seat, coup d'état, pope-hood, and his rent-free apartment all gone.

"It is better to dwell in the wilderness than with a contentious and an angry woman." – Proverbs 21:19" Imahuffin muttered darkly.

That night, sitting his ex-backyard, high on methamphetamines and stuffing his face with 'Cheetos', Imahuffin descended into hallucinations of a blistering future; visions of apocalypse, salvation, and sitting in the lap of Jesus swirled before him in violent orange-colored hues.

Two days later, Imahuffin crawled out from under his ex-back porch with the words: "Jesus saves" carved painfully into his flesh with a ballpoint pen.

Imahuffin, homeless and unemployed, needing a change of scenery, and having no clue where the bloody tattoo came from, decided this was a message from Jesus.

Imahuffin knew the Little Angels Orphanage; outside of Yelm, Washington had an old yellow school bus painted with bright red

balloons to cheer up the sick little kids going to medical appoint-
ments. Just the thing he needed to pursue his spiritual calling.

Springing from ambush in the garage of the orphanage, Imahuffin had little trouble punching out the elderly nun as she emerged
to drive. Leaping into the driver's seat, he commandeered the vehicle, much to the terror of the wheelchair-bound children in the
back, and hit the open road east to find Jesus.

Like wastebasket litter, the kids were left at various spots along
Oregon Highway 6.

~ 24 ~

CHAPTER TWENTY-THREE

This morning, the air was chewy. Coal grit, smelling like kerosene and dusty wax, was on every window sill and breathing masks now came in a bewildering variety of colors and fabrics—various chic styles came and went.

Peter Paul God-Kock turned away from the servant and stared out the quadruple hermetically sealed windows at the thick walls and rolls of concertina wire surrounding his office. The daylight beyond was a burnt orange.

But none of that mattered now. Now was the time for his return.

"I want to announce to our Oligarch we have stopped an invasion of our beloved United States. Get Barcelona on the hotline! Immediately! Tell him an armed attack by a swarm of Kocks has thrust itself over and over into the Motherland!"

He, Peter Paul God-Kock, was about to join the elite. He would take this situation and own it as he quickly pieced together his strategy for his reinstatement to the Oligarchy. His smile was wide and joyous as he contemplated his plans. He would make this alien invasion seem so brutal and dangerous it would make 'War of the Worlds' seem like 'Mr. Rogers Visit to the Neighborhood'.

Kock leaned forward over his desk, glaring at the Myers The Butler." I want Barcelona only, as he is the Oligarch in charge of

113

North America. No secretaries, no advisors, no fucking vassals, I want only Barcelona himself!"

Pointing at himself, he said. "I will tell the world that I, Peter Paul God-Kock, have personally and at great personal and professional risk, stopped an armed invasion of my country."

Myers, The Butler, scribbled as fast as he could, trying to keep up.

"I did it single-handedly! I saw the threat of invading Kocks and led my troops into a victorious battle against a hard phalanx of Kocks. I personally...in hand-to-hand combat with dozens of Kocks...."

Myers frowned. *God-Kock wanted this bullshit delivered to higher authority?*

The more God-Kock talked, the more extraordinary Myers' problems grew. Now he had a decision to make. There were consequences for delivering false or misleading information to your superiors; consequences life-altering for he and his loved ones. Myers suspected he was walking into a no-win position.

How do I send a report to Barcelona that Peter Paul God-Kock conquered anything tougher than a soap bubble?

Myers would have the Office of Homeland Security on his ass in a heartbeat. He cringed inwardly. *They'd prosecute me for lying to a government official in an official report if I made that statement!*

Myers was fucked.

"I am a hero." God-Kock stood upright, suddenly swaying momentarily from the change of position. "Why, I might...I might even get my portrait on the fifty-dollar bill! Or better yet, I would be given fifty dollar bills...millions of them!"

God-Kock was struck by an image of Jesus presenting him the Medal of Honor, and Jesus shaking his hand...maybe a hug...he began to lurch about the room in ecstasy.

"We must contact FOX News immediately..."

"FOX?"

"Of course! They are the voice of America! The official Department of Homeland Security Information Office!"

"But, most reverend and honored of all, shouldn't you talk with superiors first?" It was a tough situation for an advisor. *We simply cannot tell the same lie to the public we tell to Barcelona! The insult would be deadly.*

"Most glorious majesty!" Myers raised his voice slightly to get attention. "Oligarch Barcelona should be notified first, let him know what is going on before you announce this to the world." Myers gasped, trying desperately to reign in the damage. Myers and his entire family, his wife's family, and probably the innocent next-door neighbors would be blamed for these lies! Meyers the Butler realized this could be a personal extinction-level event unless he could head it off.

"I want a full-page, above-the-fold press. I want to hear my name everywhere." God-Kock continued without pause and without listening to Myers. "I want you to tell FOX I have successfully defended our nation from an all-out invasion of Kocks; Giant Kocks burst into our land, aided and abetted by Snow Flake Liberals. Penetrating Kocks, spewing their Liberal lies!"

Suddenly, he remembered. "Wait a minute! What about the fabulous jewels they carried? What about those riches! I want them!"

"Sir, they had a dull looking, Blue-Green rock. That's all, no riches! We put it in your safe along with the Sacred Relic of St. Catherine, Homeland Security Office of Antiquities wanted to store here."

Peter Paul God-Kock snapped his fingers. "Of course, a majestic precious jewel and a bone carved by Jesus himself!"

Myers rolled his eyes. Sweat poured, soaking his hood, armpits black, even his palms were perspiring. *Two old men, a washed up mercenary and three green Beagles doesn't amount to much of an existential threat to the nation. No matter how well you write it up.*

"Make sure my name is spelled correctly," God-Kock demanded. "And be sure and use that photo of me wearing a Generals' Uniform from last Halloween. Tell the public I have assumed command of the Missoula regiment of the Montana National Guard military and have repulsed a savage assault of Kocks, thousands of rabid Kocks. Hard, vicious, green Kocks!"

Myers stood silently, shaking, contemplating fate; he was feeling sad his children would never know the joys of serfdom and slavery, as he did, and his father before him and his grandfather before that. Myers family had been loyal Republicans for generations.

"Why aren't you writing this down?"

Anything in my handwriting makes me culpable. What am I going to do? This is getting crazier. Myers's fears grew exponentially. *I can't report this!* Myers thought of his family, devoted wife 'Shirley May', and their pocket poodle, 'Poo Poo.'

Kock snapped his fingers, "Oh yes, one further thing: I will be awarded the Medal of Honor."

Myers laughed out loud.

He just couldn't help it. The pressure, the stress, the fear just bubbled to the surface in raw howling laughter. Collapsing to the floor, rolling back and forth, tears streaming from his eyes, he was helpless with uncontrollable laughter.

Peter Paul God-Kock hit the panic button.

Seconds later, Myers, the Butler, was carried from the room by security forces, but now he was pleading and sobbing for forgiveness.

"Please, please, you gotta understand! You don't understand; I couldn't help if you don't know what he's like...!"

****

An hour later, there was a timid knock on the door.

"Yes!" God-Kock blearily replied. Shaking his head to dispel the cobwebs from the daydreams of his glorious and profitable future, he looked about, at first uncertain of his location. Then he remembered: he would be an Oligarch! His dreams had been answered! Because he captured the aliens, the Cascadian, the Einstein Stone, and the artifact of St. Catherine, he would be hailed as a hero and welcomed back to the bosom of the Oligarch family. It was so awesome; God-Kock teared up just thinking of it. *Me! Honored and*

Respected! Given riches and power! It was so incredible God-Kock got an erection he could drive nails with.

A paper slid beneath the door.

"What the hell?" Dropping his penis, God-Kock scurried over and picked up the paper:

"Alien Emissaries are gone.

Cascadian Invaders are gone.

Blue-Green Stone is gone.

Artifact of St. Catherine is gone.

We are gone."

The signature line was left blank.

God-Kock ground his teeth. *Jesus was clearly jealous of him! Sabotaging his return to the Oligarch levels he deserved.*

"Bink!"

A message had arrived on his personal computer: "Report to Homeland Security Main Offices, Immediately. signed: Oligarch Barcelona."

"Oh fuck!" God-Kock was astonished. "How the fuck did Barcelona know they all escaped before I did?"

It occurred to Peter Paul God-Kock that all of his carefully thought-out plans were gone. He would be going to see Barcelona empty-handed. With only his personal guarantee he had changed, and that he was once again entitled to Oligarch status.

God-Kock, though, had little hope of a successful ending to this. It was sort of like visiting a starving lion in his den and bringing him a cookie.

~ 25 ~

THE HAMMER

"I'm not an atheist. The problem involved is too vast for our limited minds. We are in the position of a little child entering a huge library filled with books in many languages. The child knows someone must have written those books."
Albert Einstein

$$\sim 26 \sim$$

CHAPTER TWENTY-FOUR

"Go! Go! Go!" Charley Bones yelled as they scrambled away from the Homeland Security H.Q., prizes in hand.

An early morning Amazon Prime Delivery Van was pulled up next to a Rite-Aid Pharmacy just down the road.

"Come on, let's get out of here." Charley leaped into the driver's seat and gunned the engine. "Come on, come on," he urged. Unfortunately, unlike the others, this Amazon Prime Delivery Van still had a driver on board, rooting around boxes in the back when Charley slipped into the driver's seat.

"Hey! What are you guys doing?" The surprised driver dropped his packages and moved forward to confront Charley.

Pawnee stuck a gun in the man's face and he stopped cold. "Chee, Brah, looks like you gots the day off."

The Amazon Prime Van Driver shrugged. The pay was shit, the supervisors were assholes, the benefits ridiculous, and the future bleak. "Fuck it! Can I come with you?" The driver pleaded. "If we lose a package, we have to pay for it out of our wages...losing an entire van load...well, I think I'll just disappear."

"Sorry, dude, we have a mission. Can't take recruits off the street, you know?"

"Dude," He pleaded, "You don't know what management is like. They are going to go hard on me for this!"

The disappointed Amazon Prime Van Drive hopped out and everyone else piled in. He waved forlornly as they drove away.

Pawnee Painter, Doc Betters, Muh, Jee, and Yaz settled among the boxes and packages, getting comfortable as Charley floored the Van.

"You did well, Yaz." Pawnee complimented the young alien. They had the Einstein Stone. Pawnee turned it this way and that, trying to study it in the dim light of the Van. "It doesn't look like much." The surface of the stone was dull, pitted, not the gem-like smooth appearance he had expected. It was the most curious shade of green-blue, kind of bluish teal, he'd ever seen. But here it was, he held it in his hand, weighing, evaluating it. Decades spent seeking this stone, years of devotion, study, searching, and now finding. Pawnee felt a deep well of satisfaction and pride within him.

He held up the shin bone of St. Catherine, and then he held up the Einstein Stone: A shard of old bone and a dull rock. Now what? His thoughts turned to his son. He had accomplished his goal, finding the prizes, but what comes next? Where was his son?

Yaz, lying back on a soft fifty-pound bag of dog food, asked. "Can I look at that?"

Pawnee handed it over.

Yaz looked closely at the carved, sacred shin bone of St. Catherine. He slowly began decoding the bone's scratches, carvings, and marks. This surprised him because he did not know ancient languages or artifacts. But somehow, he looked at the bone, and the scratches became letters that became words. A chill went through his body. Turning to his backpack, Yaz pulled out a small silver box, opened it, and began entering numbers and codes into it. He studied the screen, looked at the shin bone, looked back at his instrument, and shuddered.

Who knew a leg bone from the fifteenth century could make such a difference! Yaz was deeply impressed. *The 'Teaching Stone' now called 'Einstein was real and in his hands.*

In the stop-and-go traffic of Indianapolis, Charley made the best speed he could in their getaway. But the streets were jammed with people, now parked in crazy herringbone patterns, staring up the sky. Charley estimated there must have been thousands of phone images of the shifting ribbons of light; reds, greens, blues crossed the sky in a majestic kaleidoscope of colors.

Pawnee and the three beagles were sprawled on various boxes and packages in the back. Doc rode shotgun in the doorway, sitting on a fifty pound bag of dog food

Yaz fiddled with the dials using his opposable claws, stared at the silver box, tweaked dials again, stared a second time. He tapped the small device with his claw, then against the side of the van. He studied the screen again.

"Oooh, this is nasty," Yaz looked up from his calculations. "Ah, this is so not good it's probably bad, real bad."

"What does that mean?" Charley didn't like the sound of the alien's voice, as it held a growl he had not heard before.

"Well, we should...you know...find cover...fast" Yaz looked more closely at this instrument. "Sooner than soon." He looked out the back window at the billowing clouds glowing in nearly fluorescent shades.

"Say what?"

Muh and Jee stared at Yaz strangely.

"Humans," Yaz said, "The Shinbone of St. Catherine held a warning. Disaster and hope in equal measure will appear simultaneously when the Einstein Stone is revealed." Yaz studied his hand computer again. "So I checked our environmental scans and found this...." He held up the tiny computer screen it was filled with scribbled.

"Dude, we have no idea what that says," Doc squinted, but the scribbles didn't become any more straightforward.

"Oh, well, it says that your Sun is preparing a little gift for you. In a Coronal Mass Ejection Event, a massive flare is about to erupt straight at your planet, and if my calculations are correct, it could end your civilization."

Complete silence in the Amazon Prime Van, just the rumbling of the wheels on uneven pavement.

Charley looked at Doc. "Did he say that? The End?"

Doc's face went ashen. "My Indica crop is just about due for harvest...my best strain yet...Ah called it 'Doc's Dope '... it'll couch-lock a rhinoceros."

"Doc, we have more worries than that."

"That, Charles, is very much a matter of perspective! My hybrid has been years in development. crossing this strain and that..."

"Chee, dis da truth? Solar Flare?" Pawnee immediately thought of his son, wondering if he would see him again, but quickly shut down his feelings. The mission comes first.

"WE have solar flares all the time. What makes this a problem?" Charley wondered, carefully steering around a crowd of people gawking up at the sky.

"There is a mine, looks like an old abandoned coal mine," Yaz continued, "This concrete path we are on is Montana Interstate 15. This runs into Interstate 90. stay on 90 East for six miles until Home stake Lake recreation area. Now it gets tricky: take Lakota Trails road to the cutoff of Bluff Rd and Blue, go East on Bluff Rd for two miles, then left onto Maribel Lane Rd, Right on Cedar Alley Rd, left on...."

"Cut to the chase. Where are we going?" Charley demanded.

"Why, a coal mine? To protect us from radiation. it's called The Alexis Neala Mine!" Yaz replied.

"But...?"

"Don't listen to him," hissed Muh, "he's a know-nothing, a middle child. Probably dropped on his head as an infant."

"This kind of solar flare... you're scientists rate it an X, probability level...oh, not good...level 8 I believe." Yaz reported glumly, "We need to get deep."

"Shut up, Yaz!" Jee joined in. "This isn't your job! This is classified need to know!"

"This kind of intensity, if it hits in the right places...." Yaz told them sadly. "You guys are going to lose everything. Get your clubs and fur hats. It will be back to the stone ages, boys!" Yaz thought a little levity might lighten the bad news and he didn't want to mention the complete sterilization of the human race as one possibility.

"Yaz, I'm telling you, stop it this instant. I am Muh, I am the leader of this mission, you are compromising this mission by...."

"All right, buddy, that did it!" Jee was incensed. Fighting for leadership was tough enough, and Jee had no time for delays. *There is a schedule to keep, a goal in life.* He grabbed Yaz and tried to wrestle the instrument away. "Give me that, Yaz; I'm more qualified than you!"

"Enough!" Charley intervened and separated the two quarreling aliens. "Think about what we've seen in the sky lately, guys? Does any of that look normal to you? This shit is serious, and we don't need some bullshit quarrel." He turned to Yaz. "Tell us what we need to know, right now, everything you know."

Yaz beamed at the opportunity of a lifetime. "Well, I really should say how honored I am that you have chosen...."

"Talk now, brag later," Charley muttered darkly.

Standing tall on his cardboard box, Yaz reveled in his new role. Relieved that now, finally, he could speak and be heard at last. It was a dream come true.

"E.M.P.!" He nearly shouted the words, so eager to begin. "Electromagnetic Pulse! Earth, nations, civilization, all of it, say goodbye to your civilization. An Electromagnetic Pulse will fry every circuit board, every computer; everything electric will be a crispy critter. Cars, trucks, planes, trains, T.V., Internet, you name it; anything run by electronics and computers is toasted. And this bullshit network you guys call an electric grid." He laughed. "It'll fry like Rastafarian hair on a hot plate. You guys are fucked."

"You've broken the code of silence!" Shrieked Muh. "We'll be outcasts, doomed to wander backwater planets like this one. Are you crazy?"

"What code of silence?" Jee asked. "You didn't tell me about a code of silence," he whirled on Muh.

"Of course not, then it wouldn't be a code of silence!"

"This Solar Flare she due soon?" Pawnee was still studying the sky.

"By my calculation, we have enough time to get there, but can we get deep enough in the mine to prevent solar radiation damage to us? Don't know."

"What that little guy is saying makes sense if you think about it," Charley explained to Doc. "The weird sky, the weather, those invasions of space temperatures into our world, all of this means something." Charley pointed at the Sun. "That is what it means. Now let's go!"

At that moment, the sky above them turned to a shade of purple and pink, none of them had ever seen.

"I suggest we get to safety right now!" Yaz said, holding up the silver instrument pointing at it. "Your planet is going to take a beating very soon. You must drive faster if you wish to survive."

~ 27 ~

CHAPTER TWENTY-FIVE

"When something vibrates, the electrons of the entire universe resonate with it. Everything is connected. The greatest tragedy of human existence is the illusion of separateness."

Albert Einstein

A solar flare is about to hit the Earth?

Charley Bones did not understand what that would mean: Aurora Borealis to the equator?

Yaz seemed sure this was a dangerous event, even to the point of changing our civilization. Charley thought the world could sure use some changes. When he was born, he saw himself as an American. He thought Americans stood for freedom for all races and all people; he felt his Nation stood for fairness, justice, honesty, giving people a fair deal. Spreading Democracy around the globe. He Thought as an American that peace and freedom were the goals of his people.

The problem is none of that turned out to be true. Charley's life and travels had taught him the truth. Disaster Capitalism fueled the American Way: Cheap hamburgers, outrageous sneakers, and wall-to-wall T.V.s were available because other humans suffered from low wages, dangerous working conditions, grueling hours, all made worse by U.S. interference in their elections and Government operations. Every day he directly benefited from the suffering of another human being. His lifestyle was purchased at the direct, brutal expense of some poor unfortunate person who lived in a nation weaker than the U.S.

Charley Brown Bones thought about the disparity and the hypocrisy that formed his life. *What true and what is nothing but a convenient mythology justifying brutal reality?*

Suddenly an old memory sprang to mind. A relic of his past caught Charley like a swirling eddy, pulling him from the mainstream of his thoughts.

****

An Loc province, South Vietnam, August 1970.

Sometimes Long Range Patrol missions started poorly and ended the same way. The noise they had made on insertion to the jungle was troublesome but unavoidable. So they had to move quickly away.

So far, so good.

Sergeant Charley Brown Bones signaled his five-man team to move ahead. They were widely spaced and crept down beside the muddy trail cautiously but as rapidly as they dared.

Charley looked around. It was a typical tropical afternoon of the monsoon season. Suddenly the rain, like turning on a water spigot, fell in a drumming, drenching curtain for twenty minutes then stopped abruptly, followed by a 'wool-blanket' humidity that suffocated him. Charley Bones felt all the energy leave his body as he struggled up the slippery side of a rice paddy dike southwest. of the twin hamlets of Nui Ba Din and Nui Ba Den.

Ten minutes later, bedded down in a suitable hide, they settled in for the night, an observation post overlooking a well-run V.C. trail.

"Sarge," Bones turned to his scout and interpreter, Vietnamese Ranger, Nguyen Trang, "We'll settle in here, you okay?" Nguyen had been with Charley Bones for six months, a long travel time in enemy country, firefights, running for their lives, and always on alert for that next bullet or bomb. Nguyen was an educated man, rare for Vietnamese. As a pilot, he was shot down early in the war and broke his jaw. He was never allowed to fly again. He became a Ranger to continue the fight and was perhaps the bravest man Charley ever knew, risking his life many times for Americans and Vietnamese alike.

But Nguyen was troubled, and Charley needed to find out why.

"What's wrong, Nguyen?" Something heavy was weighing on the Ranger. He seldom made eye contact anymore, often preferred solitary or the company of only fellow Vietnamese. No Americans.

Charley couldn't imagine a worse place to ask personal questions. The bush was business, and everything else was secondary. But Nguyen had missed some signs back on the trail that one of the other Rangers was very lucky to find; signs of recent V.C. movement here. These were not signs they wanted to miss.

"Nguyen, whatever is bothering you, get rid of it or get past it. We don't have time for this shit." Charley was harsh because every detail became important when death resulted from a moment's hesitation or lapse of focus.

Nguyen looked angry at first, his dark eyes and features clouded. He placed his arm up against Charley's, and their skin color was nearly the same.

Charley Brown Bones was a Potawatomi Native on his mother's side and a Lakota on his father's. He was not full blood but had inherited very native features.

Nguyen looked down at their side by side arms and said, "You and me, we are same-same, yes? You and I are native people, yes? Then why do you help the White man kill us? Didn't he do that to your people?" Nguyen's university education had included American history. He continued, "Didn't the white man try to exterminate you? So why are you here helping the White man exterminate us?"

Charley was stunned by Nguyen's comments. Like a light switched on in a dark room, Charley Brown Bones was enlightened to a reality he had not understood.

Until now, Charley believed he was an 'American Indian,' and the past had nothing to do with the present. He had lived his life ignoring the history of his native people, and the traditions and ceremonies were quaint relics of the past to him. Like an African-American or Asian-American, he was an American Indian, a Potawatomi-American, so he was an American who happened to be Indian. But were the two compatible?

American Indian is an oxymoron, he realized. *Like 'Military Intelligence,' 'Old News' and 'Silent Scream.' To be a Native man, he could not be an American because the two were contradictory.*

Nguyen's words brought a realization a he had not made before: Vietnam wasn't about liberating anyone. Vietnam was about geopolitical games and money, so the Vietnamese people's freedom had nothing to do with it. Just like the United States policies toward the Native Americans were more about genocide than assimilation; eradication, not acceptance.

Who am I fighting for? Which side am I on?

Once again, Charley Brown Bones felt that jarring disconnect between who he knew himself to be and how his society saw him.

~ 28 ~

CHAPTER TWENTY-SIX

Suddenly, a large yellow school bus with bright red balloons swerved into their lane. Charley had to twist the steering wheel quickly to the left to avoid a collision. A man hanging out the back window made an obscene gesture with one hand, waving a Holy Bible with the other.

"Woah! You asshole!" Charley snarled at the driver of the school bus.

As their Amazon Prime Van pulled alongside the Yellow Bus, the driver leaned out the window and glared at them. He appeared to be barely controlling his rage while laughing manically. He made eye contact with Charley and shouted something,

"Lord...smite...heathen...pineapple..." It was hard to understand the words, but the driver seemed convinced they were necessary.

Charley was amazed, "Doc, that guy must have fifteen crucifixes hanging around his neck!"

The Yellow Bus driver struggled to get a crucifix back in the bus, then slammed the window.

Hanging out in the wind behind the wild-haired, Bible-thumping, crucifix covered, bus driver were men and women screeching Holy Bible verses, King James Version, of course, and waving weapons.

Charley backed off the gas, keeping well behind the school bus as it weaved in and out of its lane. The bus with bright red happy balloons all over it would accelerate then slow, accelerate then slow. Occasionally Charley saw a gunshot come out of the bus, and he backed off further. "Going to give you some room, crazy man." Charley was confident the fool would do something unexpected.

Fortunately, the school bus suddenly accelerated, the distance between them increased rapidly on East I-90 until it disappeared around some curves ahead.

"I hope to fuck we don't meet those assholes again," Charley muttered and gradually began to relax a little.

Fortunately, the traffic was nearly nonexistent along this stretch of the highway.

"Charles," Doc interrupted him. "If ya'll done making friends with the other travelers, I think you need to take a break, get some rest. I can drive." He had been watching Charley and could see him nodding, losing focus from time to time.

"I'm fine."

"Charles, your anger is getting worse. Time and again, I tell you, 'Charles,' you get riled up too much. Calm down! You need to sit back, relax, smoke weed, chill out, dude. Now I have this serious strain of Sativa, I call it "Doc's Dream," you need some of that."

"I'm fine."

"You are not!"

"I'm fine! But we can switch, okay?" Charley was tired of being nagged. Besides, he had gotten angry again, and he had promised himself to keep his infamous temper quiet.

They switched seats, Doc settling into the driver's seat and Charley onto a still-warm bag of dog kibble.

"Now, I want you to follow my medical advice. Whatever you do, stay away from strong Indica's. Your mood is far too grim, to begin with...."

"Doc, leave me alone."

"But...as your personal physician...."

"No!"

The dog food was comfortable; Charley leaned back, shut his eyes, and started deep breathing exercises. Ignoring Doc was his best defense.

"Shit."

Charley opened his eyes at Doc's exclamation.

Suddenly coming up on the right side, the bright yellow bus with cheery red balloons came alongside them.

"What the fuck?" Charley was alarmed. The yellow bus had stopped off someplace and now here they were again.

But just as quickly as the bus appeared, it disappeared, turning a hard right into a highway rest stop area.

Charley leaned out the window to get a better look. The yellow bus slammed to a skidding stop in the Rest Center, disgorged its human cargo, and they came out firing automatic weapons.

"Holy Shit, Doc!" Charley watched as people were being shot right where they stood, while most were running blindly in all directions.

The rest stop was a chaos of carnage.

"Go Doc go, floor it! We've got to get away from that god damn bus!"

Doc was staring in the rearview mirror, shocked by what was happening behind them.

"Pawnee, Yaz, anyone!" Charley yelled into the back. "Where the hell is that turn-off?" He wanted to get them off this road before that school bus rolled back in their direction. Those people were vicious killers.

Pawnee grumbled. He had been napping soundly curled up on attic insulation. He stretched and looked out the front window. "See, next left, go there."

"Yes," Yaz called out, climbing up to the front of the Van for a better view. "Go next left, then find Turkey Hills Road, go right and stay straight until Alexis Mine Road. Turn to the left, and there we are. Not far!"

"Hey, orphan!" Muh called to Yaz." How come you know of a mine around here? You've never been here, right? Or is this another place you've snuck off to when our backs were turned? Traitor!"

"Well, while we were incarcerated in Butte, I took the time to better my education," Yaz replied. "They had want ads in the newspaper for people to lead tours in this old abandoned coal mine called The Alexis Neala Mine...I remember it, that's all."

Muh thought about that. *Does Yaz remember stuff? Who knew?*

"You'll look peaked, son, you sick?" Doc drove carefully, following Yaz's directions closely. He gave Charley a sly look. "Y'all get sick. I can't help you, and I have decided ya'll a poor patient. Don't follow the Doctor's orders. So I'm firing your ass. Find another to care for your various medical issues."

"My medical issues? What medical issues?"

Charley looked exhausted and far too pale, but Doc decided on a tough-love approach. *Charles wouldn't listen to sound medical advice,* Doc reasoned, *so I will deprive him of my services until he wakes up and cooperates.*

"You'll need a doctor," Doc explained, as he turned left onto Alexis Neala Mine Road, then another left into the parking lot. "Ya'll better dial 911 as I have hung up my stethoscope for good."

"You have a stethoscope? For medical marijuana patients?" Charley wondered what kind of game Doc was playing now. *Every now and then, Doc gets an attitude.* "Your dope that strong, you worry they won't have a pulse after a bong hit?

"Ah shall not dignify that outrageous characterization with mah reply!" Doc sniffed as he placed the overheated Amazon Prime Deliver Van in Park and slid open the door.

"Damn Doc, your speech impediment is getting worse, not better." Charley climbed out the other side.

Doc squinted at Charley as he came around the front of the vehicle. "Y'all calling my charming Southern accent a speech impediment? You Yankee! Y'all insulting' my heritage? Better hope civilization ends, or I'm going to finish it for you."

~ 29 ~

CHAPTER TWENTY-SEVEN

"Time and space are not conditions in which we live, but modes by which we think. Physical concepts are free creations of the human mind, and are not, however it may seem, determined by the external world." Albert Einstein

"Price, get General Figg on the damn line! When are we going to shove missiles up that black bitch's ass?"

"I have just spoken with the General and have two exciting pieces of news for you." Price Wayne replied calmly. Talking with General Figg was like talking to a petulant insecure teenager, and it was exhausting. Every conversation with Figg consisted of bitching, moaning, complaining, and whining about how his life sucked.

"I asked you a question, Wayne! Answer the goddamned question first!" Barcelona had decided Price Wayne needed a reminder of who was on the boat.

Price Wayne was getting sick and tired of Barcelona reminding him of who was who on the boat. "One hour and forty-two minutes left before we decimate Seattle, San Francisco, Los Angeles, and Medford, Oregon," Wayne answered promptly.

Barcelona, number Three of the Forty, smiled. "Excellent...but why Medford, Oregon?"

"Figg received a traffic ticket in Medford. He had one missile left over, so he figured why the fuck not. He's never paid the ticket either."

Barcelona nodded his head in approval. He appreciated employees who grasped the apparent solutions: *Vengeance was necessary to keep the little people subservient.*

"Good initiative, peons, are so replaceable," Barcelona said expansively. "You could learn a thing or two from watching your superiors make these crucial decisions. Death is very educational."

"I am sure it is...depending on perspective of course. Anything else, sir?" Wayne replied quickly, wanting to remove himself from Barcelona's presence immediately.

"Make it so," Barcelona heard that on Star Trek and felt a kinship with Jon Luc Picard: *Commanding a massive ship, exploring the unknown, solving crisis after crisis, facing danger but always thinking of my crew.*

Barcelona lifted his Kaenon Polarized Sun Glasses and peered at the diamond sparkles off the sunlit seas as a gentle wave lifted his luxury yacht and then replaced it, calmly, quietly. A dolphin playfully chased a flying fish. A gentle breeze stirred the soft, deep blue Adriatic sea, and he could smell the roasting of meat for his summer lunch.

Staring up at the sky, his conversation forgotten, Barcelona was amazed at what he saw. "Wow!" The colors were beyond all experience. It looked as if the entire sky was puffing its cheeks, clouds billowing in and out of existence, their shredded remnants scattered across the fire-red sky.

A moment ago, the sky was light blue. Fluffy clouds dotted the horizon, but now, the blue was gone, and a red-orange haze that grew denser, more intense, covered the sky. Suddenly, like a stone thrown into a pond, a ripple effect spread across the sky, East to West, the ripples held veins of crimson and violet. The sky was growing dark and malignant overhead.

Then a blast of light, crimson-yellow, followed by a lightning bolt of deep blue, powered a swirling, biting wind that seem to come from all directions. A ripe stench of ozone filled the air. Barcelona's ears popped at a sudden spasm of air pressure surge through him.

Then everything stopped.

The vibrations from the engines under his feet ceased.

Suddenly, the world went quiet, no sounds, and no air movement. Just the slap of waves hitting the boat, there were no birds in the air anywhere Barcelona looked.

The sky turned a flat gray, no color at all.

But no engine noise? No phones? Have I gone deaf? No, he could still hear sounds, but not the sounds he was used to.

The boat was just drifting.

The supply, heavy-lift helicopter quit flying and dropped like a brick into the sea.

"Sir, we have a problem!" Price Wayne rushed up, sweaty and red in the face. "All communications are out. We have no way of sending a distress signal. No phones, no internet, no radio, no satellite communications. Engines, computers, navigation, water distilling, air conditioning, food storage, all the amenities, all the necessities gone. What will we do?"

Barcelona thought about the situation. It occurred to him that he had nothing to worry about for the simple reason he was blessed. Life would always grant him his wishes.

"Why, we do nothing, help is on the way even as we speak." His faith that his loyal servants would back him up was absolute. A combination of bribery and fear worked wonders with motivation.

Barcelona strolled casually up the gentle slope of the stairs to the top deck. Settling himself into a chaise lounge under the shade of an awning, he picked up his expensive whisky, sipped carefully, and smiled. "Man, that shit is good."

Price Wayne thought, *Enjoy your $12,000 shot of booze. It will be your last.* The rich and pompous had everything they wanted;

Patek Philippe Worldtimer Guilloche watches, Aston Martin and Maserati's, $100,000 shopping sprees; Personal homes on every continent, and a fleet of yachts to get them back and forth. For Price Wayne the endless list of their possessions was nauseating; *So few could have so much and so many, so little. How odd, I never thought of myself as a bleeding heart liberal,* he mused, *but clearly, some crime is so egregious it is unmistakable as anything else.*

"They will be out looking for us anytime now." Barcelona looked at Price Wayne over his sunglasses. "You are fretting, Mr. Wayne, and this is insulting to me. I am Barcelona Philippi Manjesto Rodriguez! I am the fourth wealthiest man on this planet! I am number four of The Forty! I am far too important not to rescue! Believe me, we have nothing to worry about, so relax, and go tell the chef to cook up a feast! Refrigeration is out, so let's have a party! Booze, drinks, laughter. When then find us, we will be fat, drunk, and happy."

As he settled in for the feast, Barcelona considered his conversation with Myers the Butler. Myers was a confidential informant for years. "How very curious," Barcelona muttered. "A Blue-Green Emerald?" Myers had filled him in on the recent activities out in Butte, Montana. "Green Beagles?"

Barcelona felt a chill, a premonition.

~ 30 ~

CHAPTER TWENTY-EIGHT

"Time does not exist – we invented it. Time is what the clock says. The distinction between the past, present and future is only a stubbornly persistent illusion." Albert Einstein

The Sun that gives Earth Life is a complex nuclear furnace of ionized gases wrapped by an intense magnetic field. Currents of gas whirl around the Sun, creating powerful magnetic lines that become twisted and tangled, like nests of Boa Constrictors, huge, muscular, and writhing. They potentiate each other to produce massive columns of violently ionized gases.

Occasionally, this nest of magnetized snakes becomes so tangled, so intensely bonded they create a 'Dark Spot', the fancy scientific name for what appears as a dark spot on the Sun. As the tangled lines grow more tightly wound and the Dark Spot grows intensely darker, the energy inherent in the magnetized currents creates a heat bubble of such enormous complexity it compresses the magnetic hydrogen and helium gases to the point of explosion.

A massive plume of superheated, ionized gases erupting from the Sun is a Coronal Mass Ejection (C.M.E.). An event that can stretch far out into the stellar void, harmless except when it hits a solid object like The Earth.

At 16:30 September 30, 2022, Greenwich Mean Time, a massive C.M.E. struck the Earth with a mighty hammer blow of ionized gasses and solar plasma that punched right through the protective envelope of the atmosphere, impacting the planet itself. Like striking a bell, the reverberations of the C.M.E. created a planetary geomagnetic storm rapidly circling the globe, producing an intense, broad-spectrum Electromagnetic Pulse (E.M.P.).

Everything dependent upon computers stopped instantly: All lights, water, communications, Internet, transportation, food delivery, medical services, rescue services, G.P.S. navigation services, Law Enforcement, government programs, banking all were silenced. Corporate communication collapsed, Financial centers around the globe went dark, and everything dependent on computers chips rendered inert by the E.M.P.

Within minutes civilization depended on the computer chip disappeared, and millions died.

$$\sim 31 \sim$$

CHAPTER TWENTY-NINE

"The intellect has little to do on the road to discovery. There comes a leap in consciousness, call it intuition or what you will, the solution comes to you and you don't know how or why." Albert Einstein

Charley Brown Bones was the first to exit the mine shaft and walk into a new world.

They came out of the deep dark coal mine into the open-air majesty of a celestial magic show, an Aurora Borealis on steroids. Charley stopped, stunned with wonder as the entire sky was illuminated by radiant colors of blue and green, streaks of ochre painted the wispy clouds racing overhead.

It was an experience for which there were no suitable words.

Charley Bones stopped and stared.

Doc followed, carrying Yaz. He stopped beside Charley, and they both stood silently.

They watched as the sky danced; colors swirled, shades and images and lightning fought for command. There was a strong scent of ozone everywhere. Clouds scudded by at hyper speed, forming and dissolving, like fast forward on a video. The light flickered with the dramatic cloud movement, and it seemed as if a soft gold aura was radiant.

Charley Brown stood still. Unaware of anything around him but what was directly overhead. He was stunned by the magnitude. Everywhere he looked, the entire Cosmos seemed to glow with sapient energy, a pulse in the heartbeat of the solar system.

This was overhead, but beneath his feet, he felt a deep pulse coming from the Earth that vibrated his bones. Crows above them were circling as if lost, unable to determine direction, cawing loudly.

"We are in a different world, Doc."

"No shit, Sherlock," Doc nodded, wishing for some magic mushrooms right now.

Pawnee carrying Muh and Jee emerged, blinking his eyes at the celestial fireworks. The two beagles were barking and wriggling in his arms in disagreement.

Pawnee had inadvertently picked up Jee before Muh, and this was a grave and insulting decision, violating Muh's internal sense of decorum and chain of command.

"You watch yourself, buddy," Muh warned darkly. "You are under my command. I can have you punished!"

Jee narrowed his eyes, not liking the threat.

"We will see about that," Jee muttered.
****

A lone coyote stared at them from no more than twenty feet away, unafraid, curious in fact; ears were up, tail held straight out, muzzle pointed toward them, scenting the air. Suddenly, he became aware of Muh, Jee, and Yaz. The coyote stared with rapt fascination, his nose twitching, ears alert, body held frozen, ready to run or attack. Slowly he crept forward toward them as if to investigate these strange new 'dogs'.

Pawnee set the complaining Muh and Jee down and the coyote loped a little closer.

"Hey! Hey!" Muh shouted, "pick us up now!"

"That thing is going to eat us! Save us!" Jee demanded.

Pawnee obliged, "Chee, you no like you brother?"

"I don't like anything that wants to eat me." Jee retorted.

It occurred to Pawnee they had never asked these three if 'dog' their actual physical shape was 'dog'. "You appear as dogs, but is that what you are?"

"Certainly not! We are, of course, honored to be in this disguise, but this is not anywhere near our real body shape."

"So, what do you look like?"

"We are gorgeous, of course, absolutely stunning for our people," Jee announced. "But you wouldn't appreciate the ooze."

Pawnee decided that conversation was as far as it needed to go. He looked around at the world. Everything seemed different, the same green for the trees but in a slightly different shade. What else would be different? He wondered.

Joining up with Charley, Yaz, and Doc, they checked out the Amazon Prime Van. No, go, wouldn't even turn over. They had to walk down the mountain.

At Brown Mountain Coal Rd and Little Creek rd SE, Charley Brown Bones and Doc Betters met their first citizen while walking ahead of the others.

A small family; man, wife, two kids, two dogs, and a 2019 Subaru were sitting silently beside the road. They were still, paused as if waiting. The man was outside the car sitting against the driver's side wheel, the woman inside, head bowed down, unmoving in the passenger seat.

The two kids, a boy and girl, stared solemnly back at Charley from the backseat, no expression on their faces. Their eyes were open with curiosity, but they made no sound, just sitting, looking around them fearfully. Only the dogs showed any sign of recognition, wagging and yapping to be let out. The people paid no attention.

"Hello? Hello?" Charley called out. Pawnee and the three little green aliens were about five minutes behind them. "Are you guys okay?"

The man turned to look at Charley but said nothing at first, then his eyes drifted farther to the left, then all the way right. His eyes, bright blue, were unfocused, and he looked as if seeking the direction of a sound.

"Hey!" Doc tried to get their attention. "Hey, you guys okay?" He waved his arms.

"Easy Doc, don't spook them," Charley told him. These people were in shock of some sort, and he wanted to avoid startling or stressing them any further. "Hi, folks," Charley began again, moving toward the car slowly but gradually. As a cop, he'd had many years of practice approaching strange vehicles with strange people inside.

"Do you know what happened?" The man finally asked, eyes making contact with Charley, his voice vague, and his speech slow.

"What do you mean?"

Charley wanted to hear what the man knew first. He needed to evaluate these strangers to see if they needed help or presented a danger. Old cop behavior. They appeared dazed and confused but not harmful at the moment.

"We were driving along...going somewhere..." The strange man paused and looked around as if unsure of everything. "Then, then everything...was different." He looked slowly at the car. "The car is dead, computers, phones, nothing works." He paused and looked at the sky for a long time.

"Sir? Sir?" Charley tried to get his attention back. "Are you alright? Are you hurt?"

As soon as Charley uttered those words, Doc was on duty.

"You hurt?" Doc was beside the man, taking his pulse, lifting an eyelid, tapping on the guy's forehead. "Can you feel this? What is your name? Do you know where you are...how many fingers? Do you know what the date is today?"

The man flinched.

"Doc? Doc, slow down." Charley called out, trying to get his friend to lighten up a little.

Doc stopped. "Nothing physically wrong with them, Charles. Just kind of blank."

"Where were you coming from?" Charley asked, trying to get some kind of honest response from the man.

"I Don't know."

"Who are you?"

"Don't know."

"Do you need any help?

"Don't know."

"He won't be of much use to you for a while," Yaz said, coming up quietly behind Charley and Doc.

"What's wrong with him? What's wrong with all of them?" Doc asked. "They don't seem to be injured, but they are not all right."

"That's kind of hard to say," Yaz answered, his tail wagging slowly with thought.

"A clear answer would be nice," Charley told him. "There is enough confusion as it is."

"I wasn't ducking the question," Yaz said quickly, "Just that these kinds of events are different for different species and different individuals. Some people are unfazed, while others are blanked out. If I hadn't taken you down into that coal mine, you could be like our friends here, drooling and scratching, with no clue. This pulse may have tripped their reset buttons." Yaz couldn't think of another analogy that worked. "Just like a computer."

"The Electromagnetic pulse," Pawnee said without hesitation.

"That is what hammered them."

"They could be like this for days, maybe...longer," Yaz said sadly. "Sorry."

"What the hell are you saying 'sorry' for? What is holding us up? We have a long way to go." Muh arrived in bad humor. His authority, his command, had been shredded by outright rebellion. Yaz was responsible. "We are the superior being. They should be crawling on hands and knees to thank us for saving their miserable human skins!"

"Yeah!" Jee responded. "How come we have to walk all this way? They should carry us! We are the more advanced species you know!"

"Hey, Doc," Charley said, "I got a better idea. Know how to rig up a dog sled?"

"I don't know, Charles. They've got short legs."

"So I take it that's a no?"

~ 32 ~

CHAPTER THIRTY

A small fire flickered among the pines, shadows danced and a full moon blended with the Aurora Borealis, giving silver highlights to the shimmering greens and blues.

It has been a long hike from the mine down out of the mountains.

"The question is what now?" Charley stared at the fire then looked at Doc and Pawnee. "According to Yaz's instruments, this monster E.M.P. may have burned every computer chip in North America. America is toast, almost literally.

"And that means cars, boats, airplanes, all services, the internet itself, all communications; everything is probably down across this entire continent." Doc found all this hard to absorb. Somehow the magnitude of this was too large, too unreal. To consider the loss of life was impossible, and he refused to allow that in his thoughts. Doc wouldn't run from trouble, but he didn't want to invite it in either.

"Dis going to change da world power structure for sure." Pawnee mused.

"You think?"

"So, again, what do we do?" Charley asked.

If things were as bad as Yaz seemed to think, the idea of sitting on his front porch sipping beer, eating B.B.Q., while playing with his dogs was long gone. A suddenly intense sadness hit him hard.

The enormity of his loss, not just his, but the loss of everyone, was staggering.

"I'm just wondering what we do now. Continue? If what Yaz is saying is true, everything could be moot." Charley asked in a low voice.

"Chee, Brah, our mission was to get the shin bone of St. Catherine and use it to find The Einstein Stone." Pawnee dug around in his backpack. "Well, here they are; the bone and the rock."

"We were supposed to bring the Einstein Stone back to President Chowder, and I suppose we should..." Doc handled the bones of St. Catherine delicately.

"Whoah, whoah, pull in that runaway wagon!" Jee was on his feet. "You can't just take the Einstein Stone and do what you want with it! What about us?"

Muh knew time was running out, both on his role as leader of the mission and the mission itself, and he had to speak out now. "I as the command leader of this expedition," Muh pulled himself to his full height, fur raised, tail held ridged straight out, adopting his best authoritarian stance. "I demand the return of the Einstein Stone and immediate obedience to my galactic authority!" He used a bark modulator, creating decisive and commanding tones in clear English. "We have a mission to accomplish, and time is now short. You, humans, are ordered to do as I say!"

Charley was annoyed by this incessant whining. "Taking orders from a pet? I don't think so."

"We are not..."

"What do you think?" Charley asked Pawnee, ignoring Muh. "Where should we go from here?"

"I worry for my son, Clay," Pawnee said slowly, thoughtfully. "You have Einstein Stone, you have shin bone of dis saint, and you don't need me now. Clay needs me and I must find him." The changes in the world had reminded Pawnee that of all the adventure, excitement, and grand and glorious events of his life, nothing was more important than his son. Nothing mattered but the love he held for this boy.

"So, you're going to find him?" Doc asked. He looked at Charley. It was time for them to make some decisions too. Was Cascadia or the United States still in existence? Had anything changed? Had everything changed?"

"What do you say, Doc?" Charley asked. "Do we head West? See what is going on?"

"You'll call it right, Charles," Doc said, "maybe it's time we went home."

"No!"

"No?" Charley stared at Yaz.

Everybody was looking at Yaz.

"What do you mean, 'no' Yaz?"

Yaz wasn't sure why he was talking. But something was compelling him, driving him to speak up. "You're task is not done. You have the Einstein Stone, you have the shin bone, and you must now go East, to Cahokia Mounds, in Illinois." Yaz pointed in that direction. "The Sun's has set the stage. Now you must complete the ceremony at Cahokia Mound."

"What the hell is a Cahokia Mound?"

~ 33 ~

CHAPTER THIRTY ONE

"Our separation from each other is an optical illusion." Albert Einstein

Life had changed.

Scanning the horizon, Barcelona looked for his shadow yacht, maybe a Coast Guard rescue, but he saw nothing but water and an empty horizon line, day after day of nothing. Even the seagulls had left, and they tasted horrible anyway.

Barcelona sighed, floating listlessly somewhere in the Mediterranean Sea on his Mega Yacht. Life did have its difficulties.

All food was gone, no sign of rescue, no communications with the outside world, no power, no electricity, no drinking water, and Barcelona's Mai Tai supply was now exhausted.

The situation was grim.

Whenever Barcelona felt blue, he turned to his reflection in the mirror to reassure the world was still as he believed it to be. His face always calmed him, giving him a sense of reality. Handsome, debonair, beautiful people are blessed, uglies are cursed, and his thoughts brought comfort.

Showing his teeth in a strained grin, he took stock on himself. Fabulously wealthy and powerful because of his innate perfection, plus a genius ability to be flexible; he could bend with the wind, turn with the tides, and take victory from the jaws of defeat. Barcelona frowned at himself but couldn't hold it long; his innate sense of self-love always came through when he was troubled. More than mere self-confidence, Barcelona knew he was blessed. He could not fail because he was a miracle of creation. His responsibility was to become as rich and powerful as possible, God's will.

His stomach reminded him of hunger, but Barcelona knew this was not the end despite the threat of starvation. Not for him. Not for Barcelona!

"I have been blessed by God to achieve great things." He said to Price Wayne.

"Pardon, sir?" Wayne wasn't sure he heard right. His hunger was so insistent it drowned out anything else. Wayne was reasonably sure loyalty was overrated at this stage of his descent into infamy. The situation seemed dire, and he wasn't entirely confident Barcelona was still sane. On the other hand, adrift in the ocean with no hope of rescue and no food, maybe insanity was sane.

"I cannot fail!" Stretching his arms to embrace the heavens, Barcelona admired the glorious golden rays of the sun. Sunsets and sunrises made him weep with the awesomeness of nature, proving his rare and gifted sensitivities were finely tuned.

Watching the clouds slowly bleed their vibrant peacock colors, he felt such a stirring of his soul as if God had reached out and touched him. Bracing against the slow lazy roll of the oceans' dance, a lone Man O' War floated high up against the deep blue sky, and the scent of the sea was strong.

"Since I am God's chosen, I must be worshipped," Barcelona loved the sound of that. Like a lightning strike, he realized his life had just changed forever. The ramifications of being a deity sharpened his mind with potential.

Price Wayne, fascinated by the spiritual passions of his employer, watched carefully for sudden violence or bleeding stigmata that may erupt.

"If People worship God," Barcelona spoke out loud, his voice rising in passion. "They must serve God. Who is God? What is God? Am I God as well?"

Wayne wasn't sure where this was going, but the hairs on his neck stood up.

"My people worship me; I provide for them, I am life or death to them. Doesn't that make me God?" Barcelona was silent a moment. "Yes! I am sure it does!"

The profound revelation for Barcelona was a horrible premonition for Wayne.

Suddenly, Barcelona sat up and snapped his fingers. "Why didn't I think of this before?" He turned to Price Wayne with a self-satisfied smile on his face. "All our problems are solved! The answer is right in front of me. I can't believe it. It is so simple, so natural, and so...efficient."

"What answer?" Wayne asked carefully.

"Cannibalism!"

"If Cannibalism is the answer, what the hell was the question?" Wayne was stunned to disbelief. *When somebody thinks cannibalism is a good idea and they make eye contact with you...run.* Wayne took a quick step toward the cabin door.

"Sir?" Wayne paused, half-turned to escape, and half turned to find out what Barcelona had in mind.

"Are you suggesting we...cook the crew?" Price Wayne asked in astonishment.

"Make Hamburger Helper out of the help! You bet I am!" Barcelona tucked his hands in his pockets and swayed with self-delight.

"Oh." Wayne realized he was at a curiously unexpected turning point in life. *Cannibalism is one of those situations not covered by school guidance counselors.*

"Price Wayne," Barcelona commanded. "Turn on the intercom so I may address the crew."

"Okay." That was all Wayne could say. His mind raced with implications as he turned a switch for the ships' intercom.

Barcelona cleared his throat and spoke into the microphone: "Attention, Attention," his voice echoed throughout the ship. "This is your Majesty speaking. I know we have had trying times, tough times, but we have pulled together...."

Wayne was impressed with the volume of shouts, screams, and wall pounding that erupted from the cabins. He was very glad he had locked all the cabin doors.

"We have fought as a team, we have struggled, sacrificed, we are 'one for all and all for one!" Barcelona knew the little people loved encouragement. "I want you to know how incredibly proud I am of you...."

The pounding and shouting grew in intensity.

"I am proud of every one of you as a father loves his children. Please give yourselves a big hand." Barcelona applauded into the microphone.

The cacophony of banging and thumps and shouts rose to a fever pitch, meaning one thing to Barcelona: His people loved him.

"Great men have great responsibilities," He continued, very impressed with the intensity of the crew's adoration for him. "The leadership of great men is a gift to Civilization itself. Civilization cannot exist without great men to guide and nurture it. There are great men, and there are little men. Each has a role in life. Each has a part to play in this grand drama we call human existence!" Barcelona, proud of his stirring words, was coming to the good part. He paused to clear his throat and to emphasize his wisdom. "Each of us has a duty to this world; a duty to life itself. There are laws of nature, strong laws, good laws, laws that cannot be changed, laws that have guided living beings from the beginning. But of all the natural laws, one stands out as primary, the foundation for Civilization itself. This law is: 'Kill or be killed, without this immutable law the heart of Capitalism would cease to beat!"

There was a pause in the racket coming from the cabins, and then the banging and hollering started again, louder.

My goodness, it sounds as if they are breaking up furniture and beating on the walls. Most remarkable. Barcelona was impressed with the energy, dedication, loyalty, and love his crew demonstrated with their sacrifice. *Destroying their living quarters just to honor me!* A small tear formed in his eye from the magnificence of their loyalty.

"Thank you, thank you," was all Barcelona could say, so choked with gratitude and honor, he could barely speak. "You are all just wonderful."

Turning to Price Wayne, Barcelona said, "I am sorry for my show of emotions." He explained. "But I am just so overwhelmed with the love of my people for me."

"Oh?" Wayne cocked his head to hear this one. "What makes you think that?"

"Didn't you hear all of that noise? The crew was very expressive, shouting their messages of support, showing their love and respect for me. The volume of noise, their passionate hammering on their cabin walls, all dramatic gestures of loyalty and love."

"Any possibility the noise is because they've been locked in their cabins for three days?"

"Nonsense," Barcelona couldn't imagine they would complain about a little thing like that. "Now, here is the plan...."

~ 34 ~

CHAPTER THIRTY-TWO

"Cannibalism," explained Barcelona. "Is a misunderstood survival strategy employed by humanity since we learned to eat meat," Barcelona explained to an ever more curious Price Wayne his plan for the survival of the fittest.

I once saw Bear Grylls eat a banana slug, and I thought that was as extreme as it got. He began edging toward the door if this was more threat than explanation.

"Of course, you, as my most loyal and faithful servant, will be spared. The rest of the crew will be, sadly...harvested." Barcelona wondered how competent Price Wayne was at butchering. However, practice makes perfect, Barcelona reasoned.

Price sighed. "Oh?" He stopped edging. *Well, let's just see where this leads.* "Immediately, my Master."

Price Wayne considered himself a realist. *It is what it is.* As long as he was reading the menu and not on the menu, he'd wait and see how things progressed. *We're stranded on a boat in the middle of the ocean. Who is going to know?* Wayne told himself.

But what if someone does find out? The thought came unbidden to his mind. *What's this going to look like in the history books? The Donner Party had a major public relations problem,* Price reasoned. Now that he was in the situation, he could understand their thinking.

Cannibalism is a difficult concept to explain to people not actually starving, he realized.

So, hoping to lessen his culpability in this heinous crime, he took his newly created shopping list with him, carefully ticking off each stop. At each cabin door, he shouted: "Good day to you, sir or madam, shortly you will be fetched for dinner. Please be cooperative, thank you very much."

Wayne reasoned the crew and staff would be more docile if they thought they were being fed instead of being feed.

Wayne prayed his good manners and respectful politeness would balance out his eating of human flesh.

Sadly, the grand cuisine change did not go off as smoothly as Price Wayne had hoped. The crew and staff became remarkably argumentative when they discovered the menu was very personal.

So Barcelona, being the generous and compassionate Master he knew himself to be, decided to settle the matter quickly to lessen the confusion of the men and women who served him so well. Confident they would, of course, make the right choice, he once again stepped up to the microphone.

"Please, I realize this may be difficult for some of you, but you must see it from my perspective: I own you. But, I am a great and magnanimous master, so I leave the choice to you. Stay and be with us always, or you may leave. The choice is yours."

Barcelona winked at Price Wayne. "You see, I allow lesser being the freedom to make life choices. I am the best of all leaders; A benign dictator and I care about my people."

"We're in the middle of the Mediterranean Sea, 1500 miles in all directions to dry land. Where are they going to go?"

To Barcelona's deep sadness, they all chose to swim.

Barcelona was surprised and so disappointed, troubled by their lack of loyalty. "I don't understand they were so eager before?" He vented his sadness to Wayne.

"Some just have no concept of faith, my honorable and respected greatest of all Holiness." Price Wayne shrugged. "So what now? They won't come out of their cabins anyway."

Barcelona smirked. "You are so naïve," he told Wayne. "Like all Billionaires, we live with the knowledge that humans are jealous of us. People always want to take something from us, and it is simply not to be allowed. So it is standard procedure to install a gas system throughout the boat that renders everyone immediately unconscious; prevents such embarrassments as mutinies, riots, and wage demands. We gas them, drag them to the kitchen, and there we...stock the freezer."

Price Wayne admired the foresight and planning, despite the despicable brutality.

****

Unfortunately, conversion to cannibalism was not as simple as it seemed.

There were no cookbooks for cannibalism on board, and Price Wayne was an awful cook.

In desperation, Barcelona pulled his chef, Wing Top, from his gas-filled cabin, revived him, and informed him of his new good fortune.

However, cannibalism, being a new form of cuisine to Wing Top, had a steep learning curve, and he struggled at first. Being a practical man who didn't want to become a soup, he was strongly motivated to succeed. Trial and error proved specific recipes were better with certain humans; the Purser, for instance, was far tastier in Veal Parmesan than in Stir Fry and the Chambermaids should be cooked medium-rare, not well done.

Wing Top proudly announced after only a few short days he could identify which humans were better baked than fried.

Wayne didn't know whether to laugh or cry.

~ 35 ~

CHAPTER THIRTY-THREE

Bessie May Chowder had been shot down.

Jade Bi'ch Hai Bones, Personal Security Director for the Cascadian President was angry and embarrassed she had failed her duties. Jade and a protection detail had been in a separate aircraft, flying behind Chowder when they heard the mayday call.

It didn't4 take long before they learned she was alive but captive and being flown to Indianapolis for interrogation. Jade Bi'ch Hai Bones vowed to regain her beloved friend and mentor, so she did all she could to follow. Bailing from her official Lear Jet and utilizing her wing suit, she traveled a considerable distance, flying silently and secretly over the border of Cascadia before pulling the ripcord, winding up somewhere in western Idaho, United Christian States.

Hanging in her parachute harness, she could see the lights of the town below were bright and welcoming in the fading twilight. But, suddenly, the sky lit up with forked and branched lightning; raw flashes of crimson and purple split the sky, illuminating the land below her, which had suddenly gone pitch black.

As she floated down, Jade tried to puzzle out what had happened. Where did all the lights go?

A whooshing, hollow sound grew louder; it was coming from above her. The sounds grew louder and louder until a United Air Lines 727 plunged past her, engines silent, the lights were still on inside the cabin. A young mother, holding her infant child, stared out, and her eyes met Jade's, just for that incredibly brief second as the jet plunged to its doom.

***

"HEY! Hey!" Jade wrestled with her sleeping bag, struggling to wake up. "Wow, shit!" She sat up, her face in her hands. "Fucking nightmares." The eyes of the young woman haunted her; sadness, regret, rage, acceptance, all within that brief second.

Getting out of her sleeping bag, Jade Bi'ch Hai Charley stared at her hands. They were roughened and scarred. She sighed.

Her horse whinnied softly and stamped a hoof.

Glancing around quickly to ensure there was no immediate threat, she allowed herself to relax a bit. It had been a long hard ride, and there was no shortage of desperate people out there who would take her horse, to eat, if not to ride.

She shook her head to dispel the sticky terror of the dream.

The world was now a very different place. It had taken Jade over six months to get from Idaho to Indiana, although those designations no longer applied. She had no idea if the United Christian States or Cascadia was even active any longer, and no one knew. Without the Internet, phones, television, radio, rumors were given the same weight as fact, confusion and chaos threatened to, and had, descended into savagery in some communities.

There were many different names for this situation; the Solar Flare that wiped the planet clean of political lines and boundaries: 'The HAMMER' became the most popular. However, the Fires had their name: 'God's Torch.' But for the longest time, few knew what had happened, and this ignorance created a vacuum into which poured violence and chaos as different factions fought for supremacy

The massive fires ignited by The Hammer, still burning months later, created huge clouds of thick smoke, making navigation difficult. It was easy to lose orientation and easy to be trapped by flames. Several times Jade and her small band of survivors came close.

Worse were the radiation zones: The EMP melted huge commercial nuclear reactors across the land as none were hardened against such an event. Jade was well aware that profit came before life in old America, and profit was God. Profit margins would suffer from this expense if these plants were protected against EMP.

Idaho, Utah, Wyoming, South Dakota, Minnesota, Illinois, each state blessed with multiple Nuclear Power Plants, now had multiple, vast areas so poisoned by radiation fungus wouldn't live there for 50,000 years.

Jade had encountered dying areas: trees brown, no animals, no birds, no insects, just a barren stretch of land for miles surrounding the power plant. The few people still in these areas were sick, radiation burns, hair loss, blindness, all of it horrid for her to see and helpless to change any of it. Organized medical care was wiped out when the computers and Internet disappeared.

Her journey had been one of deep sadness despair as she witnessed the devolution of society. Some communities held together helped each other, tried to maintain civilization, others just went straight to violence: might made right. Jade had witnessed humanity falling off the cliff, back into a primordial sea of primitive instincts and brute demand.

~ 36 ~

CHAPTER THIRTY-FOUR

"Hey, Jade," a woman's voice called out.

Merry Sue was an older woman, late fifties, exhausted and starving, but still aware and determined to survive. "Kids need to rest for the night. Can we camp over there?" She pointed to a small copse of trees beside a small flowing creek.

Jade nodded, and the three adults, Merry plus her husband and her brother, traipsed over and began to set up camp. Both men were named Bill: To keep them straight, the husband was named 'Missourah Bill', the brother 'Alaska Bill'. The tiny survivor family proceeded to start a fire, get wood, and begin preparation of the meager supply of tin foods. The three children sat quietly, hunger and exhaustion claiming their energy.

When she first met them, lost, hungry, city people, forced to flee into the country in a desperate bid to find food and safety from collapsing Civilization, they had no weapons, no skills, no equipment, and no luck. Without cells phones and 'YouTube' Videos, they had little practical knowledge like building a fire or splinting a broken limb. Jade had adopted them shortly after The Hammer hit. They needed her, and she needed them.

"Hey, you kids, get over here. We need to get washed up." Merry was tough and resourceful but had her hands full trying to keep three small children safe in this new world. Missourah Bill, her husband, was a good man with no hand-to-eye coordination and couldn't hammer a nail at gunpoint. Merry's brother, Alaska Bill, a dark, taciturn man, was far more than he appeared; quiet, unassuming, polite, but very watchful. Jade liked Alaska Bill; he might be the most capable of them.

"Missourah, Alaska," Jade called out. "Gather more firewood, okay? It's going to be cold tonight." it was late February, and winter on the Great Plains was no joke. Intermittent rain and sleet had plagued them for the past week.

She could see Susan had the children cleaned up and ready for supper. Jade turned away as hot tears filled her eyes. They had so little food to share with these children, and two of them orphans just as she had been in Vietnam decades ago. She ladled the soup from a thin, dented pot, shaking her head to dispel old, rotten memories from long ago. The odor of the soup, primarily onions, and beets, reminded her of similar meals in Saigon's mean streets and bustle in 1968.

As she got her small fire going again, heating tea, overseeing the children sipping soup, she thought back to when The Hammer hit. Carefully she poured herself some nettle and lemon balm leaf tea and settled back against the small log.

She breathed a sigh, and then sadness hit her hard; tears welled up. She got up and moved away from others, feeling vulnerable in her grief. The eyes of the young mother from the doomed airliner haunted her nights.

"I guess it doesn't matter," Merry asked Jade, settling down, staring into the yellow campfire. "But why are we headed East?"

Jade didn't know how to answer that. But the last she knew, President of Cascadia Bessie May Chowder, was held captive and headed toward Indianapolis, Indiana. "I am looking for a friend, Merry, someone I admire and respect very much, and I plan to rescue her."

Merry didn't answer. She thought of all the dreams and hopes she had before The Hammer; raising her babies, loving her husband, living on a small farm, peace, contentment, happiness. Merry looked down at her torn, soiled clothing; her stomach growled as all the food went to the children. She worried about Missourah Bill and her brother Alaska Bill. Both were thin, too thin. Merry was concerned they would fall ill and felt helpless to care for them. Looking at Jade, Merry felt intense fear Jade would leave Merry's little family, take off on her own. Merry knew they had little chance on their own, at least not yet. They were learning. Merry quietly removed herself from the fireside to cry in private, concerned her tears would upset the children even more.

Merry sat in her tent as the tears flowed and took a long deep breath. *Stop it! Get hold of yourself!* Merry had those children now to protect and raise. One was hers, the other two belonged to someone else, but none of that mattered now because they were a family. The most vital and most enduring form of human relationships. She gritted her teeth. *Come on, Merry,* she scolded herself. *You have duties, responsibilities. Get to them, and stop feeling sorry for yourself.*

Merry closed her eyes. A fierce and indomitable dedication to keeping these children alive grew powerful and warm in her chest.

She deeply admired Jade because Jade was brave, while she was not. It troubled her she might fail these children, and fear gripped her.

~ 37 ~

CHAPTER THIRTY-FIVE

"We are souls dressed up in sacred biochemical garments and our bodies are the instruments through which our souls play their music." Albert Einstein

Charley worried about Pawnee.

Pawnee was different, quieter, and almost reticent to talk. He wanted his son, but Pawnee had stayed with them, not splitting off to look for Clay, almost as if he was reluctant to leave the group, and to Charley's knowledge, this was highly unusual for such an independent cuss. Something was off about Pawnee, and Charley worried it would blow up on all of them.

"Pawnee, you have first watch tonight," Charley called out. They had established order to their march east. Pawnee usually took first watch but was known to stay on watch all night.

In the Seven months of moving slowly Eastward, mostly at night, they had encountered whole communities of welcome, hard-working, compassionate people mixed with areas of bloodshed infested by power-mad little men with an apocalyptic vision of grandeur.

The curious American belief that freedom is a byproduct of bullets created free-fire zones of gunplay as one idea of 'freedom' clashed with another from community to community.

It had been hard travel, and their encounter two nights ago with a band of outlaws had been brutally harrowing. Grocery stores, hardware, any store of value had been looted long ago, so now it was a matter of finding what you need in the community. Most communities, small towns, stayed with law and order, internally guiding themselves, people cooperating, and trying to maintain civility as well as safety; they pooled their resources so everyone could eat, be clothed, and housed. On the other hand, gangs of well-armed right-wing terrorists located in razor wire compounds ringed with booby traps would emerge to roam the countryside stealing and killing anyone weaker than they.

Charley quickly checked his pack for ammo, getting very low. That meant going into a community and stealing or bartering for it. Bartering was always the better choice as districts would expend a lot of ammunition protecting their ammunition from thieves.

"Hey, everyone, check your bullet count. Let me know." They all had become hyper-alert, wary of sudden movements, noises, anything that appeared unusual.

Charley threw his pack beside the fire and sat down beside Doc, who stirred a small cooking pot. Charley wasn't sure if it was supper or some kind of shellac.

"See you in the morning." Pawnee often kept watch all night, without waking the next person, just because of the beauty of the night sky, and it was time to think, to plan, to consider; What had happened to the world? Where was Clay? What has happened to him since The Hammer? He knew he should have left already but just couldn't. Something held him here, some feeling of necessity, and a suspicion that the quest they were on was more significant than he had realized.

Pawnee took up station, in the dark, where he could watch, listen, and think.

Charley, watching Doc stir the thick grey liquid, bubbles oozed slowly as it heated up. "That shit eatable?" Charley asked.

"Well, that depends," Doc replied. "You a big fan of glue for lunch?

"So, where are we?" Charley asked. He looked down at his boots and wondered if they would last out the week. They had started out walking east but had quickly found horses were ideal for the new American world. Riding a horse for hours on end was an experience that took Charley by surprise; it was excruciating. Two weeks into their journey, though, all the humans had adjusted well to horseback travel.

The three green beagles and the horses were a different story entirely.

"We are on Illinois Highway 12, somewhere close to a little place called Farmingdale," Doc called out, reading the map.

"Hey Yaz, where are we going again?"

~ 38 ~

CHAPTER THIRTY-SIX

Noises.

Jade Bi'ch Hai Bones turned quickly to the source.

Voices, male, growing closer. Jade couldn't make out what they were saying; only the tone sounded urgent, commanding.

Damn, they found us.

Clouds of smoke from the fires drifted through, obscuring her vision, hiding the threats surrounding her.

"Hey," she whispered fiercely to Merry Sue, "Quiet, get the kids and get them undercover over there." She pointed to a fallen tree, a hiding place. Grabbing her gear and stuffing it into her battered leather backpack, she swung onto the back of a piebald sorrel she'd found wandering lose a week ago. "You stay here; out of sight, I'll lead them away." She said to the Bill's. "Stay together, and out of sight, I'll get rid of them."

Riding out of their small campsite, she crossed an open meadow into a small grove of trees. She dismounted, holding the horses' muzzle and reins to keep her quiet. This was a poor hide, but the only one around. A cliff ended in a small hill overlooking her position to her left. In front of her was a wide-open stretch with no cover. She had to draw the enemy away.

"Shit!" She knew better than to trap herself, but she was exhausted. It had been a long, confusing and heartbreaking journey.

Jade reasoned she could make a break for it across the meadow, but she had to time it so they would see her but still be too far to kill her. The weather was spitting rain; squalls would brush through every few minutes. She would wait; maybe one would be heavy enough. Fat chance of that.

"Hey!" a male voice called out. "Look over there! No! I said over there. Look where I'm pointing, you idiot. I saw someone over there."

Another male grumbled something in response.

She had seen the type before. Gangs of men: no women with them, men armed with assault weapons, pistols, knives, even swords, strapped with ammo bandoliers, wearing every manner of camouflage military uniforms and equipment.

The styles varied from Forest to the jungle to the desert, but they all wore camouflage.

These gangs were everywhere, roaming in quasi-military outfits usually led by the most brutal and meanest of them. No law, no society, no restraints.

In the months of her travel in UCS, Jade had personally killed twelve of these degenerates so far but had two new knife wound scars to show for it.

~ 39 ~

CHAPTER THIRTY-SEVEN

"You saw their tracks, Godamnit! That there was a horse!" the first male voice was gruff and nasally.

"Okay, okay, Gordon, we hear you, now quiet down, you'll spook them." A second man spoke up.

"Is it a stray?" A third voice.

"Fool! Do you see any strays around anywhere? Naw, horses are far too valuable. Look how deep the tracks are; no, she's being ridden. Now hush the hell up. If you hadn't lost the tracks, we'd be home by now!" Gordon complained.

Just then, a heavy blanket of rain swept through, obscuring her vision.

As the rain lessened, she peered from her cover; Jade counted six of them. In her experience, these men never traveled alone, and as packs of feral dogs, they would attack anything anywhere, anytime. There was no restraint, no mercy, no laws, no civilization, and no code of conduct.

It was kill or be killed with little trace of compassion or empathy. She knew even the children were not safe. There was an incident of whole towns being subjugated to slave conditions by locals who rose with their stockpiled weapons and became defacto leaders, areas where guns were the only criteria for power. America was a land awash in weapons, mainly in the hands of people whose only real expertise is with a knife and fork. Jade had contempt for pretenders.

The leader of this bunch, Gordon appeared to be a large man in his early 40's, roughly bearded, with long wild hair, dressed in woodland camo, utility vests bulging with ammo packs, and carrying an AR15, he studied the ground, following her trail. She decided to call him 'Fat Man'. She hadn't seen many fat people lately, now that the entire national and local food networks were gone and the grocery stores emptied by looters.

Starvation was gripping the land.

"Split up," Fat Man said. "You four go that way, up that hill, the trail splits up there, so keep your eyes open for her. Look for tracks. We'll stay heading this direction, see if we can pick up the tracks again."

"Oh-oh, this is not good," Jade realized if they kept moving up the hill to the left, they would be looking down on her position. The others will walk straight into her position, and the only way out was a wide-open stretch with no cover. Sure to trap her in a pincher movement. She was reasonably sure they didn't know her exact location, which was good. Checking her weapons, she made sure they were ready; A Winchester 310 Shotgun, two pistols, two knives, and brass knuckles. But she only had two shotgun shells, and six rounds of ammo left.

Jade moved to settle her horse and took the reins, keeping the mare quiet. If the two kept going up the hill, she'd have to make a run for it. But, they could walk over the hill rather than along the crest. She knew there were multiple trails up there.

She could deal with the two coming on her right. She no longer needed to worry about attracting their attention.

She lay down on the ground and sighted her shotgun, wishing it was a rifle. She would take down the leader first, and then the guy on the right, who acted as if he knew what he was doing.

Maybe they would stand close together, and one round would take them both.

Suddenly a thick blanket of sooty gray smoke drifted in on the breeze. Jade waited for it to drift through.

Just then, out of the smoke, she heard the zip of a heavy-caliber bullet, .308 maybe. She ducked down as the report of the rifle sounded. "Okay, they have seen me! There are two in front," she muttered to herself. Another round zipped past, this time from above. Looking up, she saw two of them, one sighting his rifle for another shot.

"Shit! Shit!" She said, turning to her horse. She had to leave and leave now.

The horse screamed as two rounds hit, a spray of blood misted the air, as the mare fell, heavily impacted the ground, thrashing, and grunting, then a final gush of blood, and she lay utterly still.

"Fuck!" Jade hated to see that, and she had come to like this horse, had traveled many miles with her.

The two up on the hill began moving fast to get another shot at her. She knew that four total were up there, and that was a lot of firepower coming down on her.

This was a tight place. Sometimes the only way out of a tight place was straight up the middle.

Looking out, she saw that Fat Man was alone in front of her, frightened and firing almost continually at anything that moved. She had no idea where the other guy went.

Then she heard his weapon lock back after his last round. Jade knew Fat Man was an amateur by how long it took him to change previous magazines. So she had to move, fast and deadly.

Jade rose from her hiding place; glancing left and right, she did not see any other men, so she rushed Fat Man as he struggled to change magazines, hoping to take him down quietly.

But she hadn't realized how close the men were. As soon as Jade broke cover, the other man armed with an automatic weapon also stepped out. He was right there all along; she just hadn't seen him.

"Hey! Stop!"

He had an AR15 pointed at her from twenty yards.

Standing fifteen feet away, Jade had her AR15 pointed at Fat Man's face.

It was a standoff.

"Looks like it ain't your day, little lady," Fat Man grumbled with a sly grin. He'd stop trying to reload. "They are four more up on that hill, an' they're headed down now. So you want to give that gun up and be nice to us?"

The other man chuckled.

She could hear the others making a noisy descent toward her location.

"You can't kill all of us, pretty lady."

"I don't have to kill everybody. Just you."

"Oh," Fat Man was amused. "What does that mean?"

"My AR is pointed at your head, fuck-face. I don't give a shit what your men do or don't do. I'm going to kill you. Regardless of what happens to me, you, asshole, are a dead man. So, here we have it: Your men kill me, I kill you. No shit: Guaranteed."

Jade held Fat Man's eyes, and she meant every word of it. Suddenly, he didn't appear confident, so she pressed the point.

"If you want to live today, Fat Man, well then, that is a different matter. Which will it be?" Her weapon was aimed and ready, her finger on the trigger. "Do we die together today?"

"Ah, hold, hold...." He muttered. "Hold your fire," he told the others, who had joined them by now.

"I suggest," She spoke with hard words to make her will be known; show herself equal to them, strength to their strength. "If you decide to remain alive, you lower your weapons and back the fuck away from me!"

Jade had no illusions these killers would just go away regardless of how tough she sounded. She counted on the fact that there were other, far easier targets out there. No predator wants to be injured killing prey, not when there are alternatives. She just had to make herself dangerous enough they would leave her alone.

'Fuck you." Fat Man muttered. "Let's go, we can get this bitch later. We got better things to do."

She didn't lower her weapon until they were well away.

"Shit!"

No horse.

She went in search of her small gang of refugees.

****

That night, their small fire had burned down to dusty ash when the four men pounced on Jade without warning. One hit her hard in the head, and her struggles ceased.

Missourah Bill had been on watch and was startled awake by a Humvee with all lights blazing crashed through the underbrush to illuminate everyone in the small clearing.

In no time, Susan, Missourah Bill, Alaska Bill, and the children were rounded up and standing, huddling fearfully as the armed men invaded their camp.

"Okay, Gordon, we have her, now what?"

"My guess is she is a trained fighter and tough as nails. I think Barcelona will want to see her."

"Who?"

"Shit, you don't pay attention to anything. Barcelona is taking over; he'll have an empire here soon.

"What about God-Kock?"

"Who?"

"Okay, where did this Barcelona come from?"

"From what I hear, Barcelona is the leader of the Forty, and he is rebuilding society, going to remake America, only this time better," Gordon replied calmly. "Remember, a free society is an armed society. Barcelona knows that he supports us; he will ban all Liberals from camps. If you don't follow the Party, you are an enemy of the Party. It is the only way we can maintain our American God-Given Freedoms!"

"So what next?"

"We're only about fifteen miles away from one of the national guard posts he set up; we'll take her there, turn her in. My guess there is a reward."

"What about them?" One of the men asked Fat Guy.

"I don't care, shoot 'em or let 'em go, doesn't matter." Gordon looked the miserable little group over. "They won't survive long anyway." He snorted. "Hell, let them go, be more fun to bet on how long they stay alive."

The men had a good laugh.

"What do you think Barcelona is going to do with her?"

~ 40 ~

CHAPTER THIRTY-EIGHT

"It is enough for me to contemplate the mystery of conscious life perpetuating itself through all eternity, to reflect upon the marvelous structure of the universe which we dimly perceive, and to try humbly to comprehend an infinitesimal part of the intelligence manifested in nature."
Albert Einstein

"You seeing what I am seeing?"

"What do you figure they are up to?" Greg Prichard asked. "Is that the Wayne guy?"

The Hamilton Inn just off Indiana 421 and Interstate Seventy Four was well lit by a smoky, irritable diesel engine in the early morning.

Clay Park Painter recognized Price Wayne. Couldn't miss him, the guy was as colorless as a sheet of copy paper.

"What do we do about this Wayne guy?" Newell another new recruit, asked. "Weren't you supposed to meet up with him?"

"Yeah," Clay responded, sighting carefully with his binoculars at the lineup of old, battered Humvee's beside the hotel. They were Humvee's from a wide variety of military units by the looks of the badges and Unit ID on them.

"Before The Hammer," Clay explained. "Guy named Price Wayne contacted Cascadian Special Services regarding an Oligarch named

Barcelona. One of the wealthiest men on this planet. The information we received was connected to arms dealings, enough dirt to go after Barcelona in the courts anyway. I and what was a hand-picked team came clear across the continent to find out." Clay held the images of the five men who had left Seattle with him. Two were dead, the other three missing. The Hammer had changed everything.

The Lead Humvee backed slowly out and was approached by a contingent of military types all enthusiastically escorting a large, very squat man and what looked like a vampire with him.

"Price Wayne, no skin pigment."

One by one, the Humvee's filled and began jocking in the parking lot, Barcelona's vehicle assigned to the middle of the pack.

"Back before The Hammer," Clay said as they watched the vehicles leave in a convoy. "When the United States was still intact, the nation was ruled by Oligarchs. Price Wayne could have given us precious information against these horrors; we could have maybe stopped them somehow." President Bessie May Chowder had told Clay it may be a chance to take down one of The Forty, which would be the equivalent of killing Osama Bin Laden, John Wilkes Booth, and Lee Harvey Oswald with one bullet.

Before The Hammer.

Maybe the rich are right, after all, Clay wondered. *Perhaps their wealth protects them against everything, even climate change.* The thought of that sent a spike of depression into his brain.

"So, Chief," Newell had hung out here long enough, and he needed to know. *Is this guy going to do something or just fart in the wind?* "What is our mission?" He gave Clay a long look. "You know why I am here," Newell pointed at Greg Prichard, "I know this man is solid. So what is up with you?"

Clay smiled. It was touchy getting complete strangers to see themselves as a unit; even a small one.

"Barcelona is evil. That level of wealth for one individual is evil, and that much power in the hands of one man is evil." Clay's smile widened, "And we need to take this motherfucker down."

Clay didn't know what else to do. After The Hammer, after his final two men were killed in a Republican Guards ambush, he sat for two days in a wrecked R.V. off Kansas Highway 24 outside of Rossville, contemplating what to do. It was all too overwhelming, too much too soon; he could not absorb all the loss. *It is all lost, everything. just go home.* See what he could do there. But, inside him, there was a voice that kept saying: the Mission.

Clay studied the two men. He had met them just inside the Virginia Border, liked them, and they tagged along with him to find Barcelona.

Decision time.

"Alright, Greg, Newell, how about this?" He told Prichard. "Tag along with me to follow Barcelona a little longer. I want you to see what this creature really is. Then you will understand why I am here. Then you will understand why you are here."

"This convoy has C.B. radio communications aboard each vehicle." Clay explained to them. "We listen in, we follow."

"Then what?" Greg was fed up with the East Coast, The Hammer, and everything in-between. "Will you take me to Cascadia?" He had joined Clay Park Painter because he admired the man and because he seemed to have a sense of direction. Clay seemed to know what his mission was, not just floundering around like the rest of humanity. Greg wanted to focus on his life, meaning, and a sense of purpose. So far this was all just words.

"Prichard for Christ's Sake! We're probably going to get killed tomorrow; let's worry about today. One day at a time. Now calm down." Newell told him.

Greg Prichard nodded, still unsure if he'd made the right call to go along with these guys. But for now, friends with weapons seemed to be a good idea.

"Saddle up," Clay ordered, and they climbed into their Humvee, immune to nasty EMP's, and stolen directly from the Air National Guard Armory at Filmore, Kentucky.

~ 41 ~

CHAPTER THIRTY-NINE

They had set an ambush.

"There! Just rounding the curve there." Greg Pritchard pointed. A white van with black lettering said: 'Barcelona meats' came barreling around the corner far too fast. The driver was completely unaware of the spike strip Clay's men had laid across the road until both front tires were shredded, and the van went out of control.

The white van swerved left, right, then hit the curb and somersaulted onto its back, sliding another fifty feet into a neighborhood pool. The back end broke open, its contents spilled along its path of destruction.

"Damn, sir, look at that, meat! Right from the Meat Wagon!"

Clay couldn't believe it. There were packages of real meat, hamburgers, steaks, roasts. All packages up, stamped with the name 'Barcelona Meats.'

"Get that, and let's get out of here before someone comes along." Meat like this was worth its weight in gold.

Clay and his men grabbed as many packages as they could and moved off into a hide they had in the hills nearby. He was very disappointed they found no notes, no documents, and no information of any kind: Just the van full of meat.

Quickly his men had a fire going. It has been a long time since any of them had tasted steak or hamburger, and they were very eager to get them cooked.

Newell came up to Clay carrying packages of meat. "Sir, I was a butcher for twenty years, I have cut up nearly every tame and game animal there is, but I don't recognize these cuts at all."

One of the packages was stamped: 'Calf roast.' Another said: 'finger bone BBQ.'

At first he couldn't believe it. But then lessons of The Hammer kicked in. That was when Clay Park Painter realized Barcelona was in the human meat packing business.

"Don't touch it! Don't eat it!"

"Barcelona meats," Clay said with disgust. *So this was going to be the source of his new wealth?* The Wealthy were going to feast on the bones of the poor, literally.

****

Price Wayne sat on a hard wooden seat in the back of the WWII vintage Deuce and a half and vowed vengeance on God for forcing him into virtual slavery under Barcelona. Wayne didn't think it was entirely God's fault. After all, he, Price Wayne had agreed to employment, well paid, got to travel in luxury, sample various narcotics from around the world. *No, it wasn't all bad. But the cannibalism may have been a step too far.*

In Wayne's opinion, *God sending that EMP from the Solar Flare fucked things up.*

"Hey, Wayne!" Barcelona shouted into his headset, "did you remember to pack my hemorrhoid pads and medication?"

I have an A.A. degree in Business Management! A person with my advanced schooling shouldn't have to put up with this shit! But since The Hammer, quality, well-fed employment was hard to come by. Yet another reason to blame God, he thought the Supreme Being was fumbling the ball. Price Wayne wasn't a religious man, but, like many, he found it convenient at times.

Price Wayne badly wanted to be away from Barcelona; the time on the yacht was something he couldn't even think about. He just wanted out. He vaguely recalled sending some sort of secret message to Cascadia; *that lovely little Bessie May Chowder.* He so hoped she got it. But then the The Hammer hit. Now nothing was normal. So he was going to play it out. He must think of some sort of sabotage that would in some way lessen his culpability for the brief foray into cannibalism. He wasn't yet a vegetarian, but he gave it strong consideration.

"Price Wayne?" Barcelona called out, leaning back from the truck cab to peer into the rear of vehicle. "Have you the contracts we will need to establish our meatpacking business in the Midwest?"

"Yes, sir, absolutely, sir!" Wayne had no doubt they could sell the meat; people were starving in all this chaos. Just for a moment, he wondered if he, Price Wayne, was responsible for a new and significant shift in human nutrition; Cannibalism as the new norm. He found it curious that being famous and infamous were interchangeable depending on perspective.

"Good, good, every shipment is money in the bank." Barcelona was a happy man. He was off that God forsaken yacht, vowing to never again set foot on water. Now this new venture to bring in the gold and silver! *The only overhead we have is capturing and processing the meat. We don't have to feed them or take care of them. Just go out, round them up, and ship them to slaughter.*

Price Wayne felt his stomach churn.

"Of course, I have made arrangements for you to share handsomely in this little venture," Barcelona told his faithful minion. Barcelona knew that keeping servant rewarded with gold would ease any qualms he might have for turning his fellow creatures into cutlets.

"Wonderful, sir, certainly, thank you, sir," murmured Price Wayne. *Of course, this could turn out to be lucrative,* Wayne thought. *Maybe I don't need to bail so quickly. I'll just stay until I see how the business goes. Get a little more money, and then I am out of here for good!*

~ 42 ~

CHAPTER FORTY

"The intuitive mind is a sacred gift and the rational mind is a faithful servant. We have created a society that honors the servant and has forgotten the gift."
Albert Einstein

"Chee," Pawnee Painter remarked. "Yo buggahs look busted, fo' real." He held a steaming cup of chicory tea in his right hand and a cocked 44 .cal handgun in the left, as Charley Bones and Doc Betters, returning from a clandestine search for food and ammunition, trudged wearily into camp, shrugging off backpacks and weapons, then collapsing by the fire.

"Pawnee, I don't want to hear your bullshit." Charley just ached, tired, thirsty, and dog-weary of the day. "And put that away; I don't relish getting shot after all we've been through."

"Can't be too careful, no."

"Did you guys see that sunset tonight?" Yaz called out.

"Chee, that was a marvelous thing."

"Since the world caught fire," Doc added. "Sunset's have been spectacular."

"Now, y'all got any of that chicory left?" Doc asked, not entirely sure he wanted it. But hot and warm and liquid sounded pretty good.

180

Pawnee pointed at the dented little pot slowly roasting over the small fire.

Muh and Jee were nose to nose arguing over the last marshmallow.

"Do they ever not fight?" Charley asked.

"See this scar?" Doc pulled up a pant leg. "One of the little suckers bit me. Got that trying to stop them. Since that happened, they are on their own, dude."

Pawnee stared at their map, thankful they had gotten through the past several days without incident. Sidestepping any possible confrontation with roaming bands of bad guys, they abandoned State 36. Going south on Old Highway 36, also called Mechanicsburg Road, was a small lake on their left, surrounded by a thick stand of trees. It was an excellent place to lay low for the night.

Land Rovers, Jeep C.J., old V.W.'s, vehicles that contained no computer chips were protected from the EMP, keeping many communities alive. But, two days ago, they learned another bitter truth: National Guard Humvee's were also rescued and were in the hands of outlaws or, worse, wealthy oligarchs building new empires.

Checking into his backpack, Pawnee counted his remaining rounds of ammunition. Ammunition was always a problem for them because they had to go into towns and steal it:

Still, Indianapolis was getting closer. Although Pawnee insisted this was their next stop, Charley wasn't so sure it even mattered anymore.

"Look around Pawnee, what is left?" Doc said with disgust. "Even before The Hammer hit, this world was in deep shit. Pandemic, out-of-control climate collapse, religious zealotry, tyrannical politics, overpopulation, pollution, and guns all over the place. The United States had become an armed camp purposefully divided by Oligarchs. The Oligarchs constructed legislation that only favored them by seizing government control and preventing the citizens from voting or protesting. 1% of the U.S. Population controlled 99%

of the riches, which was still insufficient. America and Americans were fucked by the rich and powerful."

"What you point, brah?"

"I don't know," Charley shrugged. "Just complaining, I guess."

Doc pulled the straps off his worn shoulders, poured himself some tea and sipped it, then put the cup down. "Damn, I miss coffee." He wanted to spit because the stuff tasted like old athletic sneakers but didn't want to insult Pawnee. He sniffed the cup, and the inside of his nose felt coated with turpentine. Doc gently set the cup down.

"So we are headed to Cahokia?" Doc mused. "What then?"

"Do not know."

"Well, then why are we going there? Following the directions of an alien dog?

"We have duty." Pawnee explained. "I mean, brah, what else is there? We find something important to us, and we do it. The rest of the world goes about its business. We can only do what we can do, brah, the rest we let go of. Duty is why we do it."

"Sounds simple."

"No, Brah, is hard, very hard. It is easy to talk of self-discipline, much harder to do." Pawnee realized he was also trying to convince himself they were following some plan. Since The Hammer, Pawnee found himself questioning many things, including his allegiance to duty over family. It seemed to him that the only true commitments there could be were to the family, not the government, not corporations. The idea he had lived his entire life devoted to the wrong purpose was heavy on his mind.

"Pawnee, you have the first watch, or is it me?"

"I have it," Doc answered. "I sure do miss my easy chair."

The creature comforts were few and far between, but Pawnee missed his son, Clay, most of all. The Hammer wiped out all communication, and there was no way he could find Clay now. Before leaving Cascadia, Pawnee found out Clay was somewhere in the U.S., Probably on the East Coast. Rumor was that it has something to do with infiltrating The Forty, but there is not much to go on and no way to find him. Pawnee had been guided by duty to others all of his life; now, he wasn't sure if that made sense. Nearly overnight, what had been familiar and usual became either moot or dangerous.

"How about cleans sheets, freshwater, and grocery stores," Charley added. "Or walking down the street, knowing law and order keep you safe?"

"A tall Mint Julep, deep-fried turkey, and several bowls of Indica weed," Doc added.

"Doc, you're a hippy hedonist."

"You're just jealous because I'm uninhibited."

"Uninhibited? Christ, Doc, you're habituated! You're addicted to marijuana."

"I am not! I quit, haven't I?"

"Oh, and I supposed the crash of civilization didn't have anything to do with breaking your supply line?"

"I was going to quit anyway. Besides, ditch weed is awful."

Charley tried to relax as much as possible on the hard ground. Beat from their journey, he just wanted to lay there and watch the flames. Dusk was settling in, throwing brilliant colors across the sky, as the sun drifted to the horizon, slowly fading into night. They took turns setting up their defenses for each camp, and Charley had become more and more concerned. It seemed as if Pawnee was missing things, signs that he could not have missed before. Pawnee didn't seem to be as focused as he had been. When Pawnee came out of the mine several weeks back, he was different. It seemed incredible to Charley, but Pawnee seemed hesitant, unsure of himself.

"What find, you?" Pawnee asked. He pointed at the small pack Charley carried.

"Old maps, sort of beat up, but useful. Some candy bars...a can of peaches." He handed it over to Pawnee. Their search of the abandoned gas station was quick and uneventful, and they found little value but did not have to fight for it.

Pawnee showed them his dirty and battered map. One side of it was badly scorched and barely readable. He peered at it closely in the wavering firelight. "Less see...we stay on this road, yeah? When we hit Mechanicsburg...heading East...."

"Hello, the camp." A voice called out of the dark.

Everyone froze.

~ 43 ~

CHAPTER FORTY-ONE

"What I see in Nature is a magnificent structure that we can comprehend only very imperfectly, and that must fill a thinking person with a feeling of humility. This is a genuinely religious feeling that has nothing to do with mysticism." Albert Einstein

His .44 caliber handgun pointed at the newcomers, Pawnee Painter moved swiftly to his right, out of the firelight.

Doc moved left, and Charley dropped to the ground, his weapon out, ready to fire.

Three tiny green aliens stood still, mouths open in shock, and then quickly scrambled out of sight.

"Identify yourselves!" Charley called out, his AR15 locked and loaded, ready, "who are you, and what do you want?"

Charley, Doc, and Pawnee were well-armed by now. AR15, pistols, and ammunition were looted from a National Guard Armory in Nebraska.

"We are just looking for a little food, that sort of thing." The voice out of the dark replied.

"Who is we?"

"Myself, wife, three kids, my brother in law, that's it."

"Approach the light." Charley wanted to see for himself what this was about. He kept his rifle ready.

"I'm Missourah Bill, this is Merry, my wife, that's Alaska Bill. Our kids," The man in the lead said. "We're just looking for food, a little rest, that's all. No harm."

"Okay, approach the fire, keep your hands in sight."

Two men came into the firelight first. Both in their mid-30s, one blond, and light, the other dark with a bitter scowl. A woman, white-blond hair, slender, rough-looking, led three children. Two of the children were Black.

"You are a curious group. Did you say Missourah Bill and Alaska Bill?"

"My fault," Merry spoke up. "Alaska Bill is my brother, Missourah Bill is my husband. It's saved us a lot of confusion."

Charley observed that Missourah Bill was a short white guy, and Alaska Bill had dark eyes, hair, and skin. Charley saw no sense in discussing that and just said, "Makes sense, I guess, rest yourselves."

Doc and Pawnee remained standing, weapons ready.

The two men and the woman guided the children to the fire, and they all sat, warming their hands.

"What's your story? What do you want?"

"Food. We are starving." The woman replied. "For the kids if not us."

"Sure, Doc, get the kids some of that soup."

"What about us?"

Charley looked them over. Food was scarce, and the children would be fed, but adults were another matter. "We will make sure you are fed and protected if need be. We can spare enough."

Charley saw Pawnee drift out farther to the right to check if more people were out there. In the past, a few earnest beggars appeared in their firelight, polite, sincere, innocently asking for food while armed friends hid in the dark waiting for an opportunity to charge.

Pawnee was cautious, careful, and merciless.

Charley said. "Regretfully, we do not live in a civilized world any longer." He held up his AR15 rifle taken from the dead hands of a Nebraska National Guard Soldier, probably only 20 years old or so. "Food is scarce and safety even more so. Tell us what you need and keep your hands in sight."

"Okay, simply put, we need help." The dark man said, giving a shy smile that changed his features completely. From bitter, dark sullen came sunshine. "How about we pay for our food with stories? We have stories we can share for food." The darker man said softly. "We've traveled a long way, from Oklahoma to here, where ever here is. We can certainly entertain you with tales of wonder."

"Sure," Charley said; although he had few illusions, these stories would have any surprises but, it would be their contribution to the group. They wanted to barter for food and momentary safety, which was acceptable in a world where these were rare and valuable.

On this journey, Charley thought of the old ways, the ways of his Potawatomi people. How they lived, how they cooperated, how they survived. In the old ways of his native people, travelers and guests to your camp were fed and protected. No harm could come to them while in your camp. Of course, if the visitors turn dangerous, later harm was allowable, but generosity always came first.

Charley thought about that and decided the old ways were his to follow or not. There was no overarching civilization to demand he comply. Today, right now, was utter freedom he had never known. *My entire life has been lived under the rules of civilization, the restraints, the compromises, and the need for cooperation. Even my goals and dreams were set by the modern world. All of my expectations for life were created to please society, not myself. I went to school and learned what they wanted me to know, went to war to defend the country, got a job, saved money, waited for vacations to have fun, served my community my family, did my duty to my nation. Now what?*

"Sit, eat, and tell us tales of wonder." Charley Brown Bones said to the travelers, "please share what little we have." He had the freedom to follow his native ways, the Potawatomi; no more capitalism, no more individualism, today he was with his tribe, and the tribe was everything. He would follow the old Indian ways.

Over Chicory coffee and thin soup, the strangers regaled them with stories of their travels; the crazies, the strange people, the odd ways people had developed for coping with a world turned upside down. They were a mixed group as many were. The couple had just delivered their young son to daycare when The Hammer hit. Initially trapped by enormous fires, they escaped, fleeing the city to find safety. They were not alone; others were already there, stealing food, medicine, and clothing; they often came close to being robbed of the few morsels of food or items they carried. America had become a lawless land.

Their mortality rate was horrendous; they had started with six adults and six children; in the past three months, they lost two adults and three children to gunfire, dog attacks, accidents, or the person just wandered off, never to be seen again. America was an even more dangerous place than it had been before The Hammer; whatever thin veneer of civilization that existed in America disappeared completely for millions.

"So here we are, survivors of our little gang," The woman explained, staring deep into the fire. "Me, Bill, Bill, and the three kids...our baby son, and then the little one, Angela." The little Black girl beamed when her name was called. "the other one is D'renda." The second small girl gave a shy smile.

"What now?" Charley asked the small family."What is your next move?"

"What else? We carry on, we are family now, and we will survive. Just what humans have done our entire existence; we face the world, protect each other and hope for the best." Merry had a calmness that belied the fear in her belly.

"Pardon me," Alaska Bill, putting down his bowl, said. "Do you folks hear of a guy named Barcelona in these parts?"

Pawnee looked at Charley and Doc. "That name familiar."

"Barcelona? What about Barcelona?" Since crossing into Indiana, there have been rumors about an Oligarch setting up a new empire. Barcelona was one of the oligarchs that controlled the old U.S.

"Jade said..." Merry began. "...she believed this guy was a major threat..."

"What?" Charley perked up. "What did you say? Did you say 'Jade'?" Charley interrupted. His heart beat faster. "Jade?" he repeated.

"Jade Bones," the woman said with a somber look. "Yes, Jade was with us for several months. She was a real kick. Good hunter. We...ah...lost her last week...."

"Jade?"

"Why Charles Brown Bones," Doc burst out laughing. "Your Jade she comes a-callin', brother."

Charley sat dumbstruck. "I'm Charley Brown Bones," he said.

"She shares your name?" Missourah Bill asked Charley.

"Her name is Jade Bi'ch Hai 'Bones'. My wife...my ex-wife."

"Oh, holy shit! Jade?" Doc was happy for his brother. "Cool Beans, brother!"

Charley didn't know what to think or say. *My Jade? She's here?* He felt like he's been belted with a baseball bat.

Doc reached over and touched his friend's arm. "Charles, this is quite a blessing for y 'all." Doc knew well how much Jade meant to Charley. He often wished he would have met someone like her. Doc wished his life had turned out more like Charley's in some ways. Not just in his love life either. Charley was a man of strength and compassion in ways that Doc could not imitate. He admired his friend for his solid sense of self and his dedication. Doc always felt as if he was just struggling with not making so many mistakes, trying not to harm others; he felt overwhelmed most of his life. *Ah am an actor following a script; ah cannot read and do not understand.* Doc wondered why no one else felt that way.

"Tell me about Jade, please." Charley urged the newcomers.

"Well..." Merry told of a stranger they met, a woman in a parachute who they found tangled in a tree. "Jade," the woman said fondly. "Is probably the strongest woman I have ever met. I don't mean just physically. She is a real leader."

"How was she?" Charley wanted details. "Was she ok? Injured? What was she doing here? Parachuted from where? Why?"

Alaska Bill told them Jade Bi'ch Hai became their protector and guide almost immediately. "I've done some hunting, I was in the Army, but she is a category way beyond me."

"Where is she? What happened to her?" Charley demanded.

"We were just outside of Martinsdale, Indiana," Missourah Bill added. "We had a nice camp, a small fire, Jade had hunted rabbits, and we were enjoying our first full meal in weeks."

"That's the thing," Alaska Bill took over. "The Homeland Police, or whatever passes for them, have her."

"What?"

"We were harming nobody, minding our own business, and they attacked us."

Missourah Bill and Merry nodded.

"They took Jade by surprise, just jumped on her before she could do anything." Missouri Bill said.

"They put us on the ground, zip-tied," Merry added, tears formed in her eyes at the thought. "The kids were terrified. They were so scared." She cleared her throat. "We couldn't do anything. Anyway, they searched our camp, took anything they wanted...."

"What about Jade?" Charley asked.

"They took her. As soon as they realized she wasn't just another refugee, they interrogated her, but that went nowhere, so they took her."

"Where?" this was the big question Charley had to know. "Where did they take Jade?" The thought that he might see Jade again in this lifetime stirred Charley in ways he couldn't imagine.

His heart leaped, his gut felt hollow, the only woman he loved, and she was near.

"We have no idea, it took hours to get free of those damn zip ties, and all the while, the children were crying and screaming...." She looked down at the children who sleepily drank soup, quieted by exhaustion and fear and the unknown.

"Maybe we might know," Missourah Bill began, "some of the soldiers were talking before they left. Up north, Indiana, there is a strong man; up north, Indiana, supposedly, he has bribed or threatened all of the National Guard units to join his 'army.' They were talking as if he were building a damn empire up there. Guy named Barcelona."

"He has her?"

The three newcomers nodded.

~ 44 ~

CHAPTER FORTY-TWO

President Bessie May Chowder and Jade Bi'ch Hai heard the jail door creak open. Both turned toward the sound defensively.

Jade was on her feet fast, imposing herself between danger and her President.

Jade Bi'ch Hai Bones saw her ex-husband Charley Brown Bones walk into her cell, and she didn't know whether to scream or cry.

She was flabbergasted.

"Where the hell did you come from?" she asked with astonishment.

"Don't I always save your ass?" Charley hadn't intended to say that, and it just slipped out.

Jade's eyes narrowed.

"Wow, Charles looky here," Doc rushed into the jail cell after Charley. "We got Jade and President Chowder. Wow, amazing. A twofer."

Charley stared at Jade, still unable to believe she was standing before him.

"Jade?"

Jade, too was overwhelmed.

"Now things are getting good!" President Chowder clapped her hands. "Rescued!" She cried in an elated voice.

"Chee, enough with the reunion, we gotta cock-a-roach out of here!"

Pawnee led them out of the building and away from the prison, staying tight to the dark 3 AM shadows until they reached the horses on the outskirts of town.

"Horses?" Jade was amazed and delighted.

"We are going to meet up with...." Charley stopped himself, unsure how to tell them about the three little green alien beagles. Instead, he said, "Our camp is a few miles Southwest of here."

"We going go, now." Pawnee mounted up and was riding away.

"You're going to have to ride behind me," Charley said to Jade with a grin. "We only have three horses."

Jade looked at Charley Bones. Her heart was torn. Love surged, but bitterness remained to poison.

"Look, Charley," she said abruptly, "Ok, fine, you saved my ass," Her voice neutral, with a slight edge. "Thank you. I am delighted to see you alive and well, but don't get fucking sappy on me. I have a mission, and it doesn't include you." A blossom of sadness welled up, a reminder of what he meant to her and what she was losing, but she ignored it.

"What are you saying?"

"What? You weren't fucking listening?"

"I was listening," Charley fired back, falling into an old familiar pattern. "But you weren't saying shit, so I didn't bother to remember it."

Jade Bi'ch Hai Bones narrowed her eyes, a sure sign of trouble.

Charley saw the look and was puzzled; once again not sure of what he said to get her so angry.

"I said," her voice was low yet sharp. "Get the fuck on the other horse with Doc. I'm taking this one for myself and Bessie May. You deaf?"

"Ok," Bessie May Chowder decided this love match had gone on long enough. "The whole world changes, civilization disappears overnight, and you two keep doing the same act. Chill out."

Even though Charley Brown Bones was alive, Jade thought he looked exhausted and was far too thin. The past few months had been tough on her as well as everyone: The Hammer, imprisoned by an egomaniacal fool, finding Bessie May Chowder there, being rescued by the love of her life, walking in to save her ass. She did not know what to do about Charley now. She loved him, but they were not together for damn good reasons.

"Charley," she touched his arm, an unconscious gesture that came naturally. "I am sorry to be so abrupt. Yes, it is good to see you, and we have much to talk about, but not now, not here, not this way. I am tasked with protecting this woman, and I will obey that obligation. You ride with Doc; President Chowder and I will take the spare horse."

"Oh." Charley didn't know how to respond. He understood, sort of. Charley was certain she was saying far more than he understood, like most things between them. Women had complex, mysterious nuances to their language he often missed, every single time to his detriment.

"I don't want to ride with ya'll. Go steal a horse, you Yankee carpetbagger."

"Doc!"

~ 45 ~

CHAPTER FORTY-THREE

The journey of Peter Paul God-Kock from Butte, Montana to Indianapolis, Indians was treacherous and difficult as The Hammer had devastated America. But, the summons he received from Oligarch Barcelona, delivered by armed troops in a Humvee convoy, made it clear the invitation wasn't RSVP.

Peter Paul God-Kock trembled with uncertainty as he sat anxiously waiting for Barcelona. As a God, he was naturally above the law and could do whatever pleased him. That is how he ran his corporate businesses and his family. But Oligarchs made him nervous.

"Will...will he be long?" Peter Paul God-Kock asked Price Wayne.

Wayne looked up from his Lego construction project, irritated at the interruption. Carefully placing a tile on his authentic, Great Wall Of China Lego set. "He will be here when he gets here; shut the fuck up."

God-Kock nodded miserably; it was humiliating and unseemly for 'God' to be kept waiting like a cold call salesman.

"Excuse me?" he raised his voice slightly so the servant could hear him. "Excuse me?" he said louder. "I need to go to the restroom?"

Price Wayne looked up at God-Kock. "Shut the fuck up."

God-Kock wriggled a finger into his ear. The man could not possibly be speaking to him. *No one talked to God like that!*

God-Kock leaped to his feet, rage filling his face with blood; he was on the verge of showing this stupid peasant what kind of hell a God can bring when suddenly Barcelona swept into the room.

"So God-Kock, we meet at last." After walking in from the outer office, Barcelona gave the bulbous, bloated, white-haired fool a thorough inspection. "You look just like I expected you to look," he said to God-Kock. Taking off his elegantly sewn, hand-tailored combat jacket, he dropped it. The coat was caught well before it hit the floor and expertly impaled on a waiting hanger by a swift servant.

God-Kock preened at the words from Barcelona. "Yes," he replied honestly. "I am quite handsome." He stood up so that Barcelona could see how strong and debonair he was. His hair was neatly coiffed, glued by cement-like hairspray, his girdle was tight, and his leak proof underwear was perfect.

"Ha! You're a wealthy buffoon." Barcelona laughed, walking past God-Kock and into his office.

The blood drained from God-Kocks face; the thought another human being would insult him so directly to his face was stunning. *Doesn't he know who I am?*

Barcelona loved the expression on God-Kock's face. *Here was a fool who thought to be divine, facing a being who really was.*

"Follow me, and make it snappy I don't have much time for your bullshit."

God-Kock stared in horror at the affront.

"I have traveled by land from the East Coast, and I am here to get this place in order. I am in charge here, building an empire out of this disaster, and I need you to be the front man."

God-Kock blinked in confusion. "Me?"

"I am looking at you. I am speaking directly to you. Who the fuck do you think I'm talking to?"

Now God-Kock was confused. "But I'm...I'm God...I am supposed to be in control...I'm..."

Barcelona ignored him as the mindless chattering of servants. "I am here with National Guard and regular military soldiers I have recruited along the way, building my new army. I have twenty Humvee's, all battle-hardened military equipment from the Pentagon. I have one hundred mercenaries, blooded with kills to serve me. Currently, I am in contact with National Guard units in four states who have pledged allegiance to me."

"You?" Fearing facing a challenge to his throne, God-Kock desperately tried to conjure an incantation that would smite Barcelona into a penitent beggar. He tried desperately to recall the words from 'The Ronald Reagan Book of Spells and Incantations.'

"Arrggh woof!" God-Kock waved his arms and expelled a lungful of air at Barcelona to bolster his magic spell.

"What the fuck are you doing?"

God-Kock could see his powers were not in top form today.

"Sit down; you are making me nervous, twitching and muttering like that."

Price Wayne roughly assisted the now silently spell casting God-Kock to a chair and stood back at attention.

"I had plans to build my new inland empire from here," Barcelona said without preamble. "My empire will stretch from here to the Atlantic."

Among the many problems he faced, the most pressing was the six nuclear power plants that had melted to radioactive goo in nearly every state of the Midwest. Barcelona realized Indianapolis, indeed, every state in which Conservative politics held sway, was either poisoned by nuclear waste or overwhelmed by so many guns that chaos was all that could be accomplished there. The only way for Barcelona to actively resurrect a viable Capitalist society would be to take away all the weapons. To do this, Barcelona would need a fall guy, a minion who would take the fallout, both literally and figuratively.

Barcelona looked at God-Kock as if evaluating used house slippers.

"Well, I have a special assignment for you," he began. "I am selecting you to be my Governor for the area of Indiana, Missouri, Illinois, and the surrounding areas.

"Me?" God-Kock considered this offer. On the one hand, it was a return to power and influence, and on the other, it was insulting to offer a God mere employment. "I will, of course, take this under consideration," he stalled.

"Fuck that. You are hired. "Barcelona muttered. He'd deal with any reluctance later. "What do you know about The Einstein Stone?"

"Know? God-Kock was awkward at answering questions because people had stopped asking him anything years ago.

"I know I don't know what I know, but I do know...something...," he gave a weak grin. "Did that answer your question?"

"What? Do you know where I can find the Einstein Stone or not?" God-Kock stared back in confusion.

He turned to Price Wayne, "Get the information out of him with as much bloodshed as you can. Just don't kill him...yet."

"With pleasure, sir," Price Wayne hated to hear that command. For Wayne, it had been a long, extraordinary journey, and he had no idea at what point he gave up his soul, but he noticed his conscience was much quieter.

P.P.God-Kock, profoundly stunned to the center of his soul, felt the blood drain from his brain.

I'm not immortal?

Barcelona watched as competing and contradictory expressions crossed God-Kock's face. *Fuck me, this guy couldn't butter bread. He is perfect.*

The thought that he had lost his immortality caused God-Kock to sob uncontrollably for six hours; questioning had to be abandoned as senseless.

~ 46 ~

CHAPTER FORTY-FOUR

"Nothing that I can do or say will change the structure of the universe. But maybe, by raising my voice, I can help the greatest of all causes — good will among men and peace on earth." Albert Einstein

"Chee you people slow-poke, for sure," Pawnee pointed toward a series of small hills a few miles distant. "We need to get there before they know da prisoners are gone." He urged his horse to speed up a bit.

Charley Bones and Doc Better rode tandem on an increasingly irritable mare called "CupCake." Sheets of rain fell, occasionally interspersed with brilliant moments of blue sky and golden sunshine, only to be covered by sweeping rolls of gray clouds with more rain; it was another day of unsettled weather.

Since leaving Indianapolis under cover of night, they had ridden steadily and quietly out of the surrounding suburbs, avoiding drawing attention to themselves.

Riding their horse just behind the restless CupCake, Jade sighed, "Getting out of jail was a bitter-sweet moment."

"My dear," Chowder replied. "Getting out of jail is all sweet, no bitter about it."Bessie May knew Jade was referring to Charley Bones. The two had begun arguing the minute they were on the horses.

"President Chowder, ma'am," Charley suddenly slowed CupCake, which caused the horse to lay back her ears and snort. "Can I ask a question? Before The Hammer, you were in Seattle? How did you get all the way here?"

She covered the state of Cascadia when she left, and then Bessie May described the shoot-down and her capture "When Jade was thrown into my cell, I was just as shocked as when you walked in. That was a jail cell of surprises."

Charley, trying to rein in the ever more stubborn CupCake, struggled for a moment, and then looked at Jade. "And you, what happened?"

She told him of her journey but in brief, narrow terms.

"Anyway, don't worry about it; I'm fine." The last thing she needed now was Charley Brown Bones hanging all over her with concern. She thought Charley looked very rugged, handsome in an old-man kind of way.

"Are you all right, Jade? Are you hurt at all?" He asked her. He thought she looked lovely. A trifle pissed off, but gorgeous nonetheless. "You could use a bath and a haircut...a good meal...."

"Leave it alone!" Jade replied in a stern voice and immediately regretted it. She knew she was blowing this. Inside she was furious. All of the events of the past six months arose in her mind, and what stood out most was an overwhelming sense of vulnerability. Captured and imprisoned like an animal, Jade's sense of self as a free and independent human was slapped from her. Resentment fueled her anger, and she primed for an explosion. To top it all off, Charley Brown Bones, the man she hated and loved most in the world, was back in her life, and she had no idea what to do about that.

If only it had been anybody else to open that jail door, she thought furiously. But her heart melted at the sight of Charley. She hated it, but she couldn't deny it.

"Okay, fine trying to be a nice guy," Charley was embarrassed and insulted. She wasn't more open and welcoming. "Jade, we haven't seen each other in a long time, so much has happened...."

Charley shut up, and he knew when to back off. "Of course, you have your reasons...for being a bitch," he said placatingly.

Jade Bi'ch Hai Bones' eyes narrowed.

Charley realized he wasn't quite as placating as he'd hoped.

Jade had a habit of striking first and feeling apologetic later. Not one of her more endearing qualities, so Charley guided 'Cup Cake' away from Jade's striking range just in case. Jade has several different layers of rage; he knew all too well. All of them are painful, some even deadly. Besides, Doc would be pissed if she killed CupCake.

"Both of you, simmer down," Bessie May told them. She admired both of them, but, like much in life, she was puzzled by the complexity of their relationship. We humans want and need love, but then we sabotage ourselves, denying the very thing we crave most.

"Sure, ma'am, I can contain myself if fathead here does," Jade replied.

They rode along in silence.

"Charley," Jade said, finally. She guided her horse close to his, and Charley gave her a cautious look and moved CupCake a bit farther away. The horses' eyes widened with surprise, and she whinnied her displeasure.

Jade wanted to reach out and touch his arm, but she resisted because physical contact had always been her undoing with him. She was close enough she thought she could smell him: a peppery, masculine smell now mixed with horse sweat, which was oddly erotic to her surprise.

To get her mind off him in that way, she said more harshly than she intended, "Well, chubby, where are we headed?"

Fuck! She scolded herself. *Take it down a notch!*

"Sorry...uh, Charley, let me try again. How far is the camp? Do you have supplies, weapons?"

Charley Bones wanted to explain the three little green alien beagles awaiting them at their camp, but he knew Jade well; she hates science fiction, never trusts strangers, and is allergic to fur. Charley decided not to warn her.

This was going to be fun: Jade squaring off with Extraterrestrials. Jade hated dogs.

$$\sim 47 \sim$$

CHAPTER FORTY-FIVE

"Look!" Prichard pointed.

"Why are they rounding up all these people?"

Troops were herding more people toward the waiting trucks, lines of men, women, children, some carrying suitcases, backpacks, infant carriers, all straggling out of the various neighborhoods at gunpoint from Barcelona's men.

"Holy Shit."

That summed it up for everybody.

Clay Park Painter and his band had been following Barcelona from Virginia to Indiana, three weeks of travel, every step of the way an education, watching him rebuild an empire. Barcelona went from one military base to another, one National Guard unit to another, lining up firepower and support. He would find a powerful state militia, official or not, and hire them. At each stop, he left behind someone he could count on to be obsequious to authority above and ruthless to those below.

Barcelona sure knows violence and force are the approved, time-tested, traditional methods of empire building. Clay watched with growing horror.

"Slow here," Clay told Prichard, the driver of their stolen Virginia State Highway Patrol Humvee. He could see the Barcelona convoy up ahead, probably a mile or so, had stopped, the trucks idling, plums of exhaust rising in the damp evening air.

While they sat and watched, Clay continued. "Barcelona, the Oligarch, is one of the men responsible for the economic enslavement of humanity." Clay explained to Prichard. "He is one of the obscenely wealthy men responsible for the destruction of our climate and our world, and the fucker is once again loose to kill."

"Whatever we do, gentlemen," Clay looked back at his men in the rear seat of the Humvee, "That fat thug represents the most destructive of human behaviors; avarice and ego. Barcelona is a psychopathic sociopath. We are going to take this fucker down."

Initially, Clay had been concerned about forming this small unit into a coherent military group. A tough thing to do with complete strangers. But so far, Prichard and Newell had worked out fine; both now dedicated to ending Barcelona.

The column belonging to Barcelona loaded the new transports, and then, engines roaring and blue diesel smoke pouring up, the trucks began their mournful journey again.

"Now, first thing," Clay told them as they traveled, lights out, in the gathering gloom of night. "We are outnumbered and out-gunned. But we are no longer observers. We are assassins. Barcelona must be stopped. There is no other moral option." He pulled out his maps of the area. "Here, this next left." He indicated a State highway splitting off from this Interstate. We need to get ahead of these guys, find more firepower."

****

They were east and south of Indianapolis, Indiana, near a little town called Pipe Town, off of Old Highway 87, having taken side roads around and now in front of the Barcelona death march.

"Hey, look," Greg slowed the Humvee.

A hand-lettered sign was nailed to an electrical pole. "Private Property, do not come near!"

"Doesn't that just reek of curiosity?" Greg laughed. "Look another sign," He pointed farther down the road at the head of a driveway.

This new sign said: "Private Property, DANGER, you will be SHOT!"

"Well, well, our friend here seems to be pretty insistent. I wonder what he's hiding?"

They counted six signs, warning others to stay away, lining a narrow dirt path. They pulled over and got out; the scent of bacon frying was barely there, but they could follow it until they found what looked like a large hill of grass with a thin stream of dark smoke drifting up from a crooked metal chimney pipe.

"Well, well, what do you think of that?"

"I think we have found a well-armed prepper holed up in his den, sir. Sort of like a fat-rich rat in his nest." Greg grinned at the prospect.

"Shall we relieve him of his burden? Lighten the load of his worries?" Clay smiled back.

"Like most preppers, this one believes sufficient ammunition, food, water, and nasty disposition would keep him safe from intrusion. Like most preppers, he's dead wrong." Greg observed. A seasoned combat infantryman with service in Iraq and Afghanistan, he knew the folly of believing in firepower as the answer.

"Doesn't matter how many guns or how much ammunition, you can only shoot one at a time. Small groups of well-armed people can defeat large ones, but they have to move and hide, strike and run; defending a fixed position is a disaster." Prichard explained.

They took the man and his sloppy family within an hour, relieving him of most weapons and ammunition, a bit of food, and a warning to reconsider his beliefs. Clay personally tore down the bright yellow 'Don't Tread on Me' flag, flying next to their 'Trump 2024' signs.

As they loaded their new provisions, including eight AR-15s, six 'Bull Pup' shotguns, twenty handguns of assorted make and caliber, and more ammunition than they could carry into their Humvee, Clay told his men:

"Look at this silly yellow flag! They don't realize the cause they support has already stomped all over them! What they believe is real is nothing more than propaganda designed by their own side to hide the truth. Millions of people were deceived into believing a lost election was won despite all factual evidence to the contrary."

"Imagine millions of people believing a deadly virus is just a hoax, a trick by Liberals to deceive them, even as they die from it!" Newell shook his head, "how incredibly fucking sad."

****

"What is this about?"

Clay didn't know, but they would find out.

They caught up again with Barcelona's convoy around the University Heights subdivision of Indianapolis. Barcelona's men surrounded a small apartment house and drove out the tenants at gunpoint, loading them into rumbling old farm trucks.

Over the next four days, they watched as Barcelona's men went around the city gathering up homeless in a large crowd of men, women, and children, loading them into his farm trucks and taking them to a warehouse storage facility for holding.

"Where are they going with all these people?"

Clay had an idea but was terrified to say it out loud. The truckload of meats they had ambushed told a tale of horror.

"We need to stop this," Newell said softly, with urgent intensity.

For two weeks, they had watched the herd of captured humans grow exponentially with the addition of several fully loaded farm trucks coming in from the countryside carrying wild-eyed, frightened people.

Then Barcelona organized the trucks into one long convoy, and they set out north toward Indianapolis.

Quickly becoming Clay's right-hand man, Greg Pritchard managed to steal a 1950 Divco Milk delivery truck, 'Dagostino Milk' in barely legible red script on the faded yellow paint, from a careless antique auto collector. This ratty old vehicle made a perfect cover.

Clay divided his men between the National Guard Humvee and the milk truck, and they took off in pursuit.

The trail of tears in Barcelona's wake was unmistakable and easy to follow right up to the door of Philco's Meat Packing plant in the old Marion County Fairgrounds, Northeastern of Indianapolis itself, about three miles from the City Center.

"Here we go," Clay knew the goal of this convoy but wasn't going to say it out loud.

They watched as the old farm trucks, filled to the edges with frightened human beings, rolled through the guarded gates, onto the fairgrounds, and then into a vast Quonset hut building. There was no sign on the building other than 'BUILDING A-2'. All ten trucks disappeared inside with their live cargo.

With his two Humvee's parked outside the Fairground offices, Barcelona got out and went in.

Prichard said softly. "Clay, man, you know why they got those people, don't you?'

"Yeah. We know what 'Barcelona Meats' means.

Curls of thick black, sooty smoke began to rise from several pipes in the back of the building.

"Their starting up the ovens."

The smell of roast pork was slight, but growing stronger.

"Those people are the product: steaks, roasts, ribs; they are going in for slaughter."

Two men came out of the Quonset hut and hung a sign over the door; "Barcelona Meats."

~ 48 ~

CHAPTER FORTY-SIX

"We have to rescue these people!" Prichard vowed he would not let this pass.

"Ok, ok," Clay said breathlessly as he gathered his men outside. "We got this down, next step," pointing to the map. "First we take care of this business, and then we find out how to stop Barcelona."

"What do you mean 'stop him'?" Newell demanded. "We free these people and kill him. Simple."

"Not quite." Over the past few weeks of travel, they had consistently picked up CB radio calls indicating Barcelona was seeking something precious to the South. He had already dispatched a four Humvee convoy seeking a group of travelers that might have this treasure. Clay had seen Price Wayne, but there was no way to contact him at this time.

"We got to get those people out of there first, man!" Newell said with rising anxiety.

"We will, we will," Clay reassured them. "First things first. As near as we know, there are twelve guards on that meatpacking plant, and they are almost all pointed inward. Barcelona is far more worried his meat products will escape than he is with their being rescued. We hit them, get those folks free, and then we kill Barcelona."

Everyone liked the plan.

The only flaw came at seven fifteen that evening when Barcelona loaded up two Humvee's with his men, including Price Wayne, and set off south, down Interstate sixty-nine.

'"Let him go. We can follow." Clay told them.

They hit the Quonset hut facilities the following day at 3 AM, a perfect time because the guards were sleepy at their lowest biorhythm, unaware of the threat until too late.

They freed four hundred and twenty-two men, women, and children from Barcelona's meatpacking plant and told them to scatter, spread the word of what Barcelona is up to. Clay was pretty sure the survivors would organize themselves into an underground resistance faction to stop this horrendous evil. He wished he could be a part of the action, but Barcelona was on the move again, and Clay knew his responsibility was to take this man down as brutally and thoroughly as possible.

~ 49 ~

CHAPTER FORTY-SEVEN

"The finest emotion of which we are capable is the mystic emotion. Herein lies the germ of all art and all true science. Anyone to whom this feeling is alien, who is no longer capable of wonderment and lives in a state of fear is a dead man." Albert Einstein

The dawn was just struggling through the early morning mist when Pawnee led Bessie May and Jade into the camp.

Charley and Doc had urged the reluctant CupCake ahead to get the camp ready for everyone. By the time Pawnee and the two women arrived, Doc had put together a robust fire, and coffee was boiling. Charley had asked the three green beagles to hold off meeting the new people until everyone settled, so they wouldn't startle the women.

Zee argued, but they all agreed to step away from the fire until called.

"I don't know. Are we just fooling ourselves?" Bessie May Chowder began as the five humans gathered around the small flickering fire. "But something tells me the Einstein Stone maybe just a wild goose chase. I think we have bigger, more realistic problems at hand."

Charley was watching her closely. She had aged remarkably. At four foot nine inches, Bessie May Chowder was small, but now she was a tiny, white-haired gnome. Only her eyes held the fire of intelligence.

"I realize our lives have been radically upended by all of this." Bessie May stare into the flickering flames. "Mine certainly has. Considering all, what are our priorities now? Does Cascadia even exist as a nation? Does this UCS? Look around. Our civilization has crumbled, local communities are doing their best to survive, but we are back to the Old West. Guns are more prevalent than law. Does it make sense for us to chase after a myth? The Einstein Stone may not even do anything at all. It is what? A magical stone? A cure-all? Do we need to rethink the mission now that The Hammer has hit? Sincerely, who and what are we with our society in ruins?"

Pawnee nodded. He understood changed priorities. Clay, where was Clay! True, the world had changed, but Clay had not, his son. He had to find his son. Chasing after The Einstein Stone seemed senseless, but then something Bessie May just said changed his thoughts. "Society in ruins." He repeated.

Pawnee had sought the bigger picture all of his life, wanting to know if his presence made any real difference beyond his personal world. He wanted to know his efforts meant something to the world or was just a drop in a vast ocean of others.

Pulling his backpack over to him, he undid the straps and then pulled the sacred objects out: The Einstein Stone, a raw Blue-Green Emerald, and a white bone, St Catherine's holy relic, carved intricately.

"Wow!"

For the next few minutes they passed around the Blue-Green Stone and the holy bone.

"So this is what we are chasing?" Jade fondled the stone.

"I am amazed and I am in awe of you gentlemen," President Chowder told them. "You did it! You found the Einstein Stone!"

Jade laughed a short, sharp sound. "Yes, here they are! Now what? It seems like the very reasons we needed these sacred objects is now moot."

"No, it is not moot or useless," Bessie May disagreed. "The reasons we sought these treasures, the imminent collapse of our society, is here. It has happened. The struggle now will be to recreate society, a just society."

"I stay with you for now," Pawnee rumbled, deciding. He had a choice. To go look for his beloved son, having no idea even where to begin to look, or he could stay, complete this mission as far as possible. "I find Clay when this mission is done." He arose, "I go stand guard now." He left before his tears could show.

The words of his loyalty struck Bessie May Chowder deep, creating a rising tide of loneliness. She studied the fire intently, emotions running strong and swift. Deep in her inner self, she longed for someone to hold her, keep her warm, share her thoughts and love, and be her companion. She missed Frederick so intensely tears came hot and fierce. Just as quickly, a sudden tsunami of rage rose so bitterly it nearly choked her. The injustice of life could not be ignored; Children, abandoned, cast aside, left alone in a world that just couldn't care less. Her entire life had been a challenge; too short, too Black, too female, too bright, and too poor. She knew failure, and success, but every step of the way, every damn moment, every single second, she longed for someone to recognize, then cradle and love the small, scared girl that lived within her. Of all the people in her life, only one knew what she felt: Jade, another orphan.

Bessie May felt cheated. She never had the chance to pursue her dreams because she had been forged by a racist, misogynistic, class-stratified society like a sword is repeatedly heated and beaten until it is solid and tough and sharp.

Doc saw Bessie May tear up, saw her inner struggle, "Ma'am, we are here for you. Night and day. The only time you need to be alone is when you need to be."

Charley Bones and Pawnee Painter nodded at her. Jade placed a comforting hand on her shoulder.

Bessie May Chowder looked around the faces that glowed in the firelight and realized she may have found the first family she'd ever known. This gave her a premonition, whether of joy or sorrow she did not know, but something had shifted, something was different. She gave them a soft smile, "Thank you," her voice gentle, 'that means so much."

"Bessie May," Jade said softly. "Whatever the world is right now, we have each other. We are a family; you belong here with us, and we with you."

Charley smiled at Bessie May. "Our first task is to stay together. We have your back, always, Bessie May. We can worry about our destination later. Now we need to focus on us. We need to bond as a family...."

"Bonding like family, are we? So why the fuck are you humans keeping us locked away like scurrilous pets?" Muh led Jee and Yaz into the firelight, tired of waiting in the dark to be introduced to the new humans.

"Oh my God!" Bessie May Chowder exclaimed in astonishment, "What in the world do we have here?"

"Hiya Toots!" Jee called out to Bessie May.

"What the fuck is that?" Jade was on her feet between the ET's and Bessie May. "Green beagles? Talking green beagles?" She had her weapon posed to take them out. "What the fuck is going on here?" She not only hated dogs, but their color was the most awful puke green she'd ever seen.

****

Bessie May, fascinated and curious about the alien beagles, talked with Muh and Jee while Jade stormed off into the night to calm down. Charley thought it went as well as it could. Jade didn't shoot the aliens.

Pawnee was still laughing at the scene.

"Doc, we need to get the horses watered and fed," Charley told him.

****

Muh, standing beside a nervous CupCake, glanced up suspiciously. He didn't trust them: Horses. They seemed to be plotting something and he doubted their loyalty.

"They have long ears," Muh said, pointing.

"So?"

"Long Ears are a sign of nefarious plotting and underhanded behavior!" Muh said with righteous indignation.

"What?"

"Everybody knows that. It's because they hear things they shouldn't."

"Do you ever seriously listen to yourself?"

"Do you think the horses like me?"

"No one likes you."

"Do so."

"Do not."

"Guys," Charley called out, "get away from CupCake! Go bother something or someone else."

****

"When are you going to steal the Blue-Green Stone so we can be on our way to Indianapolis?" Muh hissed at Jee as they stood aside, watching Jade and Doc tend to the horses.

"Me?" Jee was surprised. "Why do I have to steal it?"

"It is my command."

"Get the other guy, the traitor, to do it?"

They both looked over at Yaz, sitting comfortably beside the fire, who wondered why they were staring at him.

****

"Everything is energy and that is all there is to it. Match the frequency of the reality you want and you cannot help but get that reality. It can be no other way. This is not philosophy. This is physics." Albert Einstein

Staring into the flickering flames, Yaz grew sleepy, his eyes heavy, he drifted into a dream world:

Earth count was the year 1407 AD; the sun was bright overhead as Yaz crossed the immense playa of beaten red earth, but then he stopped, starring upward. In addition to the sun was another bright, glowing object in the sky. *A Super Nova?* Yaz was amazed, the celestial explosion was impossible to miss even in broad daylight.

Everywhere he looked people were moving about, getting food, talking, laughing, playing games, building this or that structure. Children ran and played, dogs barked, the air was filled with the hum of satisfaction, an aura of festive joy, scents of sage and pine and flowers followed his movements.

No one seemed to be even interested in the Super Nova, as if it was a normal event.

Yaz was amazed at the health and vigor of these humans. Yaz, Muh, and Jee visited the Earth earlier, over a thousand years earlier. A century ago, the humans in the Middle East were mean-spirited, argumentative, money-grubbers, challenging, and difficult people, nothing like these cheerful beings before him.

Yaz knew he was on a different continent, but the difference was so profound it was as if these were different species of humans.

The huge efficient megalopolis, filled with thousands of happy residents, was named: Cha Oka.

Over the next few days, Yaz traveled about the huge urban environment of Cha Oka and saw penguins' skin, seal bone, whale oil from South America and musk ox meat, polar bear fur, and salmon from the Arctic North. There were beads and fine masks made by people from what would be known as Japan, finely carved bone figures depicting Vikings sailing the seas. Yaz had no idea humans had developed such a widespread and dynamic civilization. And most strangely, there were no weapons. Yaz saw nothing that indicated war or killing. They hunted meat but not each other.

"My Friend!"

Yaz turned around and saw a well built mature man approach him. The man was decorated with feathers beads; his face was painted ochre and blue. "My Friend!" he repeated. "Welcome, welcome to our village."

Yaz knew it was more than a village. There were thousands of people in full-time residence, many building mounds around the area that seemed to stretch for hundreds of acres. Each mound was built by the hand-labor of men and women dedicated to this task. No slavery. No coercion. No force. Millions of tons of soil were delivered in woven baskets to build hundreds of sacred mounds. Different mounds; small ones, peaked ones, some lined up like a snake, others like a turtle, but each had different astrological, astronomical, cultural, spiritual, and environmental meanings. A vast wall of posts outlined the central plaza, and he could see the most prominent mound was a massive mound of earth, rising hundreds of feet in the air, multicolored with layers of different soil types, so it was impervious to weather.

"What is that?" Yaz pointed at the most prominent mound: four soaring terraces rising over a hundred feet in the air interconnected with both steps and arched ramps to form this structure. Intricate buildings of wood posts and bark occupied the various levels.

"That is our most holy place, the focus of our prayers and our lives," the man known as Watchful Raven replied with pride. "This whole place is called the 'City of the Sun', and this major mound is 'The Sun Center'; it is where we connect with our Great Creator."

Yaz stared in awe at the massive accomplishment.

"Come with me; we have our ceremony ready. My friend, I am known as Watchful Raven; I welcome you to our ceremony. You are the first of your kind to be with us."

Yaz followed Raven past the central mound, weaving in and out of a community of homes; well placed, well-coordinated housing with broad streets and clean walkways. Each house, every building was constructed with a unique method; The ground was scored with deep lines marking the building outline, wood and sticks were laid in the excavated pits to form the walls, then covered with a mud wattle construction with a thatched roof. Every building of the hundreds of building were all aligned precisely, forming a well coordinated, planned community unlike anything found across the continent.

Cooking fires glowed in the early evening mist as people moved harmoniously between heavily thatched roof homes, tended the communal fires, busy with their day-to-day tasks. Columns of grey smoke rose to mingle with a heavy mist coming off of the three rivers nearby. The sounds of contented laughter followed their progress toward a long building set apart from the others.

"Is this where your Kings and Royalty and rich people live?" Yaz looked around but couldn't see any grand palaces or homes.

Watchful Raven laughed. "On my no, my friend. We do not need Kings or royalty, and there are no rich people. Why would we have that? Wealth breeds insanity greed and war. We are all equal here, my friend. If we share all, there is no rich, no poor, there are only happy people. We have learned that avarice and ego are the twin demons of evil. These are destructive of all life. Greed and an attitude of entitlement are poisons to the soul."

"But don't you want more than the other guy? Don't you want a bigger hut? Faster horse? More women?"

Watchful Raven stopped laughing. "You are our guest. I will allow you this one indiscretion," he said somberly. "Women and men are equal, there are different duties and responsibilities, but one gender does not control the other, that is madness. As for bigger and better things than the next man? Why? What would that gain me but the anger and envy of others? Why would I need more? To make myself feel good about me? I already do. I have a nice place to live, food, friends, and enjoyment. Why introduce greed and envy? No, we are civilized here. We work together to make it better for everybody. I do not know where you come from Yaz, but we are a modern, sophisticated people here, and we have achieved a just and egalitarian society."

"But what about your criminals? What about cheaters and liars and thieves and murderers?"

"If all things are available to all, then where is the incentive to steal or cheat? No Yaz, we are not saints or without our flaws. We have disputes. We have the normal things human beings experience. But we see the world differently. Rather than see someone's actions as a crime, we ask what is missing to cause them anguish."

"Say that again?"

"Yaz, we all have personal possessions', things we hold dear to our journey through this plane of existence. Not all things are shared in common. Suppose someone takes something belonging to me, then a responsibility is incurred. They must give it back or compensate me for it. But more importantly, we do not punish. We seek to find out what was missing in that person's life they needed to steal? We answer that question, so the person does not need or want to steal a second time."

"You know," Yaz mused, "When my brothers and I visited this planet a long while back, humans were being told they were sinful at birth and needed to be saved."

"Saved? From what? Are you telling me a newborn being is capable of evil? This is a curious idea."

"Well, it seemed to be a central fixation with some of the desert dwellers. They seemed to believe in this book, see, and it told them they were bad to the core, bad from the moment they appeared and only God could forgive them."

"Who wrote this book?" Raven said suspiciously. "It sounds unconscious."

"That's the thing, the desert dwellers told us nobody wrote it. Their God created it and...."

"Their God? They own this God?"

"Well, yes, you see, they are the chosen people. According to their beliefs, God has selected only this one faith over all the others."

"Really?" Talking Raven looked puzzled. "Then they completely misunderstand the concept of God, yes?"

Yaz found himself in a predicament. Sure the Old Testament of the humans was pretty specific to this point. "Christians, Muslims, Jews all firmly believe they are the only true sons of God and have killed each other for centuries to prove it."

Talking Raven nodded, "Oh yes, now I understand, and I had forgotten this. Yes, nearly every religion created by humans has two things in common: Creation of a human evolved God and their special status under this God. Because they believe as they do, many humans consider themselves the 'Chosen people' of this self Created God. Humans create a strong figure to protect them. Their God is always a parental male father figure. In other words humans create an anthropomorphic God, jealous, angry, and vengeful, while being loving and compassionate, and then proceed to worship his human attributes."

"Yea, so, that is exactly how I heard them address their God."

"Problem is, A God modeled after human behavior and emotion is not God, but a projection of human ego."

Yaz couldn't bring himself to admit he and his brothers added to the human insanity of the times. *We were drunk, on vacation, and young, first time out on our own;* Yaz recalled their first visit to Earth. He thought of the trouble they caused, their arrogance, and their teasing of primitive humans to play with their egos and fears. Suddenly Yaz felt shame at their deeds.

Talking Raven just looked at Yaz for a moment as if reading his thoughts. "Interesting." He said softly. "And incredibly sad.

Yaz looked around him to see if anybody else was there. He looked back at Talking Raven whose eyes had never left him.

"Huh? Me?"

"You see, Yaz," Talking Raven said softly, "we see human beings as capable of great good, great compassion, and that is what we seek to encourage in our civilization. We emphasize these as our highest values, and we live them. To share with another is always our goal. We seek a win-win in our dealings with each other. We seek to have the other person do as well as we. That is the most important thing. The highest honor of our people is to sacrifice your life for another. Our greatest leaders give away their possession so they may lead with their heart and mind, not their ego. Our society is based on human beings sharing, not money, not possessions, not power, but on the capacity for people to grow and love and experience life. We see all life as equal, all life as entitled to live, all life is necessary for all life to thrive. We are not put on this planet to grow rich; we are here to learn how to be better human beings."

"Yeah, those other guys in the Middle East said that too, but they lied. All three religions are based on a class structure, with the priests and mullahs, and rabbis controlling everything. Those three religions created societies of inequality, unbalanced and treacherous because their stability depended on the exploitation of other people."

Raven grimaced. "When you follow a God created by humans all you will get are human created results. How incredibly sad, and how incredibly useful to know. You will understand this later on this afternoon at the longhouse celebration."

"Celebration?" Yaz pictured a drunken orgy. "So...ah...can anyone join in?"

Raven gave Yaz another long look. "You have a bizarre impression of human beings."

"Well, the last guys I was around were sort of crude, if you get my meaning. They told me women and children belonged to the male of the household, and the Male was the undisputed ruler of his home, and women were tortured, killed with stones thrown by their neighbors if they dared to speak out or attempt to leave abuse or even for wear the wrong clothing! Some even believe women must be covered head to foot to 'protect' them."

Raven shook his head, "Please do not tell me any more of these people. I do not wish to have such pictures in my mind."

Yaz nodded, wishing he'd thought of that.

They continued walking among the people, turning this way and winding their way across the various neighborhoods. This Cha Oka people were vastly superior to the humans they had met in the early days, and Yaz was impressed with how far the human race had progressed.

Talking Raven finally brought Yaz to a large Long House, with smoke curling up through a vent in the roof of thatch. It was initially dark inside as Yaz tried to make out the people present; gradually, his vision cleared, and he could see a small group of four, two men, two women, seated at a cheerful little fire. Yaz was sitting across from the elderly people and observed them. They were all highly decorated, tattooed with colored inks, blues, and greens, and dressed in their finest clothing, both cloth and leather. They were smiling and laughing with each other. For the two days he had been here, Yaz believed he was in the happiest place he'd ever been, on any planet, in any solar system. He was impressed with the mood of all the people; bright, energetic, compassionate, impassioned; just plain joyous attitudes.

A large man, dressed in furs and feathers, heavy tattoos on his face and arms, gave Yaz a warm welcome smile. "I am Teaches Hawk, and today we welcome our friend, Yaz, our new brother to whom we will entrust our most sacred treasure. We knew in the beginning that this could not be ours forever; we knew someday, it must be returned to its owners. This is that day. WE rejoice we do honor, we offer love. We offer respect to the Universe and pray to the Great One, the All-Knowing, and The Center. We thank the universe for love it has given us, and we know that from here, we will take this understanding and spread it out to the world. Thank you, Creator, for this great gift. It is now up to us to carry these teachings onward."

Watchful Raven placed a large, dull, Blue-Green Emerald in front of Yaz.

"We have entrusted all our knowledge of this Mystery Stone, and all our knowledge of human life and concept of God into a Codex.

This Codex contains all our knowledge of science, astronomy, medicine, and the lives of all the creatures sharing our wonderful world. There will be many Codexes' because we have much to say, and we understand our knowledge may get lost over the many generations, so multiple copies should advance future human civilizations considerably."

"But," Yaz hated to interrupt, but he was puzzled. "I still don't understand why I am here. I enjoy everything; I am impressed, but why am I here?"

****

"Hey, Yaz! Yaz!" Charley called out, "Hey, wake up, dude, we need to talk."

Yaz jolted upright and said: "Time does not exist – humans invented it - time is what the clock says. The distinction between the past, present, and future is only a stubbornly persistent illusion."

"What?"

Yaz held his head, "Ow, my head hurts."

"What was that about time?"

"That sounded familiar; that was a quote from Albert Einstein, wasn't it?"

Yaz shrugged. "I don't know. What did I say?"

Muh and Jee sat down beside Yaz at the fire.

"Dinner?" Muh reached out for Doc's boiling pot.

"No! That's..." Doc was too late.

Muh drank from the pot smacked his lips. "Needs salt."

Charley and Doc stared.

Muh just cocked his head and took another drink.

"But that's not food! That's..."

"Doc, yesterday both Muh and Jee ate a can of car wax and liked it."

"Oh, well...I guess I can find something else to bind up my boots." He showed Charley the flapping sole. "But nothing would have worked better than my glue." He looked over as Muh handed Jee the pot. Jee took a long deep drink and drained the pot.

"Bummer, dude."

"Yaz, why did you quote Einstein?"

The memories of Cha Oka swirled in Yaz's mind. "I must tell you all some things you need to know."

"What?" Muh was aghast. "No way! Shut up!" Muh couldn't let Yaz steal the spotlight.

"Quiet! Quit fucking barking!" Charley turned on Muh. "Keep quiet, or I will fucking muzzle you!"

Yaz looked uncertain but swallowed and continued gamely.

"I had a...dream, I guess. Just now. I was visiting a place called Cha Oka and..."

"Oh great!" Muh exclaimed. "You gonna share vacation pictures with us?"

"Wait a minute!" Jee didn't like what he was hearing. "You visited someplace without us?"

Yaz ignored them, and for twenty minutes, he explained his dream. Yaz was tired, but he held everyone's attention. Even Muh and Jee were attentive.

"Finally, the Ending Ceremony began," Yaz explained to every-one his memories of his last night in Cha Oka. "Great long boring speeches, lots of congratulations, and swapping of stories for hours. Between speeches, prayers, and jokes, I was offered something to drink, something to smoke, and something to huff. All of it tasted horrible, but I felt pretty good. I was having a discussion about theoretical astrophysics when the lights went out."

Yaz looked around the firelight at Charley, Doc, Pawnee; they seemed interested.

But Muh and Jee were shaking their heads. "Yeah, we thought so; it's nothing but another one of your drunken fantasies. Ya bum!"

"Next thing I know," Yaz was determined to finish. "I'm standing at the spaceport, my ride waiting, and I'm holding this Blue-Green Emerald, a Mystical Stone. I brought it back home with me and turned it over to the Galactic Council." Yaz sipped his hot chocolate and leaned back on his log. "But, I gotta say I don't remember much beyond that. I have no idea what this is about; I don't re-call anything said in the ceremony or instructions. Nothing. Those Cahokians had some really good shit!"

"Isn't this the same Blue-Green Emerald the Galactic Council gave us to return to Indianapolis, Indiana?" Jee wondered what was going on here. "Why was Yaz sent back to get this Blue Emerald thing and not all of us?"

He glared suspiciously at Muh. "Did you know about this?"

Muh, furious that Yaz had been given some special assignment, said heatedly. "This orphan is a liar! This mystical...sacred...holy stone, whatever the fuck name it is, the Blue Emerald, was given to me, and only me, by the Galactic Council to bring to Earth to apol-ogize to the Earthlings: Indianapolis, Mecca, Jerusalem, and then home! That is our sacred mission! That is our only sacred mission. I have spoken!"

"This 'mystical stone' is what is now known as The Einstein Stone?" Bessie May Chowder asked curiously.

Yaz nodded slowly. "I do not know."

He then turned to Muh and Jee. "You say the Galactic Counsel gave you the mission directives, but where are they? We only have your word! How do we know Jee and I are supposed to grovel and prostrate ourselves to make amends?"

Muh thought about that for a moment. "That is right, you can-not see them because I am the leader and only I have access to top-secret information. Compartmentalization protects our secrets, and I have spoken."

"You made up this whole worldwide spiritual trail of tears, didn't you?"

"I am the leader!" Muh replied hotly. "You are not authorized to question my decisions. Only a higher authority can do that. You are a lower...class."

Pawnee heard the aliens arguing out on his observations post. *Sound travels far at night, particularly when those alien beagles are bitch-ing at each other.*

Pawnee came into the firelight and held up his hand. "Enough. Shut up with the yipping and barking."

The aliens stopped and looked at Pawnee.

"Yaz," Pawnee said, "you have the information we need; what do you say?"

"I'm sorry my memory is so hazy. But, as I fear, there are consequences for failure. We must do this. If we don't take this Einstein Stone to Cahokia, Cha Oka, whatever its name, not only will all humanity be erased from the cosmos, but I'm pretty sure you and Jee are going to lose more than a gym membership."

"What?" Jee was alarmed. "Wait a minute! Do we have something to lose here too? That's bullshit! We're VIA's! We're just fucking visitors here; we aren't involved!"

"This is the first time anybody has spoken about the elimination of humanity" Doc didn't like the direction of this conversation. "Ya'll want to discuss that a little more?"

~ 50 ~

CHAPTER FORTY-EIGHT

"The religion of the future will be a cosmic religion. It will transcend a personal God and avoid dogma and theology." Albert Einstein

"Ya'll, we need to talk about the Einstein Stone," Doc told them.

"What are we going to do with it?" Jade asked.

Standing up on his side of the fire, Muh crossed his arms in self-importance and said, "Well, given the topic, I have an announcement."

Everyone looked up.

"Go on," Bessie May said.

Jee, on all four paws beside Muh slouched in an insolent stance; tail curved up in defiance, ears forward, cigarette dangling from his jaws, gangster-style black sunglasses hiding his eyes.

Yaz nudged Jee, "You look ridiculous. Don't you know how a mirror works?"

"You know, I've never, ever seen a beagle smoke a cigarette. Not once, and I've been around dogs a long time."

"Charley, they aren't dogs." Chowder said. "What they seem to be open to speculation." She observed. So far, this particular pack of aliens didn't seem all that special. Except for Yaz, the other two she would prefer to kennel.

"Oh, yeah, forgot. Go on, Muh, what do you want?" Charley asked.

"I demand the Blue Emerald be returned to me immediately," Muh growled indignantly. "Further, I demand you provide escort, safety, and security for my underlings and me...."

"Hey, wait a minute!"

"Let me ask you something?" Bessie May tired of the back and forth. "You told us earlier that you are here to straighten out a little mistake you made a few millennia ago. Right?"

Muh and Jee nodded.

"As you explained earlier, you are supposed to take it to the President of the United Christian States of America, right?"

Muh and Jee nodded.

"What was he supposed to do with it?"

Muh and Jee shrugged.

"You were just going to hand it over, say oops, and leave?"

"Pretty much, yeah."

"That's your answer?" Charley had reached the end of patience, which was a short rope, to begin with. "I think you're full of bullshit."

"Okay, okay," Muh replied with placating gestures. "The most honest answer is; we have no idea what the blue thingy does. Not a clue, nothing, we know nothing!"

Jee added. "Really. What he said."

"Wait a minute," Yaz spoke up. "didn't you hear me?

"Don't listen to him," Muh demanded. "He's adopted."

"What?" Yaz was dumbfounded because this had never occurred to him. "Are you sure?" *But we're triplets!* The idea was so preposterous it could be true. *Could Muh be right?* Yaz sat back down in confusion. *Who was mom?* Suddenly Yaz was riddled with more than just esoteric spiritual confusion.

"Oh, for God's sake! Focus, focus!" Chowder snapped her fingers in front of the three little green alien beagles, and they all turned to her. "What does the Einstein Stone do?"

Yaz began to question his life. His purpose for existence. *Adopted? Me?* Quickly he became lost in an existential maze of dead ends and quicksand.

"Yaz!" Chowder reached over and poked Yaz, disturbing his concentration. "You seem to have some answers. Let's hear them."

Muh howled, jumping between Chowder and Yaz, his paws wide stretched defensively. "Nooooo! You must follow the hierarchy! The chain of command! You must address all questions to The Leader! Me!" He barked excitedly.

"Except you don't know shit," Jee said.

"I know shit."

"The shit you know is just shit!"

"But it's the real shit!"

Is not."

"Is so."

"Yaz," Chowder continued ignoring the squabbling ETs. "The Einstein Stone is seen as a 'Teaching' Stone. Perhaps it is a threshold or something. Also, the Mayans believe it held world-changing consequences." Bessie May's voice held a hint of wonder. "We guess that it is based on an evolutionary step of some kind. But what? This could be huge, could be invaluable. Look around," She gestured at the surrounding countryside. "You see anything that looks like progress out there? We need help. This Einstein Stone could be the very thing to help us. So, Yaz, tell us what we need to know. Please."

"Yeah, yeah. Sure," Yaz said distractedly. *Adapted? His thoughts were stunned. Muh, said I was adopted? But, we're triplets; we look identical.*

"Orphan!" Muh sneered.

"Yeah," Jee added. "Homeless waif!" Jee added.

Yaz started to reply, and Pawnee held up a hand. He tapped his backpack. "The Blue Emeral', she here. She is going stay here until President Chowder tells me different."

"Why are we going to Cahokia Mounds?" Chowder asked Yaz.

"Why?" Yaz looked puzzled. "Because Cahokia Mounds is the Center and the apex point. The Beginning...Cahokia is the grand example!"

"They called their community 'Cha Oka...'" Yaz started to explain then stopped. *The Hammer. A huge solar event. Just like before? The Super Nova was similar to The Hammer. Is there a connection?* Implications swirled in Yaz' mind. *But I don't understand any of this!*

"Go on, don't stop now," Charley urged Yaz. "We are going where, for what reason?"

Charley, Doc, Pawnee, and Bessie May leaned forward to hear.

Jade, on the other hand, was listening outside the circle.

Yaz had just started to recall some detail about Cahokia when Jade quickly got to her feet.

Gunfire followed.

~ 51 ~

CHAPTER FORTY-NINE

Peter Paul God-Kock rode the lead Humvee like Patton in a victory parade, shouting encouragement, waving the national flag of Trump, a picture of the former President playing golf. He accepted their indifferent stares and apathy as signs of subdued patriotism.

"Thank you, thank you, my loyal subjects!" He shouted at an elderly woman wheeling a shopping cart.

"Onward to Victory!" He screamed at a very startled pair of school kids.

" Sisk boom ba, sisk boom be, who do we want to lead? Me! Me! Me!" He cried out to strangers as they passed, startling the people who had no idea who he was, irritating the people who did.

God-Kock was amazed with himself, leading the army of Barcelona like the brilliant and commanding Supreme Being he knew himself to be. Singing with gusto, God-Kock delivered his version of "Caissons Go Rolling along" while hanging out the top of the Humvee, certain his every move, every gesture, and every word was being recorded for posterity. *I'm the Napoleon of my time!*

Three Hummers behind God-Kock, Captain Marty Harasin, Veteran Team Leader, retired Sergeant Major, spoke to the lead Humvee in his microphone. "We'll pull off over here, to the right, near that section of woods. Got it?"

The driver of the God-Kock's vehicle acknowledged the order.

230

"And it's high high hee in the field artillery..." God-Kock was growing weary after thirty-five renditions of the same song, his throat growing hoarse. "The caisson go rolling...." God-Kock cried out as he noticed his Humvee steering off the highway. "Hey, what are you doing? I didn't command you to stop?"

"Sir?" as the Humvee driver slowed to take the turn, he called Harasin, "Should I keep going or laager in for the night?"

"You heard the briefing; ignore him that moron. Take your orders from me, not that dickhead. He's along as the patsy if we need one."

"Yes, sir."

The column of Humvee's pulled left off the road and into a field where they parked for the night; their fifty caliber weapons remained ready for trouble. Even armored vehicles were not safe in the new world of The Hammer.

Capt. Harasin got out of his truck reluctantly. He was growing very tired of dealing with this raving nitwit. He approached God-Kock.

"Sir, we are fairly sure the enemy is in this area," He explained to God-Kock, who had exited the vehicle, irritated haughtiness marking his features. "There was a report of contact by the Illinois Home Guard," Harasin started to explain. "A unit of old National Guard and volunteers, just south of here. There was a big guy reported. It could be Pawnee Painter, Charley Bones, Doc Betters, I don't know? But whoever it was, he accounted for two Humvee's destroyed, and he held them off long enough for the others to escape. So, if I were you, I would be careful about exposing yourself to potential enemy fire."

God Kock looked up from the makeup mirror as he turned on the battery-operated LED lights, bright and illuminating. "But I must have makeup," God-Kock demanded. "God's are different than mortals. We need more pancake foundation and eyeliner. It's just the way things are." He wanted to be patient with this mortal, but it just seemed as if he refused to listen to his superior.

Captain Harasin wondered if shooting him now would just be kinder for everybody.

"Sir, Barcelona for you," His sergeant signaled an incoming call.

"Yes, sir," Harasin took the phone and turned away. "What can I do for you, sir?"

"Captain Harasin, are you closing in on Chowder and her terrorists? I have had reports of a gang like hers roaming and killing in your area. Why haven't you killed them yet? Must I come down there and settle this matter? Get me the Blue Emerald!" Barcelona's voice was weary from issues commands. The assault on his main stockyards was very disconcerting. They would have to round up a whole new herd of humans or risk having dissatisfied customers. The business had been growing, and Barcelona was pleased with the public willingness to overlook his sources of meat products, willingness based on their continuing ignorance, of course.

"Yes, sir, right away, sir,"

"Now, is the idiot God-Kock still alive?"

"Is that a question or an order, sir?"

"Put him on." Barcelona was tired and did not feel like dealing with stupid. But duty was duty.

"We don't allow him near the microphones, sir...it has been difficult," Harasin tried to explain. When the column left Indianapolis pursuing Bessie May Chowder, Pawnee Painter, and the invading Cascadian's' they learned early on not to allow God-Kock near any form of communications device.

His certainty that all communications were for him and that every form of communications was a secret code, created in God-Koch a peculiar form of paranoid histrionics that was both irritating and likely to draw fire from the locals. God-Kock never met a microphone that wasn't his friend.

But it was the incessant singing that made them take away the microphone permanently.

Harasin, 26 years in the US Army, had his orders: bring back the Blue-Green Emerald. All the rest was expendable, including and especially, God-Kock.

He handed God-Kock the microphone.

"Don't slobber on the mike."

It seemed to God-Kock that many people must talk to themselves. *Nasty comments could only be self-directed as no one would dare insult a God.*

"Listen to me very closely," Barcelona said to God-Kock. "Are you listening? Say something!"

"Yes," God-Kock answered promptly. Please, he had the answer.

"Yes, what?"

"What what?" Suddenly, God-Kock wasn't sure he had the correct answer and began to sweat. God-Kock hoped he was covered under the same insurance policy as the Catholic Pope with Papal infallibility.

"Tell me, God-Kock, what today is, what is the date?"

"Date? No, I don't want a date." Relieved that he knew the answer to this one, God-Kock beamed with pleasure, confident now Barcelona would be pleased with him.

Barcelona looked at the microphone as if it were a snake. He kept hearing rumors of aliens with Chowder and her gang. If anyone would know, God-Kock had them in a cell before The Hammer.

"Listen carefully, God-Kock I need information."

The sounds reverberating in God-Kocks' mind sometimes made hearing in the real world difficult.

"Yes, I have our convoy moving in formation, but this Captain minion is interfering with my commands. I am God-Kock! Do you hear me! Tell them who I am!"

"Ah fuck!" Barcelona threw up his hands in disgust, growing tired of this. "Never fucking mind! Give the mike back to the Captain, now!"

God-Kock reluctantly handed the microphone over to Harasin, now thoroughly confused about what was going on.

"Harasin!" Barcelona bellowed. "Let somebody else deal with crazy. I have better things to do."

"Yes, sir," Captain Harasin responded promptly.

"Look, all you need to know is that the area around Collinsville, Illinois is important. Right down the road from you. Your mission: bring the intact Blue-Green Emerald back here or else. Questions?"

"And what about numb nuts?"

"Keep him alive. He may become useful."

"And if not?"

"Well, for god sake, don't bring him back home! Set him free; let him wander the world preaching for pennies. Sell him for scrap. I don't care!"

~ 52 ~

CHAPTER FIFTY

"I am but a humble gatekeeper for Jesus." Imahuffin told anyone who would listen.

For Imahuffin, his role in life, his profession, his very reason for existence was as a 'Gatekeeper for Jesus'. Whether the title was Priest, Imam, Rabbi, Chaplain, or Minister of God, he knew the job was to be God's Receptionist. Keeping faithful penitents from wasting God's time with trivial issues his most important duty. Of course, to be successful, he would need penitents to begin with.

A prophet with followers is considered an avatar; a visionary with no followers is regarded as a crazy, spider-eating desert dweller. Imahuffin thought sourly.

After The Hammer, with the world in chaos and confusion, Imahuffin continued his desperate journey in the old school bus, steering the venerable vehicle across the beleaguered states of Washington, Oregon, Idaho, and into Montana, no one to talk to, no one to proselytize, and no one to lead to Jesus.

Occasionally, he would stop for gas and food and rest and to steal crucifixes. In times of great stress or great prayer he would wear one of the crucifixes around his neck. Hundreds of crucifixes rattled each time the bus went over a bump.

As the miles went on, he grew incredibly bored with his sermons and even more desperate for human contact.

A few miles later, outside of a highway rest stop, a motley gaggle of ragged men, women, and one child, hitchhiking down Interstate 86, waved their "Mormon's for Jesus" signs, and Imahuffin pulled over.

"Are you Mormons?" Imahuffin asked.

One of them stuck his 'Mormon's for Jesus' sign in the door and waggled it.

"Ok, ok, don't get snippy. Do you want to see Jesus, or are you heathens like those damn Lutherans?"

Magic words.

"Jesus! Jesus! Jesus! Take us to Jesus!"

Mormons throughout Utah saw the Hammer as a sign from God they were to travel to St. Louis, Missouri, the root source of their sacred Golden Plates and, more importantly, the 'Amulet of Smith,' an object long rumored to not exist.

Thousands of faithful Mormons started, long lines of determined people, marching toward the horizon to do their duty and meet their God. From Salt Lake City, Utah to just outside Butte, Montana, the thousands dwindled to forty-two truly determined, committed, staunchly fundamentalist true believers. All of whom were angry at this obligation.

"I'm going to Indiana to meet with Jesus; you want to come on along?" Imahuffin called out to the people.

The grateful, exhausted pilgrims boarded the bus. Imahuffin slammed the door shut and turned back onto the highway, I-86 East, through the mountains and plains and then Indianapolis. Imahuffin watched the Mormons settle in; some were blank with catatonic exhaustion, others smoked cigarettes, gambled, and bragged about sex.

Imahuffin realized these two groups were divided by gender.

A few miles down the road, Imahuffin learned two essential facts: The Mormons were well armed and hungry to hunt nonbelievers. Their leader had died of an infected horse bite last week, and they were helplessly desperate for someone to guide them to Jesus.

Imahuffin had his followers.

With religious fervor, Imahuffin, gripping the steering wheel passionately, launched into a fiery sermon of blood, guts, conquest, and Jesus Christ. For 20, 30, 40 miles, and more, the Mormons were battered and overwhelmed by Imahuffin's prodigious knowledge of Jesus, with quotes, half-quotes, and misquotes from the Holy Bible; King James Version, of course.

In due course, they had just passed a slow-moving Amazon Prime Delivery Van when they came across a roadside rest stop. Imahuffin decided to test out his proselytizing prowess.

He swerved the old bus into the parking lot, slammed on the brakes, threw open the folding doors, and screamed: "Sic 'em!" Pointing at the dozen or so travelers standing around staring at them, eyes wide with surprise.

By now working into a frenzy of faith, the Mormon faithful stormed out of the yellow school bus with the happy red balloons and began to shoot everyone in sight; men, women, children, dogs, and a pet lizard. Imahuffin stared in wonder.

Awed by what he had accomplished; Turning ordinary Mormons into murders he began to wear two crucifixes at a time permanently. He was so proud of them.

"You must attack any town that doesn't worship Jesus!" Imahuffin shouted over the screaming, sounds of panicked running, and gunfire, "You must torch everything to the ground as an offering to the Lord and never rebuild this town again as it is an insult to Jesus. Sew the land with salt! Deuteronomy 13:13-19!" Imahuffin waited to see if the Mormons objected to Jesus being in the Old Testament, but blinded by blood lust, they didn't seem to notice.

'Moses of the Murdering Mormon's,' a phrase Imahuffin invented, was born.

~ 53 ~

CHAPTER FIFTY-ONE

Jade snarled at Charley, "Try not to fuck things up over and over, okay?"

"Me? You're the one who wanted the damn shot, and you missed."

"I 'missed' you moron because you're panting like a plow horse. Would you shut the fuck up?"

"Breathing! I'm breathing here."

They watched the four-point buck, enough to feed them a few days, scamper off into the thick forest of poplar and maple. The gunfire from the assault on their camp had driven off all the game in the area.

"If you tell me you want the next shot, I'm going to shoot you." As soon as she said it, she realized it was a lame attempt at humor. Damn, she thought. Realizing she snapped at him, Jade didn't want to fight. *Why am I always so rude to him?*

"That's just like you, Jade, always dependable." Charley fired back. "Always an asshole!"

Even as he was arguing with her, the fear of losing her again made his heart skip. *I've just found her.* Her clear, brilliant green eyes, thick raven's wing hair, and slender form, inside he smiled because it was more than her physicality; it was the totality of her. Beyond the sensuality, Charley Bones loved her, all phases of her. He knew what made her laugh and what made her cry.

"Don't call me an asshole, you motherfucker, or I'll gut you!"

Of course, he was far more familiar with what made her angry enough to express streaks of violent, homicidal rage.

"Jade! For God's sake, back down, okay?"

It was a struggle, but she managed to swallow her next venomous reply.

"Okay," Jade took several deep breaths. "Okay, you're right; in fact, I've thought about this. Maybe we can change things, maybe not be so...argumentative, maybe let go of the past."

Charley sensed a trap but couldn't figure it out. "Okay." That was all he knew to say in self-defense.

Sensing his wariness, Jade put her hands behind her back.

Charley had been around that block before. A head butt was always possible, so he remained wary.

Sensing his caution, Jade said to Charley as openly as she could. "It looks as if we are heading toward some kind of mystical event. Look at what has happened to our world. The Einstein Stone, these secret codes, the aliens, a nation that has gone dark and savage. Civilization is hanging by a thread. The very climate of our planet is changing in ways no human has ever witnessed!"

"Is this your happy face?"

"No, be serious. The world is a disaster. Maybe you and I can call a truce?"

"Depends."

"Huh?"

Charley hadn't meant that at all. Desperately he searched his mind for the words he meant to say. "Uh-oh... Yeah... that sort of came out wrong... I meant..."

"Oh, did it now?" Jade fired back. "You think I'm a bitch now, buddy? You ain't seen nothing yet!"

"I didn't say...." Charley protested.

The rage, always on simmer, came to a full boil. Jade jabbed him in the chest with her index finger, hard enough to bruise.

"Just like you, Charley, always blowing up a good moment! You Dickhead!" Jade furiously stalked away. She had tried making amends, but that idiot just playing games again. Her momentary vulnerability was exposed, now hidden in defensive rage.

Charley watched her go away, rubbing his bruised chest, wondering what happened.

"Well, you fucked that one up, my man."

"Doc, I didn't mean to...it's complicated."

"If there were a University that taught men and women to communicate," Doc observed. "Charles, ya'll have flunked the admissions test."

~ 54 ~

CHAPTER FIFTY-TWO

The Imahuffin School Bus O' Slaughter had made good time in its blood-drenched journey toward St. Louis. Imahuffin only allowed an occasional stop to smite the heathens, which irritated his Mormon murderers, but it did keep them fresh.

Imahuffin could see the glow on the horizon from the Nebraska border. It was St. Louis burning to the ground.

"Your Lordship?" Terry Harry, the Mormon Elder spokesman, addressed Imahuffin carefully. "Well, according to the CB chatter, St. Louis is a hellhole of fires, gunfire, robbery, assault, and prose-lytizing."

"What?"

Terry Harry, eyes alight at the thought of holy battle, said, "All the murders and firefights have brought on religious zealotry, sir, bibles and bullets: Baptists are running over Lutherans, Four Square gunning down Episcopalians, and Catholics are hunted by everyone. It's a Bible thumping' bloodbath, sir."

"Damnation, son that sounds like our kind of place. We will head to St. Louis to assist our Christian brothers in converting the fallen." Imahuffin could feel it in the air, smell it, taste and touch it. His destiny was just about to happen. St. Louis was now the Holy Grail of the new world for Imahuffin, just ripe for a strong man to reach in and grab the city by the throat and rule it.

Pope Imahuffin I. The dream was alive. He slipped another crucifix around his neck to the growing collection.

"We are going into St. Louis and clean house, rid the world of those false prophets, wipe out those who believed in a different Jesus! A false Jesus! We have been given a summons from God to eliminate the side branches and suckers so the tree of Jesus could grow straight and strong! Just like in the Whole Bible, King James Version, of course! Accept NO substitutes!"

"Kill the Liberals! Kills the Liberals! Kill the Liberals!"

didn't want to change their chant. Technically, they were setting out to kill other Christians. Not that killing a Christian or two who deserved it was a bad idea or sacrilegious or anything. But Imahuffin felt his team was on a roll, had their mojo working, momentum was on their side, and like a championship NFL Coach: when winning, change nothing. Imahuffin was so proud of his little Mormon murderers.

To keep their spirits up and to pass the time, Imahuffin swung between renditions of 'Nearer my God to Thee' and Leviticus, 'Give me that old-time religion' followed by Deuteronomy. He preached up a storm, waving his arms, seeking guidance from the heavens, shouting out his prayers, spraying the front windshield with spit for an abundant and holy future. "All human beings that are doomed lose the right to be redeemed; they must be put to death - Leviticus 27:28-29!"

"Leviticus! Leviticus! Leviticus!" The Mormons got into the swing of things.

"Listen, my followers, Listen," shrieked Imahuffin. "A sword, a sword is drawn for slaughter, polished and sharpened, to cut off the heads of depraved and wicked Liberals who dare blaspheme against Jesus! Leviticus 2-10!"

"Leeeviticus! Jeeeesuss! Leeeviticus! Jeeeesus!'

The speedometer of the 45-ton yellow school bus hit sixty-five as it went from shoulder to shoulder, throwing gravel, running other vehicles off the road, but Imahuffin, one hand on the wheel, didn't care; he was lost to the Lord.

"....and then the Lord saying kill them, kill them, kill them...." Imahuffin was running on spiritual energy. "Kill...kill..."

Terry Harry scurried forward, he had good news from the CB radio, but he was scared to death of dying in a flaming explosion of gasoline and metal before he got the chance to say it. So he did the only thing he could think of in such a perilous moment: Give Imahuffin drugs.

"Sir! You forgot your Oxycodone! I have one more pill, sir. Do you want it now?"

Imahuffin stopped preaching and stared at Terry. Then he stared at the small oval pill. "You have a what?" He'd thought he'd swallowed the last Oxy just before the Missouri Border. "Did you say the last pill?"

"I hid it from you in case of emergency," Terry replied eagerly. "Can you...ah...slow down long enough to take it? I've heard that Oxy isn't as powerful when you're traveling over thirty miles per hour, sir."

"Really? I didn't know that." Maybe that explained why his other Oxycodone's seemed to disappear so fast. Imahuffin swore he would do better and travel slower.

"Here you go, sir. You'll feel better in no time."

The School Bus slowed, 70, 50, 30, and soon even the most fevered crusader relaxed.

Terry breathed a sigh of relief. The bloody wars going on in St. Louis between the Christian Crusaders, the Drug Dealers, Organized Crime, Disorganized Crime, the Cops, the rogue Cops, Organized and semi-organized Militia's, and then the hundreds of civilian factions was too horrendous to think about.

Some American cities were lawless "last man standing" territories.

Imahuffin, the Oxycodone coursing through his bloodstream, smiled so hard his cheeks hurt and couldn't remember where they were going and why.

Terry could see Imahuffin's eyes go waxy. "Sir, you said we were going past St. Louis and going to a small Distillery in Collinsville, Illinois. They make Rye-Whiskey sir, very, very rare blend."

Terry's mouth watered. He loved whiskey.

"I said what?" Imahuffin stared at the more petite man. "We are going where?" He couldn't remember saying that. It bothered him so much he draped another crucifix around his neck.

"We are headed for Collinsville, sir. Watch for the signs. 'Macbeth Distillery Rye-Whiskey.' We have a distillery to liberate!" The thought of dying violently did not appeal to Terry Harry, but getting blind drunk on good whiskey, was a real winner.

"Remember God's very words," Imahuffin challenged his holy warriors. "A feast is made for laughter, wine makes life merry, and money is the answer for everything." – Ecclesiastes 10:19!"

"We are off!" Imahuffin announced, "to liberate a Distillery from the atheists and nonbelievers. Whiskey was made by Christians for Christians!" He announced.

He slung another crucifix around his throat and the old school bus rumbled down the road, voices inside merrily singing '100 bottles of beer on the wall' followed by 'Nearer my Jesus to thee,' as they rolled past all the exits to St. Louis.

Terry hadn't gotten the chance yet to tell Imahuffin about Peter Paul God-Kock and his army off armored Humvee's. The CB chatter was filled with reports and warnings of their attacks around the Illinois area, getting into gun battled with local thugs and rogue elements of the National Guard.

Avoiding death by random violence anywhere, urban or rural, was high on Terry's Bucket List.

~ 55 ~

CHAPTER FIFTY-THREE

P.P. God-Kock's Humvee squad was only three miles outside of Collinsville when God-Kock commanded his men to halt for lunch.

The column of Humvee's continued on unchanged.

Twice more P.P. God-Kock commanded a halt.

One-half hour later the Humvee column of four slowed and turned off the road into a parking lot.

God-Kock couldn't believe his direct orders were disobeyed. *God should not be treated this shabbily!*

He eyed Captain Harasin with evil intent as the soldier approached his Humvee. Confident now that Harasin was Satan come to challenge him. This was no different from Jesus in the desert and God-Kock being seduced and betrayed. "Get thee behind me, Satan," God-Kock muttered darkly.

"Look...ah...God-Kock," Harasin hated talking to this idiot, and he felt insulted. Twenty-six years in the US Army deployed to war zones and hot spots all around the globe, combat wounded, plenty of medals, Harasin was one week from retirement when The Hammer hit, and everything disappeared. His retirement, his release from 'the Big Green Weenie' was to be a salvation of sorts, a chance for Harasin to reconnect with his wife and children. Now all gone. Service to people like Barcelona as a mercenary was all that was left to him. Harasin felt cheated out of his just rewards and was a bitter man.

"I ordered a halt hours ago!" God-Kock protested. "Why didn't we stop as I commanded?"

Harasin looked up at God-Kock and shook his head. *Idiots,* he thought, *all my life, I've had to deal with idiots.* "We couldn't stop back there," Harasin explained slowly. "Kind of the wrong place, you know?'

"Oh? Maybe it was, and maybe it wasn't!" God-Kock wasn't going to be denied his snit. "Are you sure that's all it was? Could you be...jealous? Huh? Jealous of my innate command of military maneuvers? My genius at tactical warfare?"

"What?" Harasin wanted to just walk away, get in his Humvee and go someplace else, anyplace else.

"My choice of the camp was perfect!" God-Kock exclaimed. "Perfect! The view was spectacular. The sunrise would have been visible, and it was clean, with no dirty dirt. We must go back there and set up camp as I ordered, and that is final! I have commanded it!"

"It was the middle of a fucking bridge, you moron!" Harasin tired of the pretense.

Peter Paul God-Kock's mouth dropped open in stunned dismay at the deliberate insult.

"You don't laager a unit of military vehicles on a fucking bridge!" Harasin continued. "Now, stay off the intercom, stop issuing threats to every community we drive through and shut the fuck up, okay?"

Captain Harasin turned before engaging further with God-Koch walking back to his vehicle.

God-Koch was paralyzed with insult, and he could not believe God was spoken to in such a harsh and insulting manner. Watching the Captain walk away, God-Kock vowed vengeance. There would be a Biblical level of' smiting' in the future.

"Sergeant Halm?" Harisin said.

"Yes, sir,"

"Any sign of tangos?" Barcelona told him to find this band of terrorists and take them down. But they had violent contact with some renegade units along the way down here. Old Humvee's, four by four pickups, old jalopy cars, all manner of vehicle tried to intercept their journey. Harasin had lost nobody and intended that to continue, but they were running short of ammunition.

"Well, sir, there is CB chatter that leads me to think they are headed South, maybe East of St. Louis," Sgt Halm replied."Yes, well, we are here, Horse Shoe Lake Rd. Let us settle in for the night. I need to touch base with Barcelona."

"What should we do with rat fuck?" Sgt Sergeant toyed with his pistol while staring at God-Kock, who was carefully applying eyeliner to emphasize his commanding eyes.

Harasin thought about that. "Lock him in the Humvee with no access to communications equipment. Food, water, that's it."

"But he won't like it."

"Tell him he is in seclusion to keep him safe from evil."

"What evil?"

"The evil I'm going to do to him if he fucks things up again."

"I'll just tell him he is in seclusion because for him to hear God's commandments, he needs solitude and quiet. Like Jesus in the Desert."

"He'll believe that?"

"Who cares? He'll be locked in a Humvee."

"Barcelona on the line, chief," another soldier called out.

Captain Harasin answered. "Yes, sir, we are close to Collinsville, we have had no contact with the subjects, but we're following rumors of a group, well-armed, traveling with a petite Black Woman and a huge Hawaiian man." Harasin was lying. They were flying blind and were only still traveling South because that was the direction they started in.

"Got them! Go get them! And remember, bring me back Bessie May Chowder and the Einstein Stone, all the rest...well, you know."

"Will there by anything else, sir?

"Yes, I thought you should be informed. I have changed the name, Barcelona Meats, to Mana Meats. Like the Mana from heaven supported and nourished the holy desert people in their time of need, so too, would the meat supplied by Barcelona!"

Harasin said nothing.

Setting up, organizing, resetting the slaughter equipment and the distribution network was tough sledding. But Barcelona was a passionate man, and human flesh was the Keto Foods of the modern era. For Barcelona, it was the perfect blend of capitalism and reality: The cost of production was meager and profits ridiculously high. Not only that, but the way humans breed, Barcelona knew he would have a steady fresh supply of meat for as long as he wanted it.

Barcelona explained all of it to Harasin.

"Will there be anything else, sir?" Harasin replied quickly when Barcelona stopped to take a breath.

"Okay, okay, just make sure they know Barcelona Meats is now Mana Meats and we are in business; we will be setting up butcher shops all across the nation. And pass out the flyers as I told you." it worried Barcelona that Harasin seemed to be resistant to his business plan. Utter and total compliance was all Barcelona expected, so he was puzzled by Harasin's hesitation. *I may have to go there myself,* he mused a tickle of excitement at the thought of doing the actual killing himself. *I have grown and matured, He realized. I don't have to wait for others to kill for me; I can do it myself!* It was a new concept to him, one he had to think about seriously.

Harasin didn't want to discuss cannibalism, now or ever. "Sir, we will head out in the morning and should make Cahokia Mounds by noon. If they are there, we'll find them.

"Captain Harasin, I value your professionalism and your loyalty...."

I'm getting praise from a man who eats human flesh. Harasin sighed; he looked up at the stars. *Without light pollution, the stars have returned.* Millions and billions, a dusting of stars, he wondered what life was like on all those other planets.

"I'm just a soldier, doing my duty, but somehow things have gone sideways for me," Harasin muttered sadly.

"What? What was that?" Barcelona replied.

"Nothing, sir, nothing."

"Harasin, I just want you to know that if this all goes well, we will return your wife and children unharmed. I promise you."

Harasin wondered if being an asshole was a cosmic thing or just specific to Earth.

~ 56 ~

CHAPTER FIFTY-FOUR

"We need to talk," Muh told Jee. "This is serious."

"Serious? I'll say, you've been the worst leader I have ever ..."

"Stop it! Pay attention. Yaz has betrayed us."

"Yaz?"

"The orphan!"

"Oh yeah, him."

"When were we here on this planet the last time?" Muh asked Jee.

"The year One? No, that doesn't sound right. Earthlings have an odd way of keeping track of time. I never understood it. Like time started over after people had been around for centuries. Makes no sense."

"They base it on the death of Jesus," Muh explained. "Like time started over when Jesus croaked."

"Yeah, I liked Jeepers? Jeepers got himself killed, huh? Why didn't anyone tell me?"

"Jesus, Jee!" Muh perked his ears in irritation. "Will you get that right? The name is 'Jesus.' Not 'Jeepers.' Get it right, the humans are freaking pissy about this guy. Now, as I was saying, when we first landed here, it was in the Middle East and..."

"Yeah, I remember, we started hanging out with those desert dwellers? A little drinking, gambling, occasional camel rustling...those guys were a real hoot. They called themselves "The Chosen People."

Muh and Jee had a good laugh.

Wiping tears away, Jee asked. "So, what is your point? You said the orphan has betrayed us?"

"Pay attention!" Muh fired back. "Why are we on this planet right now?

"You mean...our punishment? Because of the religious thing? The charges by the Galactic Council that we interfered with a primitive culture?"

"Precisely. And who got this all started? Who decided he wanted to help these desert dwellers become more sociable? Who started us on this path of ruin?"

"Yaz?" Jee made a wild guess.

Muh continued. "Remember, that day we drinking at 'The Smiling Camel Tavern of Smyrna'? Yaz was so drunk he stumbled out into the street and straight into this guy riding a burro."

"Yeah, they started yelling at each other. Yaz punched the Burro in the fetlock!"

"Yeah, yeah, but after that, remember, Yaz and this guy hit it off, they had drinks, started singing some weird drinking song, they got the burro drunk, then this guys' wife shows up, and she's angry about what they did to the burro and, boy, did she bitch at all three of them: Yaz, Jesus, and the Burro."

"That kind of sounds like every night we were there...drinking, fighting, crying, everybody leaving all upset, then doing it all again the next day. Heavy shit!"

"Well, you recall the Jews were a tiny little group of angry nomads so obnoxious, demanding, pushy and insulting no one wanted them in their towns, so they finally settled into some kind of raucous community way out in the desert?"

"Yeah, they followed this book. Wow, what a book." Jee thought a moment. "What was the name of that book? Oh yeah, they called it an 'Old Testament. The Bible! Wow what a freaking book, dude! It was angry, vengeful, racist, misogynistic, nasty, loving, compassionate, tender, vicious and really incomprehensible."

"That was the problem," Muh explained. "Yaz felt the Jews wouldn't be so mean-spirited if people liked them, and people would like them if they weren't so mean-spirited. Since they followed this Old Testament, he decided a new book, a 'New Testament,' was needed. One a little bit less nasty a little more reader friendly might make them more likable."

"That's right!" Jee exclaimed. "Yaz wrote the New Testament Pamphlet! He just kind of stuck it on to the end of the Old Testament...like a sequel."

"But," Muh said ominously, "it was his next move that blew this thing up. Yaz got his drinking buddy with the Burro to pass out these New Testaments pamphlets."

"Jeepers!" Jee said.

"No, 'Jesus'," Muh said irritably. "'Jesus,' not 'Jeepers.'"

"But that wasn't his name!" Jee protested. "Translated from his language to English, his name is 'Jeepers' not 'Jesus.'"

"I know, I know, but we gotta go with 'Jesus'; these humans are pretty dead set on that name."

"Okay, okay."

"Anyway, this guy made a name for himself with those pamphlets. Nice guy, honest as anything, but a very sloppy carpenter, so he needed extra work. He started passing out those New Testament Pamphlets, and before you knew it, people started listening, following, every worshiping the guy. Who knew the guy had a talent for public speaking?"

"Jeepers did?"

"'Jesus'! Jesus, will you get 'Jesus' right? Now, where was I?" Muh muttered. "Jesus became quite an accomplished speaker, worked in a little entertainment for the crowds, and had a fish and loaves thing that wowed them. He even had a gig where it appeared he was walking on water. Boy, did that bring in the donations? Jesus had a hidden talent for publicity. He got people's attention, and so naturally, they started calling on him for special ceremonies, celebrations, store openings, things like that. The followers soon started calling themselves 'Christians' in honor of his stardom.

"Wait a minute," Jee looked at Muh with skepticism. "So you are saying Yaz created Christianity, huh?

"Well, no, not exactly." Muh looked embarrassed. "It seems this Jesus guy turned out to be some kind of Avatar. Like Confucius, Buddha, Muhammad, Jesus, Gandhi, Betty White, people ahead of their time who understand."

"Understand what?"

"That is what is most confusing," Muh confessed. "Each and every one of them taught Love, Love was the answer to the question, and Love was central to their teachings. But now, especially the most faithful, fundamentalist followers ignore Love completely; hate and anger are the prayers these days. Very strange!"

"Okay smart guy, what about the third desert religion: Islam? They came along long after we left this planet, you to know. How could we have done anything to them?"

Muh kicked dirt in embarrassment. "Time capsule." He admitted. "Look, I knew these Jew folks didn't seem to play well with others, so I thought I would help out. The Old Testament is weird, but it seemed to work well enough at first. So I left a ton of clues scattered around the Middle East, ideas buried in caves and stuff. I told them to follow the Old Testament, just follow the old prophets like Abraham and Noah, even Jesus had some good things to contribute. But they should have their own book just to give them status. I kind of set it up, and this guy named Muhammad, another good guy, an Avatar like Jesus, came along; he found my notes and files, and the next thing you know, a new religion, just like the other two, was born. Another new religion based on love and respect.

"So what about...the book: The Koran."

"Yeah, that," Muh was reluctant to admit it but also kind of proud. "I named it! I didn't write it, but I named it." Muh admitted. "It was in the Time Capsule."

"You named the seminal book forming the basis for the Islamic Religion on Spirituality after an old girlfriend!" Jee said mockingly. "That wasn't cool."

"'Karen,' but they misspelled it," Muh said defensively. "She was a nice girl too!"

"Muh, I have enough of your bullshit. Yaz isn't the only traitor. You and Yaz are guilty. I am innocent!"

"I am the oldest, which makes me the most experienced, therefore the wisest."

"Muh, the three of us have been banished to this place, but I want to point out that I had nothing to do with Spiritual Interference. I am innocent. Yaz wrote the New Testament Pamphlet, you named the Holy Koran..."

"Karen."

"Whatever! I shouldn't have to be here!"

"Well, Brother, what can I tell you? Do you want to hear how Yaz betrayed us or whine about your fate?"

Jee thought about that for a moment, not sure.

"We when our vacation time was up Jesus was just catching his stride. We all left; you, me, and what's his name. But now, while you and I were busy living our lives as decent Mf*rhf"s, what does he do? Nearly a thousand years later he sneaks back to Earth to meet with these Cha Oka fools? He even steals a valuable trinket from them!"

"Okay, so?"

"Does the Galactic Counsel know about this? I don't think so, or it would have been in the Arrest Warrants for all three of us!"

"You're right; there was no mention of Cahokia or Cha Oka." Jee thought about it. Muh was correct, something was fishy here.

"So Yaz has put our collective necks in a real sling now. When the Council finds out about Cha Oka, they won't believe we were mostly innocent. Oh no, because now we will have two counts of a 'Species Abuse,' the second one with 'premeditation'! Are you ready for that! Premeditation moves it to a new level of criminality! And you and I are innocent...mostly!"

"You know the punishment for fucking with these cultures twice!" Jee said with shock.

Muh buried his face in his hands. "We'll be too old to procreate when we get out."

"We'll be painfully unable to procreate before we get in."

Muh and Jee sat silently as the enormity of this sunk in.

"This is not good. What now?" As soon as Jee said that, he cringed, hating to give Muh a chance to show his superiority.

Muh said. "We complete our mission, that's what! We go to Indianapolis and confess we meddled with human religions. Explain that we are sorry; offer them the Einstein Stone as payment, and leave. Just like that."

"Well, that should do it," Jee mused, "But do you think the humans might be a little touchy about it all? What about all the people who believe in these religions with their hearts and souls? People are willing to die, or at least kill others, for these faiths. Once we tell humans their two favorite religions have some...alien interference, I don't think they will praise our honesty and they will become violent. Humans are odd. They believe that because a religion deals with the Sacred, that religion itself is sacred. But it isn't. Religion is about control and power, Spirit is about the Creator."

"Well it's good and bad," Muh observed. Good humans are good humans. There are Christians, Muslims, Jews, Zoroaster, Hindus, Buddhists, Baha'i, Druze, Sikh...humans have created many beautiful ways to worship and live their lives.

"Okay, great, but how are they going to deal with us?" Jee responded.

"Humans are very responsive to gifts," Muh explained. "Good people don't cause trouble, and bad people do. Bad people act out their insanity, and the good people sit on their hands and pray it goes away. So we bribe the good people outrageously and hope apathy wins. Our only hope is to present the Blue Emerald, so they don't tear us to shreds."

Both Muh and Jee looked at Pawnee's backpack that held their Blue Emerald.

"We are so fucked."

~ 57 ~

CHAPTER FIFTY-FIVE

Imahuffin and his band of merry killers stopped at a place called Pontoon beach, a place that had neither, celebrating their victory over the fiercely defensive six barrel makers and a secretary of The Old Overcoat Distillery.

"Scrappers they were!"

"Damn, Secretary got me with a stapler!"

Imahuffin grinned loosely at the merriment and took another deep pull of the Old Overcoat Rye Whiskey. One of the barrel makers had some oxycodone and meth. Imahuffin was a happy, very jittery, man. He had found a Rosary Supply Store down the street from the Distillery.

"Hey, something is going on south of us, near Collinsville!" Gary, the CB operator, called out. "A bunch of Humvee's has cornered this gang of terrorists."

Imahuffin shrugged. He was high, he was happy, he didn't care. He roped another crucifix.

"Sir, I just heard, these terrorists, they are five people; Three men, one of the huge and Brown and two women, one of them tiny and Black."

Imahuffin sat bolt upright, his addled synapses sputtering, reality fading in and out; he tried to make sense of what he just heard.

"Big Brown...man...little Black woman?"

Imahuffin blinked. Then blinked again. "Could it be?"

Cranking the engine unmercifully, Imahuffin gathered his Mormon murderers and wheeled out onto the highway heading south: Bessie May Chowder and Pawnee Painter. He just knew it.

"Kill the infidel's!" Imahuffin screamed as he raced down the highway, his adrenaline pounding. "The LORD, your God, will be merciful," Imahuffin could feel the spirit of the Lord take his soul in its teeth and shake. "OBEY ME! Deuteronomy 13:13-19!" Shouted Imahuffin.

"Smite them all, smite them all, the big and the short and the tall. Smite them all...," the murdering Mormons sang lustily as Imahuffin drove them South to Cahokia Mounds.

"Jeeesssus! Jeeeesuss! Jeeesus!"

~ 58 ~

CAHOKIA MOUNDS

"The ancients knew something, which we seem to have forgotten." Albert Einstein

~ 58 ~

~ 59 ~

CHAPTER FIFTY-SIX

"So there it is."

"It looks like a pasture with hills."

"There are mounds of earth everywhere!"

"See that big one! The largest one? Sort of square with several levels? Monk's Mound. The footprint of that massive mound of earth is larger than the Great Pyramid at Cheops. All built by hand, every basketful." The massive Mound of dirt was leveled at several points, one in front, two on the side, and the large clearing at the very top. Charley Brown Bones knew only a little about the area the Mounds themselves, but he knew nothing about the Native People who built it.

Pawnee led them into the parking lot about two hundred yards from the main, largest Mound. The day was cold and wet; showers, sometimes like a tropical monsoon, would flood the area then recede to a heavy, cloudy mist that obscured the surroundings.

"Chee, you guys settle down back, dere!" Pawnee snarled at the three aliens riding a disgruntled CupCake. It had taken close to three hours to persuade the alien beagles to ride the wary animal, and it took another hour for CupCake to accept them. Nobody was happy.

Jade and Bessie May Chowder followed slowly in the rear well back of any fallout from the explosive scene ahead of them.

"How are you and Charley getting on?" Bessie May asked quietly

"Mostly not. My fault." Jade replied. "I am so confused with him. I'm offering him the store one minute, and the next, I'm slamming and locking the front door. Poor guy doesn't know how to act."

"Jade, you and I have miserable backgrounds for loving and trusting other human beings."

Jade didn't reply. What could she say? A Vietnamese orphan in Saigon, living on the streets, surviving the only way possible. Jade knew she had been lucky, more fortunate than her peers who died early and ugly.

His name was Billy Two Bears, a US Army convoy truck driver, Fourth Transport Command, Qui Nhon Army Ammunition Dump, in Saigon for in-country R&R when Jade tried to pick his pocket, a task ordinarily easy and over with. Still, Bill Two Bears was quick and observant. Billy saw something in this stick-thin, filthy nine-year-old thief and, to the amazement of his wife and family, arranged to adopt her. Life on a dirt-poor Potawatomi Reservation in Mayetta, Kansas, was no picnic, but it beat wartime Vietnam hands down.

When she was only fifteen, Billy, his wife, their three children, and a grandmother all died in a house fire, leaving Jade alone in the world once again.

Trust? Jade thought: *Every person I have ever loved dies, or I drive them away. I gave my trust to Charley Brown Bones once. Can I do that again?* It occurred to her that trust didn't have to be all or nothing. She could slowly develop confidence: like a Venetian window blind, it can be open all the way or just a little. The more she thought about it, the better it sounded.

Jade wanted to trust Charley Bones again. But how?

"We here." Pawnee had kept on riding up to the very base of the Mound; he halted and pointed, the other horses paused behind him. "Monk's Mound," he announced.

CupCake saw his opportunity and made the most of it.

"Whoa! Hey, what...!"

CupCake, doing a fair imitation of a PRCA bucking horse, kicked out both hind legs and hopped on her front hooves, successfully throwing green beagles in every direction.

For the next ten minutes, they all dealt with the whinnying, bucking, barking, snarling, and chaos that surrounded the foot of Monk's Mound.

"Okay, okay, everybody calm now?" Charley demanded of the winded and heavily panting beagles. "You guys get a grip now?" he looked over at Pawnee, who was settling CupCake down, not an easy task as she kept trying to nip and kick at the beagles.

"What now?" Jade asked as the commotion settled down. She pointed at Monk's Mound. "What about this place? What is it?" Everyone looked at Yaz.

Yaz had no idea what to say or what came next.

~ 60 ~

CHAPTER FIFTY-SEVEN

"Why is this place called Monks Mound?"

"My guess?" Charley replied slowly. "Bigotry. The early settlers suspected these mounds were made by native people for some religious or spiritual purpose. Evidently, they couldn't stand to believe heathens had the skill and capability of such an enormous feat. So certain were they were of Euro-Caucasian superiority they called it 'Monk's Mound' which made it more 'civilized' to Christians."

"Your bitterness is showing, dear," Jade said softly. From the time she first met Charley Bones, she had learned about the Native people of North America and the deliberate, coordinated genocide conducted by the American people aided and abetted by their Government. Jade was appalled to learn the extent to which the invading Europeans slaughtered, cheated, robbed, and ruined an entire race of people.

"Adolf Hitler and the early European colonists had the same goal: Extermination of a whole race of human beings," Jade spoke softly, sorrowfully. "Hitler hated the Jews because scapegoats are necessary to create a 'superior race'. In the early years of the United States, Native People were hated for the same ethnocentric reason." Jade told them.

"What?" Muh and Jee said simultaneously.

"No way!" Jee protested.

"Americans say they have always stood for freedom," Muh added. "They say they fight to free others, grow Democracy and freedom wherever they go! Americans say they are the good guys! Hitler was a bad guy!"

"Hitler murdered and tortured the Jews for less than ten years," Charley said, a hard edge coming to his voice. "My people, Native Americans, have been the victims of deliberate, planned, and executed genocide for over three fucking centuries! But we are still here! Got that! Still here!" His rage and pain boiled out.

Jade took Charley's hand. Impressed with Charley's words, but more so by the fact that Native Americans still managed to exist, even thrive under such relentless attempts to have them exterminated.

Muh looked at Jee. "I think they have been brainwashed. These people seem to believe nonsense," he told Jee in their language so the humans could not listen in. "Millions and millions of Americans believe the exact opposite and that many can't be wrong. Millions believe the US is the greatest nation on Earth because it is the bastion of freedom, the world leader in peace and justice. They believe Americans are the free people on the planet, and no other nation even comes close."

Charley, Jade, and Doc looked on as the two alien beagles yipped at each other, green fur standing up and tails wagging fiercely.

"You want to tell us what that is about?" Charley asked Yaz. But Yaz had no interest in arguing over the self-induced delusions of an entire nation; mythology and truth are a tough blend.

"We go up there!" Yaz pointed to the top of Monks Mound. He was hurt by Muh's claim he was an orphan. Yaz had checked himself in the mirror, and he looked identical to Muh and Jee. Triplets. Still, doubt haunted him. But he had one birthmark that seemed a little different from theirs.

"Hey, pooch, wake up!" Charley nudged Yaz with his foot. "Why are we going up there?" For some reason, Yaz seemed to be having moments where his hard drive would shut down, adopting a coma-like behavior.

Yaz experienced vague memories of long ago. Shimmering with few details, he felt wrapped in a heavy fog of thoughts and words.

Cahokia seemed like a listless dream, and then came a filmy recall about magic, secrets, and civilization. An image emerged: A Blue-Green Stone.

Yaz wished he could recall more, struggling to remember. He studied the top of the Mound before them.

The Einstein Stone? What am I supposed to do now?

It was so important, but Yaz could not remember why.

"Up where?" Yaz wondered.

****

"So what are we going to find up there, huh?" Muh asked Yaz, pointing at the one hundred-foot-tall Monk's Mound. "You're supposed to be some kind of expert, arc you?"

"You're talking to me now?"

"Apparently," Jee replied sarcastically.

"Oh, nonsense," Muh said firmly. "We've always talked with you, including you in our decisions. You have been and are our brother. We are one for all and all for one! One big happy family!"

"Except you're adopted," Jee added. "You're an unwanted, unloved orphan."

Muh looked at Yaz, "We are supposed to bring the Stone to Indianapolis; why are you telling us differently?"

That was a tricky answer for Yaz, as he couldn't remember much, bits and pieces, flashes of scenes that didn't tell him much. Standing very still, hidden memories welled up like a Spring Tide, pictures and places from the past ebbed and flowed: the face of an old man appeared in his mind, his eyes kindly, and his voice soft. Yaz suddenly remembered something about the very top of this particular Mound. He looked up and studied Monk's Mound, but it wasn't called that then.

"So, oh unwanted one!" Jee probed to see if Yaz knew anything at all. "No answers? What do you know? Huh? Anything?"

"I have no idea," Yaz answered truthfully as he stared at the top of the Mound. Memories were suddenly pouring in: Cahokia Mounds, the Mound Builders, intense details swirled momentarily overwhelming him. Yaz staggered, dizzy with memories of intricate ceremonies, crowds of cheering, happy people, words and songs, and chants came to him. "But, I do know we must go up there," Yaz said, his voice hazy, his thoughts foamed with images and memories.

Zip, Zip. The sound of bullets passing close by caused everyone to duck

"Get down. They're firing at us!" Charley saw a yellow school bus loaded with men waving guns coming at them from the South.

"Doc, let's go, get to the next level." He shouted, and he reached down to grab Yaz. "You come with me."

"Hey," Yaz protested, "I'm not a stuffed toy! Gently!"

"Jade and I stay below to hold them off, you go," Pawnee called out to Charley and Doc as they started up the stairs to the first level, 50 feet above ground level.

Bullets impacted to the right and left of him as Charley charged up the steep stairs of Monk's Mound. Every step, as the bullets pinged around him, Charley kept muttering, "I'm too fucking old for this shit!"

"You ain't alone there, brother!" Doc gasped as he carried Muh and Jee like two loaves of bread, one in each hand. Muh and Jee barked with irritation at each step.

"Don't talk, run!" Bessie May Chowder was thankful she was small and a tiny target but frustrated her legs were so short as to make this a tough climb.

As the others ascended the stairs, both Pawnee and Jade fired simultaneously, then he went left, ducking behind a cement park bench, and she went right to a park bench on that side. Both had good cover, and bullets chipped and pockmarked the cement.

~ 61 ~

CHAPTER FIFTY-EIGHT

If Imahuffin ever thought the battered, yellow school bus, with bright red balloons painted all over it, was an odd choice for a mass murder vehicle, he kept it quiet.

Now, careening around a grove of trees directly South of Monks Mound, Imahuffin powered the old bus onto the field in front of the massive Monk's Mound and then skidded to a stop on the slick dew grass.

The rain had just let up, but dark clouds were already forming rapidly; a wind kicked up, swirling the tree limbs. Crispy brown autumn leaves filled the air and danced in the breezes. It was a cold, bitter day.

Jumping Jim Imhauffin, now the acknowledged leader of a band of bloodthirsty Christians, stared at the heathen dirt mounds and felt nothing but contempt. "Savages!" He smirked. Each movement brought a shifting of the hundred or so crucifixes wrapped around his neck and shoulders.

"All they could do was pile dirt!" Imahuffin snorted with disgust. "Fucking savages! White people build with cement, like the advanced people we are!" Not for the first time, Jim Imahuffin felt immense pride in his race; the Caucasian people dominate the world, first in everything, best at everything, and conquerors of everything!

"We are the chosen people!" Imahuffin screeched to his followers.

Moses of the Mormons had morphed into Mad Max, and Imahuffin was proud of his band of Christian Crusaders. He had found them as delicate, soft city people, but Imahuffin had bonded them into a vicious pack of killers through constant proselytizing, badgering, and humiliation. Looking back at his crew, Imahuffin smiled. They were toughened pirates dressed in every manner of clothing, carrying handguns, shotguns, AR-15's, bandoliers crisscrossed their chests next to the ever-present crucifixes. At the same time, smoke bombs and ammunition hung from their combat vests. They had morphed from soft hands and delicate sensibilities to calluses and killer instincts.

Jesus will be so proud! Imahuffin knew Jesus must have felt so uncomfortable among all those swarthy types. He pulled out his favorite photo of Jesus, his blond hair and blue eyes a tribute to his race, and lovingly studied the features of his God.

"There they are!" Someone shouted.

Looking up through his windshield Imahuffin saw movement; three people and three beagles were gathered at the Mound's base. Pulling out his binoculars, he studied the figures in the distance. One was a small Black Woman: Chowder!

"There be sinners ahead!" Imahuffin shrieked, "Behead the non-believers! God commands it! Deuteronomy 17:12, King James Version of course!" Revving the engine until blue smoke billowed out the tailpipe while the stench of burning oil filled the air. Imahuffin slammed the venerable old bus into 'D' and hit the gas.

"Kill in the name of Christ!" Imahuffin's war-whoop was picked up by his followers.

"Kill for Christ!" "Kill for Christ!" They began firing out of the windows toward Monk's Mound.

CHAPTER FIFTY-NINE

"Well, what the hell have we here?" Harasin couldn't believe he had so far failed to capture or kill any of the miscreant tangos. But this time, he would get them, and God-Kock wouldn't blow it.

Captain Harasin sat in his Humvee, looking through binoculars to the East. The morning was dull, grey, raining. He could see the small party of travelers begin to climb the Mound.

To his right, a large yellow school bus decorated with bright, lively red balloons accelerated toward the Mound, people firing out of the windows.

Harasin had no clue who the bus people were, but they were firing at his targets, the people he was sent to gun down. That could not be tolerated. It was now a matter of pride that Harasin kill the people he was sent to kill before other killers killed them.

"They have AR's, shotguns, hunting rifles, and pistols." Harasin reached up and patted the .50 cal. above his head. "We have these babies. Let's go shred." He signaled for his Humvee's to line up for a charge. They would cross the flat ground guns blazing and wipe out the band of renegades in a second. As they geared up to charge, a brief question popped into his mind; Harasin wondered why these particular dirt bags needed killing. Harasin cringed. As a professional soldier, he took pride in asking very few questions. I will do my duty, follow orders, and fuck the big picture. He reminded himself.

***

Two Humvee's down the line from Harasin, Peter Paul God-Kock, experiencing a significant shift in reality, blinked and blinked again, trying to figure out if bright blue Jackrabbits were normal. He wondered if the 'medication' Captain Harasin insisted he take was having strange effects. *A piece of paper with a picture of Howdy Dowdy on it? That was medicine?*

Then God-Kock was distracted by his face melting off. "Huh? What is happening?" He rubbed his face, hoping to get all the features back in the right place.

Suddenly, his Humvee lurched forward, and Imahuffin could hear the others running up their engines, several .50 cal. weapons were cocked in preparation for battle. God-Kock sat up straight in the cupola and looked out over the field. He could see a small band of people at the foot of the massive Mound of Earth; they had small creatures with them. *Pets?*

"They got poodles?" Somehow that was the funniest thing God-Kock had ever heard, and he fell against the cupola side, howling with laughter.

Captain Harasin, preparing to charge Monk's Mound, noticed Imahuffin flopping around in the cupola of his Humvee. "What the fuck is numb nuts up to?" Harasin could see God-Kock, two vehicles over, slapping the side of the Humvee, very happy about something. "Well, good, the LSD is kicking in nicely." He muttered.

"Command!" Harasin ordered. "Full speed." He wasn't going to let some drunken bunch of idiots collect his prize. "Our Rules of Engagement are hot; repeat hot!" He had to stop that stupid yellow bus from interfering with his mission.

Clouds of blue smoke and the smell of exhaust gas filled the air as the line of Humvee's accelerated into battle.

****

"Charge!" Imahuffin's' scream to his Mormon Murders echoed across the Cahokia fields. "Charge the infidels; kill them for Christ!"

The school bus accelerated toward the Mound, Imahuffin's nose pressed against the windshield. The Mormons in the back were chanting, readying themselves for the slaughter.

"Jeeesusss! Jeeesusss! Jeeesuss!"

Imahuffin could see the tiny figure of Bessie May Chowder climbing the stairs, and it felt like red paint exploded in his head.

The Mormons were firing at the Mound, shouting hosannas to heaven, and Imahuffin felt like a man truly blessed by God.

CHAPTER SIXTY

"Hold it, hold fire until closer," Harasin called out.

The battered yellow school bus was nearly at Monk Mound as Harasin's Humvee's covered the open ground, closing on the bus.

"Fire! Fire! Fire! Fire!" God-Kock flung himself back and forth in the Humvee cupola. "Kill! Kill!" He pleaded. "Kill the bee, kill the bee!" A bee the size of a Buick was sitting on the back of the Humvee. God-Koch blinked his eyes, rubbed his face, and the bee blew him a kiss.

"Shut up, you hose bag!" The Humvee driver screamed up as God-Kock began dancing in the cupola to a Barry Manilow tune playing in his head. "Captain," The driver radioed Harasin. "This freakin' guy is out of his mind!"

"Steady, steady," Harasin replied. "Save your ammunition for the bad guys, don't shoot the idiot. Yet."

No reply.

Harasin hoped his men were professional enough to follow orders. But he wouldn't blame them if accidents happen.
****

Clay Park Painter had scattered his small band across the narrow, ridged-topped mound North East of the Monks Mound, which gave an excellent view of the battlefield. They were at the intersection of Collinsville Rd and Sand Prairie Road. To his right on Collinsville were the four Humvee of Captain Harasin charging toward the school bus.

"Ho shit, what is this?" Clay muttered. They had followed Barcelona and his two Humvee convoy from Indianapolis to Cahokia, finally leap-frogging ahead to set up on the Mound. Turning to his left, he saw Barcelona now entering the Mound compound. He would be in the field of battle very shortly. Clay could not figure out who the players were and why they were all attacking that small group of people and their pets.

To the center, coming from the South, a bright yellow school bus charged straight for a group of people at the base of Monks Mound.

On the Mound, it appeared as if two people were remaining on the ground level while three others climbed to the next level.

The Yellow school bus was nearly obscured by gun smoke as it neared the Mound. Clay watched people on the ground react. Suddenly, he pushed the glasses hard against his face, and a flash of color caught his eye.

"That looks like a Hawaiian shirt!" Clay gasped. A Hawaiian shirt? Here? Then he said aloud, "Holy shit, could this be Pawnee? My father?"

"That's Pawnee!" he said aloud. "What are you doing here?" he could not believe it. After all that happened, The Hammer devastating America, he found his father. Clay's heart lurched with happiness and dread.

Just then, Barcelona's Humvee's accelerated down the road and charged onto the field, and the air all around Monk's Mound was now filled with bullets as gunfire erupted from the School Bus and all six Humvee's.

"Who the hell are these guys?" His father was in real danger.
****

Bessie May struggled up the slope to the second level and paused to catch her breath. From this level, approx. Thirty feet off the ground, she could see the attack on their position developing.

Charley Bones, Doc Betters, and three little green aliens waited for her.

"We've got three distinct sets of bad guys out there!" Chowder pointed.

"Pawnee and Jade holding defensive positions down below," Charley added. He could see the yellow bus seem to be accelerating the closer it got. Farther to the right, another group of four Humvee's was now closing on the bus.

"What the hell, more of them?" Charley pointed.

Doc could see yet another group of two Humvee's just now turning on the edge of Cahokia grounds.

"Six Humvee's and a Yellow School bus! Hell of an assault!"

Zip! Zip!

"They have cover," Doc said, pointing down to Pawnee and Jade. "But we've got the high ground, and we fire from up here. Bessie May you get to the top level."

Charley looked around, not liking the lack of protection.

"We are all exposed on this damn Mound, and there is no cover here at all. What are we doing up here?"

Doc pointed to a fist-sized rock. "Here, you hide here. I'll go get help!"

"Funny man!"

Doc moved ten feet away and lay down, his rifle pointed down the steps. "All right, Yankee, have it your way."

"We'll hold this and then follow Bessie May to the top," Charley shouted above the sound of rifle fire.

"Psst! Psst!" Yaz tried to get Bessie May's attention. "We need to get to the top right away." Much was coming back to him. The Ceremony at the top of the Mound was extraordinary and very specific. Astonishingly, the memory of the ceremonial words appeared in his mind. "We must hurry to the top before they can stop us," Yaz demanded.

Muh looked at Jee. "What the hell is he talking about?"

"You mean as the leader you don't know?"

"Sure I do!" Muh lied. "I'm just checking to see if you do. A good leader makes sure his inferiors are aware of their responsibilities at all times."

"If anyone knows about inferiority, it's you, Muh."

"Do not!"

"Do too!"

Jee had enough. It could have been the danger around them or the stress of being surrounded by humans, but Jee snapped.

"Arrggh!" Jee leaped on Muh, and they fell to the ground, locked in a tight combat embrace, snarling and snapping at each other. Within moments they were struggling back and forth until they rolled right off the edge, down the slope back down to ground level where they crashed into Pawnee.

"Ah chee, wot dis!" Pawnee was completely unaware as the two tiny green aliens slammed into him.

Zip! Zip! Zip!

"We need to get to the top?" Bessie May watched as the two little green aliens disappeared over the edge of the Mound. She turned to Yaz. "Well, all right, let's go." She picked up Yaz and climbed a hundred stairs to the top.

"Charley, Doc," She called out, "hold this level we are going to the top!"

****

"Sir! The battle has begun!"

"Well, get us the hell in there! Now!" Barcelona stated firmly but softly. He believed a leader should never raise his voice, forcing others to listen more carefully.

"I want everyone dead. Shoot anyone in front of us." Just then, a wall of rain washed through, momentarily hiding the scene. Lightning illuminated the entire area, and thunder rumbled impatiently.

Price Wayne was furious with himself. He had allowed himself to be tricked into this bullshit war, and he wanted none of it. Sure, he acknowledged a little cannibalism in his past. *Everyone has some minor indiscretions, right?* Belted into the back of the Humvee, he worked his brain, looking for a way out of this.

"Grease them all!" Barcelona thought better of it. "No, wait! Wait until we get rid of Chowder and have the Einstein Stone."

Wayne could see the logic in that. The 'fewer witnesses, the better' worked in his favor too.

The Barcelona Humvee assault began, engines roaring; they entered the battle, half his unit going to the other side of Monks Mound, the Eastside, while Barcelona attacked the Mound itself, rolling up the Westside.

The Einstein Stone was all Barcelona could think of. *Sure, I've started to rebuild my empire, but I am hungry. Just like the drive to earn my first million and then my first billion, there is nothing more important in life. Nothing! Now it was The Einstein Stone.* Barcelona's gut ached at the thought that God-Koch had the Einstein Stone in his safe but lost it.

"Sir!" Barcelona's driver said. "We have a call from Captain Ha-rasin, explaining that he will go after the Mound after he gets rid of the yellow school bus."

Barcelona lusting for Einstein Stone and had to swallow a few times, take a deep breath to calm himself. "Tell the Captain, never mind the yellow bus, I want him to join me in assaulting the Monks Mound. Get Bessie May Chowder and the Einstein Stone first, and then he can take care of the rabble."

"Yes, sir! No survivors, sir, yes sir!"
****

Peter Paul God-Kock, LSD swirling through his synapses like a backed-up toilet, struggled to understand what was going on. The fiery balloons, flying tacos, and laughing crows, were a real distraction.

Suddenly to shake off a yellow striped Tarantula clinging to his left foot, he kicked out, striking the Humvee Driver in the head.

The driver slumped unconscious.

Imahuffin's Humvee, now out of control, collided with the next Humvee to its right, rebounded, and struck the Humvee on the left.

A chain reaction wreckage occurred before Captain Harasin knew what was happening. All four Humvee's were suddenly slammed into different directions from the collisions, and his well-orchestrated frontal assault spun off target in a flurry of mud and dirt.

Harasin couldn't believe it.

God-Kock stood up on the cupola of the still moving, driver-less Humvee as it continued to rumble toward the school bus. Then, leaning into the wind, stretched out his long bony arms like pterodactyl wings, he tilted his face forward into the rain and wind, a crucifix thumping wildly on his chest and began shouting: "Jeeeesussss! Jeeeessusss!"

A Holy Roller hood ornament on a runaway Humvee. Harasin wondered why he was here and how soon he could leave.

****

Peter Paul God-Kock, tears streaming down his face from the raw, wet wind, saw the bright yellow bus with red balloons and suddenly he knew the purpose of his entire life: To Rule! God-Kock began to yodell: "Jeesus Jeesus jeesus."

It was strange he hadn't thought of it until now. Peter Paul God-Kock felt truly blessed. He dropped down into the driver's seat, opened the door, and pushed the unconscious soldier out. He vowed he would live up to his exalted, sacred responsibilities and rid the Earth of nonbelievers. Grasping the steering wheel in both sweaty hands, bracing himself for his imminent victory, he gunned the engine toward martyrdom, soon to be slaughtering infidels for Jesus.

God-Kock knew at that moment without a shadow of a doubt that Jesus loved him and had given him this special, sacred moment to kill as many heathens as he could. He had been taught all his life, "White people are the chosen people of Jesus, Peter Paul." From his ninety-three-year-old grandmother to his twin brother. They all agreed. *White people were blessed; brown people were not.* Pure and simple according to everything Peter Paul God-Kock believed.

Eyes flooded with tears at the honor of killing brown people to honor his Lord and Savior, he screamed, "I'm coming, Jesus! I'm coming!" he shouted, spraying spittle against the windshield. "Wait for me, Jesus, I am almost there!"

The Humvee traveled another twenty yards before it slowed, then stopped, out of gas.

****

"Damn, Apocalypse!" Pawnee muttered.

"Fire, damnit!" Jade shouted. She had moved off twenty yards to give a better field of fire. Firing several rounds through the windshield of the oncoming bus, she narrowly missing the mad Imahuffin but had little time to berate herself for such a poor shot as the enemy was firing back. Two more quick rounds and she took out a large man swinging a machete from the bus doorway.

Pawnee stood up and emptied a full magazine, twenty rounds, into the front of the charging yellow school bus, shredding the front tires. The radiator was blown open, and bullets punched holes through the front windshield. Suddenly, the 54 place school bus dropped bumper deep into the dirt, grinding up the grassland soil like a road plow until it came to a sudden jarring stop.

Then silence.

"Thunk, thunk, thunk" Bullets from one of Harasin's Humvee's, coming in from Pawnee's right, began hitting the broken down bus. A few of the mad Mormons returned fire at the incoming Humvee's.

Imahuffin, thrown onto the front hood by the abrupt stop, slowly slid off, crumpled to the ground, laying very still, waiting to see if Jesus was coming for him. He gave Jesus a moment to think about it. While Imahuffin lay face down in the dirt, his merry band of Mormon killers debarked and proceeded to assault the position of Pawnee and Jade.

Three were cut down immediately.

Wait a damn minute, Imahuffin rose to his feet, swaying, and then steadied himself. "I am their leader; I must lead." An image of Teddy Roosevelt leading his troops up San Juan Hill to defeat the treacherous brown people of Cuba gave Imahuffin an instant erection.

Grabbing his semi-auto shotgun painted a happy rose color; Imahuffin jacked a round into the chamber and immediately followed his rapidly depleting troop of depraved killers to the side of the Monks Mound.

Pawnee dealt with one more attackers who showed him a silhouette and then looked at Jade. She fired and then knelt as return rounds impacted the bench in front of her.

"We can't hold this position; they'll flank us," Pawnee called out.

"I know, I know," Jade called back, emptied her magazine into a small crowd of attackers, seeing one maybe two drops, the enemy was growing thinner. "I'll cover; you go to your right."

Pawnee looked, the newly invading four Humvee's had collided somehow and were now stopped, facing in different directions. Pawnee could see the soldiers in the Humvee's beginning to dismount.

He turned his attention back to the bus, so it was now or never.
****

Captain Harasin was startled to see another set of Humvee enter the battlefield. One Humvee headed for the East side of the Mound, the other the West. He spotted Barcelona standing tall in the Western Humvee cupola, putting his glasses to his eyes.

"Son of a Bitch," Harasin muttered. "The old cannibal himself has joined us." When Harasin accepted the mission to go after the fugitives from Cascadia, he wondered why they were so important. Right now, the world smashed by The Hammer, there were many other more necessary things to do. "Barcelona is here? Now I know there is more to this story."

"Sergeant, get me Barcelona."

"I've already tried, sir; he won't respond. Just a message to stay with the mission, kill or capture the Cascadian's."

"Oh really?" Captain Harasin had no illusions about loyalty. "Let's be cautious around Barcelona. Have the men keep their weapons handy."

"But sir, aren't they with us? Are we with them? Kind of?" his Sergeant asked.

"With us? Sergeant, that man is an Oligarch, an American Billionaire who rose to power by being a ruthless and bloodthirsty capitalist. Do you think he gives a shit about our lives?" Harasin added one more salient point, "You do understand that Barcelona is a cannibal, right?"

The Sergeants' face paled. "A what, sir? But isn't he one of the richest men on Earth? Why would he...?

"Does it matter?"

"No, sir! Yes, sir!" The Sergeant saluted. "It doesn't matter, sir; the men will follow you. Just say where and when."

Harasin smiled. He loved the military for one thing: his men, all the bullshit, all the stupid leaders, insane orders, ridiculous rules and regulations he could do without. The bonds of men in war, forged by death and blood, were like no other. These men would give their lives for him, and he for them. Unlike these same sentiments spoken in peacetime, it was an authentic fact of life for combat veterans.

"Now, first things first, Sergeant. let us get rid of the people on that Mound of Earth, and then we will deal with Barcelona."

"I'll spread the word; don't let anyone be taken, prisoner!"
****

Barcelona took in the scene.

The yellow bus directly in front of the large Mound was stopped to his right, now directly in front of it, disgorging weapon-waving morons. He presumed that four Humvee's now scattered in various directions to his distant right belonged to Harasin.

"What to do, what do." Barcelona was momentarily frozen when he realized his mistake. Impatience. Here he was, going into a battle with only two Humvee's, and Harasin had four. When he had dispatched Harasin to find Bessie May Chowder he was distracted and overwhelmed with decisions, and he barely even remembered sending Harasin. *Now here I am,* he thought, *out in the field under armed because of my impatience to get the Einstein Stone.*

****

Shots were being fired on all sides down around the Mound. People from the bus were firing up the Mound and left at the Humvee's. The Humvee's fifty caliber machine guns opened up on the bus, spent shells flying out behind the gunners like clouds.

On Monks Mound, Barcelona could see a man and woman at the base, armed and in good defensive positions behind cement benches. The third level was being defended by two men; both seemed to have some military training. Moving to the fourth or top of the Mound, he could see a small woman and a pet of some kind was with her.

"Sir! Sir, what are your orders!" His driver looked at the scene before him and wanted nothing more than to turn around and go home. But with a wife and kids, he needed the job.

The rain had paused; briefly, a shaft of raw shaft of startling sunlight burst through, enhancing brilliant greens and browns and tans of the trees and grasses. Price Wayne sat up in the back seat where he had slouched in depressed resentment. He could smell wet, cold rain on the varied breezes as he stuck his head out the window. It was the saddest, most dispiriting thing he'd ever seen; gunfire, men screaming, engines roaring, and a dull grey cloudy rain hour after hour. *I've got to get out of here!* Price Wayne realized he was a pacifist sun worshipper in the wrong circumstances.

Barcelona leaned back, looking into the back seat; his servant was staring out the window like a basset hound on his way to euthanasia. "Hey! Wayne!" Barcelona barked. "Cheer the fuck up!" He pointed forward to Monks Mound. "The Einstein Stone has got to be with the group on the mound." He said studying Price Wayne to make sure he was still alert and available for duty. "I want to dismount and join up with those crazies at the Mound. I want you to lead them to victory."

"What?" Price Wayne couldn't believe his ears. "Fucking Shit! What? What?" Price Wayne was overwhelmed with emotions: Terror, disbelief, and regret. "You mean me?" He said with astonishment. "No, no, you can't mean that!"

Barcelona realized Harasin, as a professional soldier, would probably have standards, a code of conduct that might interfere with the mission.

Price Wayne wouldn't know a scruple if it was humping his leg.

"Price Wayne, I shall not say this again." Barcelona roared into the back of the vehicle. "You will dismount this vehicle, go over to Captain Harasin and inform him you are relieving him of his duty. You will assume command and charge the top of this mound, killing all who oppose you! Is that clear! That is a direct order!" Wayne might just get shot right off the bat, but Barcelona didn't care. Wayne was becoming whiny.

"Oh...no...no..." Wayne had a decision to make: Add slaughter to his list of crimes, or run away and try to eek some sort of survival existence fighting for scraps of food and dying of some horrible infection in some mud-walled pit. *Stay and die horribly or leave and die slowly.* Price hated his choices.

"I'm not combat trained, sir; I have done duty mostly around kitchens, bars, some barbeques...I am fair with a boning knife but faint at the sight of dismemberment! Please sir!"

"Price Wayne, pull yourself together man!" Barcelona felt the insult deep into his bowels. *This creature refused to do as ordered! Billionaires must never be disobeyed! How else would they re-establish civilization? There must be order and consistency. Orders are given; orders obeyed.*

Barcelona pointed at Price. "Get out, get a gun, join those crazies and win me the Einstein Stone immediately or within the next ten minutes you will have your body cut up into various savory pieces, displayed in my meat counter, each piece wrapped in its little clear plastic, on a nice white Styrofoam dish: head, neck, shoulder cuts, ribs, Butt roasts, well, you get my meaning, yes?"

Price Wayne thought of his recent yacht experiences where this cannibalism fetish began.

"You bet, sir, I will wipe them out in no time!" Price Wayne scrambled out of the Humvee, delicately holding an AR15. He wanted to check to see if it was loaded but had no idea where the bullets went in, so he shrugged and began to trot toward the Humvee now parked beside the ruined yellow bus.

Price Wayne was sure he was dead meat; either way, he just didn't want his meat to be lunch. Not for the first time, Wayne realized the threat of cannibalism, by people who really mean it, is quite compelling.

****

"Hurry, it is just a little farther." Yaz was so excited. Memories were returning, and he knew what he needed to do next, but now he also realized time was of the essence.

"I'm coming as fast as I can." Bessie May looked down from the Mound. "Oh my!"

"Come on, this is so exciting!" Yaz shouted. "I am remembering everything, wonderful times!"

Just then, a bullet zipped by his head.

Ducking, Yaz said, "Come on Bessie May it will take two of us to pull this off before they get up here."

Bessie May could see a group from the yellow bus; begin to climb the left front of Monk's Mound, their weapons ready, and several opened fire.

She whistled, and both Doc and Charley looked up. They were on the second level. She pointed, and they immediately saw the bus people climbing the South face.

Both fired simultaneously, and two dropped.

The others stopped climbing and dropped to the ground. They fired a few snapshots in Doc's direction.

Then Charley turned and ran for the stairs while Doc provided cover. Charley stopped after twenty yards and turned to provide cover for Doc. They were well-rehearsed for two old guys using muscle memory from a war half a century ago.

Chowder was impressed.

"Where are Pawnee and Jade?" She fretted. "They were down at ground level, but they aren't there now." She couldn't see them, hoping they were uninjured.

Another bullet passed close by.
****

Imahuffin fired two rounds from his shotgun, which did nothing because the targets were way out of range. But the kick of the gun rattled his teeth, and he felt better.

The raging Mormons, reduced to seven in number, had spread out over the South or front face of the Mound and were receiving well-aimed fire from the second level. He could see two men up there, holding his men back, and then one ran for the stairs to the third level while the other kept his men pinned down.

"How dare they interfere with the work of the Lord?" Imahuffin was incensed with outrage.

As their leader, Holy Man, and Chaplain, he realized he was tasked with responsibilities, ordained to step up and make Jesus proud. Imahuffin could rush the enemy and die valiantly, leading his men to the glory of Jesus.

No, thought Imahuffin: *that's not right.* It was much better to get someone else to die and then claim glory for himself. Politics in the United States had taught Imahuffin that hypocrisy was a mandatory, essential requirement for power; Promise the people anything and give them nothing. Therefore, he was just maintaining tradition.

"Tradition is everything!" He muttered. "Our very civilization depends on hypocrisy, how can I throw that away?"
****

"They have no chance."

Clay Park Painter saw the whole battle heat up, and the people at the top of Monk's Mound were in trouble. Humvee's and armed men were attacking on all four sides and would be there instantly.

Clay could see Pawnee off and on, his view obscured by rain falling in sheets. The day became dark with heavy, roiling clouds scudding low overhead. He was proud of the old man, assaulting two of the stopped Humvee's. One man against two Humvee's; each vehicle held two armed men with a fifty caliber machine gun on top. Suicide! But Pawnee moved fast and took both out, a hand grenade each, in just moments.

Clay's love and respect for his poppa increased. It was a perilous move, exposing himself, protecting the people at the very top, and that is something Pawnee would do, for sure.

"We've gotta get down there, now!" Clay was going to get his papa's ass out of there or die trying. "Let's go, lock and load!"

Greg Pritchard, now Lieutenant Prichard, second in command, grinned with anticipation. From childhood, playing with toy soldiers and acting out combat with his best friend Gary, he longed to experience combat. Now it was here.

Clay, driving the Dagostino Milk Van, led the other vehicle across the road and straight at the rear of the two of the four remaining Humvee's that Pawnee had attacked. His men dismounted and spread out; Clay led them on an assault toward the armored vehicles.

Suddenly, the cupola on each Humvee turned directly toward them, the fifty caliber guns now pointed at Clay and his men.

"Oh, Shit!" Clay shouted. "Down, down!"

Clay was certain they were dead. The fifties couldn't miss at that range.

Suddenly, Pawnee Painter briefly exposed himself, threw a hand grenade-like a Nolan Ryan fastball straight into the passenger window of the nearest Humvee and ducked out of sight.

The Humvee erupted in flames as the explosive detonated.

The sole remaining Humvee quickly swiveled to meet the new threat and opened fire on Pawnee's last position. But Pawnee had moved back around the corner of the Mound, so the Humvee began to move toward him. Pawnee had nowhere to hide but had acted anyway, stopping the enemy to protect Bessie May.

Seeing his father's situation, Clay immediately attacked the remaining Humvee with automatic weapons, fire, and hand grenades.

The second Humvee swiveled its fifty calibers straight at Clay and his men; the soldier in the cupola staring down the barrel at them.

Once again, they were sitting ducks; nowhere to hide, no place for cover, and only ten yards from a weapon that shoots six-inch shells.

"Oh fuck!" Clay shouted, "Back, back," He signaled his men to scatter. Then Clay stood up in full view of the Humvee and made himself the target so the others could escape, emptying his machine gun at the Humvee just as it returned fire. Heavy, deadly rounds came at him, kicking up dirt beside him, coming so close to him he could hear them hiss by. His rounds pocked the windscreen and ricocheted off the metal around the Humvee gunner. Then slamming in another magazine, he realized he was still alive. Awash of amazement came over him as he opened fire again, this time, as he began moving away to reduce his silhouette. Bullets were flying back and forth in an ear-splitting cacophony.

Clay had no doubt he was going to die in those few seconds. He had regrets, but he had acceptance; it was the death of a warrior. He had planned for his a long time ago when he had decided to follow Pawnee into Special Forces.

At that moment, he was hit by a baseball bat blow to the shoulder that blew him backward off his feet, and he fell twenty feet down the slope to stop, supine, writhing in agony.

Pawnee had witnessed it all. He was stunned to see his son leading men into this battle. *Where did he come from? What is he doing?* Then he saw the round strike his son, and Pawnee's heart nearly stopped. He had seen the exchange of fire between Clay and the vehicles. He was so proud of his son for his courage. His heart swelled with pride, then froze with fear. Pawnee charged around the corner of the Mound straight at the Humvee, throwing his last hand grenade into the fifty caliber cupola, killing the gunner, then ripping open the door and killing both soldiers in the vehicle.

Pawnee rushed to his son and quickly applied pressure to stem the bleeding. Clay's shoulder was a mess, but he could tell the round had not impacted the shoulder directly but the deltoid muscles on the outside.

Greg Pritchard was immediately beside Pawnee and Clay, "I'm a medic," He told Pawnee, "let me in."

Medics are almost God to any combat soldier, and Pawnee immediately stepped aside but held his son's good hand. Newell was then beside them, offering help. Pritchard ordered them to move Clay over to a small stand of trees for shelter from the spitting rain.

"My son," Pawnee said softly, tears streaming from his eyes as he leaned over Clay. "My son, my son..." He was relieved when he saw how competent Pritchard was. "You in good hands, son."

"Pawnee!" Jade came rushing over. "Come on, come on, they are under attack!" She pointed as the first Humvee on the North side started to climb Monk's Mound's one hundred foot slope. "They are in trouble; we must get there now!"

Pawnee looked at his beloved son. "Yes, I know, I know...Clay, you be okay; I'll be back, my son, I will be back!" He gave Prichard a stern look. "You take care of my boy. You hear!"

Greg Prichard had no doubt this wasn't a request.

With that, Pawnee turned and moved after Jade rapidly. He had found in his life that slow exits were much more painful. Once again, duty has taken him from his son.

Quickly he glanced back. He met Clay's eyes and they held each other for just a moment. In that instant passed years of hurt, pain, loneliness, anger but especially love. Pawnee felt a flow of love for his son he did not believe possible.

Hearing more battle sounds, Pawnee saw flashes of rifle fire as they exchanged deadly force at the top of Monks Mound.

~ 64 ~

CHAPTER SIXTY ONE

"We must get to the Northwest corner!" Yaz hurried over to the corner and furiously dug with his tiny, green paws. The image of the waddle and daub holy temple that once stood on this spot spun before him. He could see the small alter, the placement for the stone and other ceremonial objects as they existed so very long ago.

Suddenly he sat up. "Wait a damn minute. We need the Einstein Stone, and who has it!"

"Oh yes, Pawnee was carrying it last I heard."

They both looked down and could not see Pawnee anywhere.

"We can't do anything without the Einstein Stone."

Two bullets snapped by from the murderous Mormons climbing the Mound.

"Yaz, we cannot stay here; we will be killed," Bessie May shouted.

"We've got to find the Einstein Stone!" Yaz shouted. He couldn't believe it, here he was on the verge of great duty, primed to do the most excellent service to humanity they have ever known, and he didn't have The Einstein Stone! Yaz felt light headed for a few moments, worried about fainting.

"Do we need it? Are you sure?" Chowder asked anxiously. The bad guys were near. Bullets zipped closer and closer, kicking up dirt within yards, then feet. She fired two rounds of her 9mm Browning, but crazies were climbing the South and a Humvee tearing up the North side. "Yaz, we need to move from here soon!"

But Yaz knew he needed to be here, doing what he needed to do. He just wished he could figure out the 'why' of it all!

Just then, Barcelona's Humvee came roaring over the edge of the East side landing and crashed down on all four wheels sliding to a stop.

Yaz ignored the threat and returned to digging. "I must prepare the site!"

Bessie May was armed with nothing more than a Browning 9mm, eight rounds left; she held her ground and sighed, waiting for a soft target.

Just then, the second of Barcelona's Humvee's reached the top level, crashing down on the heavy military springs.

All at once, Bessie May Chowder was facing two Humvee's, with .50 cal. weapons pointed right at her. Both vehicles maneuvered around until they lined up on the south side pointing north toward Bessie May and Yaz.

Bessie May didn't think her 9mm would make much difference.

"Come on, you assholes," She whispered. Bessie May knew how to handle a handgun and a knife, for that matter. The streets of Detroit did serve some valuable lessons, better than four years at Stanford Law. But this was a different world. Unfortunately, a shootout between a .50 caliber and a 9mm would likely have only one outcome regardless of education.

"We've got to find Pawnee," Yaz bawled. "We got to get the Einstein Stone! I can't do this without the Blue Emerald!"

"Get down," Bessie May said harshly. "Shut up till I tell you to talk again."

"We've got to find the Einstein Stone!" Yaz cried miserably. "Where is it? Where oh where is the Stone? I must have it! I am nothing without that Blue-Green Emerald!" Handfuls of mud came flying out of the growing hole as Yaz returned to furious digging.

"If you don't stop that caterwauling, I'll leave you to your dig and go find my friends. So far, that stone is just a rock. Nothing more. And this place is goddamned dangerous!" She fired two quick shots to her right, and someone screamed.

****

Charley Bones and Doc Betters had been fighting off the screaming crusaders of Imahuffin until it became apparent they were far too exposed. Armored Humvee's were scaling the sides of Monk Mound, and Charley or Doc couldn't do anything to stop them.

"We can't stay here!" Charley called out to Doc. Bullets zipped and hissed by, kicking up dirt and mud next to them.

"No shit Sherlock!"

Just then, they saw Pawnee race across the second tier of the Mound and disappear over the side. So they followed in time to see Pawnee attack a Humvee with hand grenades, and then saw a soldier lying on the ground with another leaning over him.

***

"Medic!" Pawnee made the call every combat vet knows to make in a time of trouble. He hoped to God that *flaky dope smoking Doc was within earshot.* Pawnee thought that John James Jefferson Betters IV was the finest combat medic he'd ever seen and that had been through years of combat. *Doc was good, gruff, abrupt, even ridiculous, but good.*

Doc was beside the wounded soldier like a Labrador in duck season.

"I've got it, bad wound, but he's okay." The medic assured Doc. "Name is Pritchard, a medic for Illinois National Guard...or was."

"Good job, son," Doc told him, impressed with the kid's skills as he worked over the down soldier. It occurred to Doc, watching Pritchard care for the wounded man, that maybe his time was passed. *Perhaps these young people can do what I used to, and perhaps even better.*

"What is going on, Pawnee?" Charley said as he ran up.

The Humvee's were burning merrily, and shots resounded from above and on the other sides of the Mound itself as a steady rain now poured out of the leaden sky, soaking everything.

"This, my son," Pawnee sat back in shock. He looked up at Charley with tears streaming down his face.

~ 65 ~

CHAPTER SIXTY-TWO

"And just what the fuck are you?"

Muh and Jee jumped and turned to the new voice.

Captain Harasin, weapon drawn, approached the mysterious creatures cautiously; green beagles were new to his experiences. These 'dogs' were suspicious, perhaps even alien, so Harasin prepared to defend humanity. He knew everything he needed to know about aliens because aliens were just like Liberals and Progressives, Communists and Socialists. They were hostile bloodthirsty demons seeking to dominate Earth, enslaving the human race! Harasin knew his patriotic duty was to murder them before these monsters destroyed all life on the planet.

This could get ugly. Muh didn't like the looks of this man. *This is all Jee's fault for questioning my inherent right of superiority and leadership.*

Muh pointed at Jee. "Take him! He is expendable!"

"What?" Jee screamed.

"Hands up! Err...paws up!" Harasin knew what to do. *Take them prisoners, torture them for the location of the mother ship, and then execute them.* He congratulated himself on his decision: *it was the only civilized way to handle this.* Harasin was momentarily grateful for the generations of humans that had gone before him, each teaching him how inferior beings are to be addressed. If history was any lesson, violence and bondage were the preferred taming methods for the lesser, colored races: green was not white.

Harasin took a deep inhale, smelling the stink of gunpowder, his weapon still warm firing at screaming Christians, the yellow school bus, and the dirt of Monks Mound. This is what he lived for! Action! Captain Harasin fondled his weapon at the filthy invaders of his homeland, trying to decide who to torture and kill first. Twenty-six years of service in the US Army had provided Harasin with a personal, even intimate, knowledge of humiliation and subjugation.

"Ah...sir?" His Sergeant was hesitant to interrupt his leader when the slaughter of hostages was imminent, but this was important. The hostages could always be slaughtered afterward. "Captain Harasin, sir? Mr. Barcelona has contacted us. He is ordered you to turn your command over to...him." The Sergeant pointed at Price Wayne.

Harasin looked at the glowing, nearly albino human standing before him, a water-logged ghost, pearly luminescent in the gray rain.

Price Wayne gave a tentative wave and a hopeful smile. He wished he hadn't lost the damn rifle. *Oh well, can't find it now.*

"Shit." Captain Harasin wanted to kill something. So far in life, Harasin felt cheated, and nothing had worked out the way it was supposed to. After The Hammer, his very nation was in ruins, so what was left for him? What was he supposed to be loyal to?

"Ah, sir, sir?" Price Wayne couldn't believe he was standing here, unarmed, defenseless, about to order a trained soldier around. "Sir? Mr. Barcelona, his Lordship? He...wants you up top? Like right now? Please?"

Harasin stared at Wayne, then at the green beagles. He thought about burying the bodies so no one would find them.

****

He opened his eyes, a cricket hung on a blade of grass two inches from his nose.

Peter Paul God-Kock picked himself off the grass and looked around. He was all alone. Four Humvee's now down to one. God-Kock felt like a boy abandoned on the playground by his peers. They had left him, laughing at him, abandoning him...a God. It was just shameful.

P.P. God-Kock was determined not to be the brunt of humor or injustice ever again.

God-Kock had no idea what he should do next. In a flash of embarrassment, it occurred to him that this wasn't normal for Supreme Beings: Supreme Beings always had the answers. He thumped himself on the head in the hopes it would shake loose some omnipotent thoughts.

Just then, a man waving a machete and wearing hundreds of crucifixes, raced by God-Kock, but then suddenly stopped and stared at him. The man screamed: "Jeeessussssssss!" At God-Kock.

"No," God-Kock answered. "I am often confused for him, but I am really..."

"No!" Cried the manic Imahuffin. "Don't you want to kill a Liberal?"

With an expression of joyful hysteria, P.P. God-Kock loped alongside Jumpin' Jim Imahuffin as they raced up the stairs. God-Kock was finding the world a fantastic place. He could not believe the beautiful colors of everything. The amazing grass, the stupendous rain clouds, and the trees were like shifting mirrors of gray-green, changing shape and color constantly. He kept getting distracted: a dandelion saying hello, Clouds fornicating, a bird kind of like a crow but with lipstick. All sorts of things were crossing his path. God-Kock began to realize he was being tested by supernatural beings, beings more God-like than God. Peter Paul God-Kock was glad he held an AR-15 with lots of bullets.

Following the fevered charge of this Imahuffin up the stairs, God-Kock experienced a strong sense of foreboding for what awaited him at the top of Monks Mound.

****

Barcelona's Humvee's were now on top of Monk's Mound, parked side by side on the South end.

Calmly opening the door, Barcelona stepped out. It was all as he had hoped. Here was Bessie May Chowder at his mercy. He was confident the Einstein Stone must now be within sight. Barcelona stared for a moment at green beagle standing in a small, newly dug hole in the Earth.

"Curious," Barcelona wondered what this was about. He turned to Bessie May and smiled. "President Chowder," He started magnanimously. "How are you, my dear?"

"I'm surrounded by a crowd of idiots and mouth breathers that want to do me harm! How the hell do you think I feel?"

Barcelona smiled even more widely. He said to his men, "Take them hostage."

Chowder said, lowering her weapon, "Okay, you got me."

Yaz looked up from the four-foot hole he had burrowed into the surface of Monks Mound, dirt-smeared his face. All the humans were facing each other in a standoff. "Wait! Don't commit violence just yet! You don't understand!" He pleaded. "All the memories are coming back, and I am being flooded; if I don't do this freaking ceremony fast, my head is going to explode."

"How fascinating," Barcelona said drolly. "The talking Beagle wants to pray or something." He looked more closely at Yaz. "What have we here? Some kind of science experiment? A DARPA Dog?"

"I am not a military experiment!" Yaz howled back. "Bring me the Einstein Stone! I must do this ceremony!" Already the images and memories were back, flooding him, taking up his entire consciousness, Yaz struggled to remain awake. The pressures of the memories demanding release were intense.

"Well," Barcelona looked at Bessie May. "The green beagle is demanding the Einstein Stone, how cute. Of course, this stone actually belongs to me. So why don't you tell me where it is?" Barcelona considered a green talking beagle has just another mystery that had nothing to do with him.

Bessie May said nothing.

"Wring the truth from them." He told his four heavily armed soldiers. "Find the Einstein Stone."

Imahuffin and God-Kock were both panting with exhaustion from the run-up 100 stairs. "Wait...gasp...I am here...gasp...to defend Jesus!" Imahuffin announced in a barely audible voice.

God-Kock was breathing so hard he was afraid his lungs would turn inside out.

Barcelona looked disgusted. "Holy shit, what have I here? The Frick and Frack of the Faithful? Buddies of the Holy Bible?"

Bessie May recognized Imahuffin, wild-looking, drooling, muttering and waving a sharp-looking machete. There were so many crucifixes on his chest all she could see was his head and arms. The man next to him looked like a happy-go-lucky concentration camp survivor.

"I'll be damned," she muttered. *Peter Paul God-Kock, the former Western Division director for Homeland Security. What is a member of the infamous Kock family doing out here? In this bizarre new world, anything is possible, and anything is likely.* She mused.

"You must turn these heathen over for immediate smiting!" Imahuffin huffed for breath. "Those are mine! I get to smite them! Mine, mine, mine!" He pointed at Chowder and Yaz. "Mr. Barcelona, sir, I believe those....beings are mine...sort of."

Barcelona chuckled and shrugged. "Yours? Maybe. Who knows? Who cares? What matters is who has them now. Me." He motioned to one of his guards. "Kill him if he does anything."

"What's 'anything'? The guard asked, fearful of Barcelona's wraith, he wanted no mistakes.

Barcelona snorted. "What the fuck do you think the word 'anything' means? Kill him if he does ANYTHING!" He shouted, spraying spittle.

Suddenly a spectral figure appeared out of the gloom and mist and driving rain.

The ghostly, vaguely human shape came nearer and nearer.

Everyone stopped, waiting for whatever was about to happen.

"Ah....sir?" a timid voice came from the figure.

For a moment Barcelona wondered if he was seeing Price Wayne or the newly-departed Spirit of Price Wayne. He shrugged. It didn't matter. "So there you are? Where the hell is Harasin?"

This was the moment Price Wayne dreaded. Harasin's last words for Barcelona were mostly death threats against Barcelona. "Sir, I couldn't find...."

"Never mind!" Shouted Barcelona, dismissively. Barcelona pointed at Imahuffin and P.P. God-Kock. "Seize them and have them bound to a tree for interrogation. Start with that one!" He indicated Imahuffin.

God-Kock was puzzled. A wave of LSD inspired thought had overwhelmed him and spinning lights appeared in front of him. *What am I doing here? Where is here? Who am I? What am I?*

Peter Paul God-Kock, ex-oligarch apprentice, ex-Director of the Western Division, Homeland Security, United Christian States, abruptly turned and started back down the stairs, quickly disappearing over the rim and out of sight.

Barcelona, Wayne, Imahuffin, Chowder, and the four mercenaries silently watched God-Kock leave. Yaz stood trembling, awash in a mystical memories tsunami to the point of catatonia.

"Where the hell is he going?" Price muttered, but not caring as it was one less to deal with.

"Take Imahuffin and break his ass." Barcelona brusquely shoves Price Wayne, "wring whatever story he has out and bury him."

Imahuffin squinted; he was pretty sure his superior sacredness outranked everyone here, and he didn't appreciate being insulted. "Now listen here...!" Imahuffin could feel these people were not in awe of him, and this troubled him. Imahuffin looked around for his trained Mormon murderers, but none were alive.

"Gag the maggot," Barcelona ordered Wayne to silence Imahuffin. "He's all yours, Wayne; I've got business with Bessie May here." Barcelona brushed his hands in dismissal.

Price Wayne pointed at two guards and said, "Keep your guns on them."

Imahuffin, on the verge of major coronary, veins popped out, face red and sweaty, grunted through his tape, "Jeeesussss, Jeeesusss, Jeesusss," staring at Bessie May Chowder like a pit bull eyes a bone. The hundreds of crucifixes shifted and rustled with each heavy breath.

Price Wayne swore this was his last day doing this. Being ordered out of the Humvee in the pouring rain to find Harasin and try to get him to obey. It was all horseshit, but Harasin was a scary man. Price Wayne was done, just get this finished, and he was out of here. As he approached Jim Imahuffin, he did so slowly, careful not to make eye contact.

Imahuffin was painted for war. Crosses adorned his forehead and cheeks, underneath the crucifixes, he wore a combat vest with a picture of Jesus, teeth bared, solid muscular arms and a challenging expression was painted on the back. Imahuffin glared at Price, at Barcelona, at guards, balanced on the fragile edge of explosive rage.

"Easy, big boy, easy," Price Wayne hated himself and Barcelona and God for getting him in this situation.

"Easy..." Wayne had a sudden vision of being impaled on a crucifix. He shuddered.

Imahuffin started snorting and hissing, so Wayne held still, waiting for some evil to emerge from this strange man. Wayne addressed the mercenary covering Imahuffin, "Shoot him if he even blinks."

The mercenary ensured his safety was off, and the weapon was on full automatic. "Damn straight," the soldier said nervously.
****
Bessie May resented being handled by these thugs. "What do you want, Barcelona? Are you lost?" She glanced over at Yaz, wondering

if he was okay. Ears down, tail drooped, Yaz looked very dispirited. She hadn't seen Charley, Doc, Pawnee, Jade, Muh, or Jee and had no idea where everybody went. Suddenly it was just she and Yaz.

She had no idea if that was good or bad.

Bessie May Chowder and Yaz were placed in the back storage hold of the Humvee.

"Where is the Einstein Stone? Answer quickly, and you will die quickly. Refuse to answer and it will be prolonged, probably involving fire." Barcelona said to Bessie May and Yaz.

Yaz, disoriented and disgusted by being manhandled like a stuffed toy, replied sullenly. "You don't understand I have a sacred duty!" he softly growled. "You'd better let go of me if you know what's good for you."

Barcelona laughed. "The fucking house pet has no sense of self-preservation at all, does he?" Barcelona stepped to the back of the Humvee and said: "I want the Einstein Stone."

"Why?" Chowder asked. "Why do you want it? What purpose will it serve you?"

"The Blue-Green Emerald called Einstein Stone? The name alone should tell you that, you dumb bitch. A Blue-Green Emerald is pretty damn rare, and I will have it. But more importantly, I want it. I am Barcelona. I can have whatever I want. I want this, I will have this. So where is it?" He held his Sig Saur to Yaz's' head. "So you tell me, or the pet gets put down!"

"What?" Jee jeered. "We are VIA's; you cannot touch us."

"Oh?" Barcelona looked amused. "So who cares if the dead dog is a VIA?"

"You cannot possess the Einstein Stone," Yaz said ominously.

"Oh?" Barcelona smirked. "Fucking watch me...mutt"

~ 66 ~

CHAPTER SIXTY-THREE

The rain was falling harder when they gathered on the South slope to discuss the situation. Bad guys held the high ground and Bessie May Chowder. Complicating matters, they were out of ammunition.

"Bessie May is up there; we have to get her back."

"What about the beagles?" Jade asked.

"Who?"

"Jade?" Pawnee pointed to the broken-down yellow bus with bright red balloons. "We need ammunition; you check out the bus, see what you can find."

"Charley, Doc," Pawnee turned to them. "Follow, quiet."

"The steep slope of the Mound provides cover for us." Pawnee explained. "They can't see us unless they look over the edge."

All three lay flat, just looking over the scene on the fourth level. "It is a good thing we are in the nighttime. Otherwise, this would be no good." Pawnee whispered softly. "We have only one chance, and that is to distract these guys, get them unsettled and see if we get an opening to attack."

"I'm not too eager to attack without bullets," Charley told him. "Do we wait for Jade? See what she finds?"

"No time," Pawnee replied. "You and Doc, you stay here, South-side, wait for my signal."

"What are you going to do?" Doc said suspiciously. "Pawnee, you probably got some harebrained stunt that involves you hanging your ass out into the wind, right?"

"Two Humvee's are parked on the Southwest side next to the stairs." Pawnee pointed out. "Da four mercenaries are guarding dis crazy guy wearing crucifixes."

"That's Jim Imahuffin," Charley said, pointing to the gaunt, stony-eyed man hung with various crucifixes: big ones, little ones, rainbow-colored, illuminated, twisted, fluorescent, and one with a strobe light like a 1960's dance ball. "He is one crazy asshole."

Pawnee studied the situation. They had left the wounded Clay with Prichard, so Pawnee was relieved his son was now safe. This Prichard knew what he was doing.

"We have no ammo, so a frontal attack is probably not a good idea." Charley just wanted to get that out there if Pawnee had some suicidal ideas.

"Barcelona our first target," Doc explained. "Take him down, and the snake is headless."

"I have an idea, me," Pawnee said softly. Since it was his plan, Pawnee chose the most dangerous job.

Pawnee explained it to Doc and Charley, and they both said, "Hell no."

"You gots a better plan? You gots any plan at all?"

Moments later, Pawnee carefully moved along the steep western slope of the Monks Mound, maneuvering himself close enough to the Humvee's for his plan to work. Charley and Doc remained hidden from sight on the Southside.

Everyone was exposed if the enemy just simply looked over the edge of the Mound. Everyone hoped this would not happen.

Peering over the lip, Pawnee observed Barcelona gesturing and threatening Chowder. Barcelona was now maybe three yards away from where Pawnee had crawled. Picking up a fist-sized stone, Pawnee Painter took careful aim and skillfully threw the rock.

'Thunk!'

"God damn son of a bitch!" Barcelona shouted, grabbing the back of his head. "Some fucking body threw a rock at me. Kill those motherfuckers!" He whirled around, seeking the source of this outrage, but it was impossible to tell in the dark.

Price Wayne ducked in fear for his life.

This is just beyond belief! Barcelona had been subjected to indignity after indignity over the past few months. *He was Number four of The Forty! Soon to be Emperor of all North America! This disrespect was intolerable.* Barcelona was going to make sure people suffered for this.

"Over there, you assholes!" Barcelona furiously pointed to the North. "That way, shoot that way." He had no idea where the rock came from, but this called for action, any action.

Pawnee watched them fire in the wrong direction and was pissed. They were supposed to come in his direction. He was the distraction. What more could he do to get their attention?

He stood up. "Hey, you dickheads looking for me?" Pawnee raised his hands in surrender, a massive smile on his face. All four guards spun around and advanced on Pawnee.

"Get him!" Barcelona snarled at his men. "Bring him up here to me."

The obvious threat was they would just shoot him. But Pawnee gambled that Barcelona would want to take personal revenge up close. Barcelona would want him alive, at least initially.

This was the part that Charley thought most risky. *They would kill Pawnee before the second half of the plan could unfold.* So Doc and he had to act quickly. Advancing to the lip of the South slope, peering over, they could see the guards were about twenty feet way facing moving toward Pawnee. Charley and Doc rose and lobbed rocks toward the guard's backs; ducking down the slope, they quickly scrambled over to the East slope.

It was a long throw, but luckily two of the stones connected with a guard skull. Startled and now very irritated, all four mercenaries turned and opened fire where they thought the rocks came from, into the dark of the Southern slope. They charged, hoping to find the culprits.

Charley and Doc quickly scuttled over to the West slope.

Once the guards were diverted away from Barcelona, Pawnee struck. Moving up the slope fast, he was on Barcelona like a giant panther.

Charley and Doc watched Pawnee go for Barcelona in a silent takedown. Barcelona got out one quick yelp and then was down.

But it would be much nicer for everybody if they had more ammunition. Charley maneuvered on the steep slope over to where he could see the yellow bus. He hoped Jade had found ammunition by now.

Then he saw her by the bus and waved.

Jade gave him the finger.

"Nice, really nice," muttered Charley. "Pawnee doesn't have time for this bullshit." He muttered softly. But Jade was moving toward him, so he hoped it was because she found ammunition.

When Jade was closer, she gave Charley a thumbs up.

"Part two of our little plan," Charley said quietly.

Jade was breathing heavily when she reached Charley and handed out spare ammunition pilfered from the bus. She said,

"Let's go, let's go." Charley urged her.

"Now, what the hell is this about?" She muttered, trying to figure out who all the players were. In combat, the 'fog of war' obscures much, especially when the others make plans she doesn't know about.

****

At that moment, Captain Harasin guided his sole remaining Humvee up the slope, landing on the top level with a splashing of mud water. Barcelona's guards whirled from firing into the dark to face the larger threat of a looming Humvee with a fifty-caliber machine gun on the roof.

***

Jim Imahuffin, seeing the guards diverted, saw his opportunity, pouncing on Price Wayne.

"Holy Shit!" Price Wayne was completely surprised by the attack and went down to the ground with Imahuffin pummeling him with his fists. A lifetime of cooking, ironing, laying out clothing, and attending to the whims of an indolent master, were poor qualifications for hand-to-hand combat. Price Wayne went down under a flurry of Imahuffin vengeance. Only a last-minute knee to the groin stopped the onslaught. As Imahuffin rolled over clutching his tentacles, Price Wayne scurried under a Humvee to hide.

Harasin observed the scene on the Mound. Behind one of the Humvee's, two men were rolling around the ground fighting, while Bessie May Chowder and some small green...creature sat beside her.

Imahuffin attacked Price Wayne, and Barcelona guards were still trying to figure out if they should shoot or not.

Unfortunately, the fifties were out of ammunition, but Harasin and his two men held fully loaded AR15's. "Fuck 'em all," he screamed, "Open fire!"

"But sir!" His sergeant protested. "Mr. Barcelona is over there; he could be hit."

"When I order 'Fire', sergeant," Harasin snarled. "You send your bullets where I tell you to, never mind who the target is. I'll deal with blowback!"

The men with Harasin all unloaded the vehicles and opened fire as ordered.

The four Barcelona guards now over on the North slope turned to charge back to the Humvee's but a fusillade of bullets caused them to drop to the ground for cover.

Harasin saw the two Humvee's rock when the fusillade of bullets hit them; mud and dirt flew up, obscuring the scene. Suddenly, Harasin felt like a balloon with the air running out. He had been an E-8, a Sergeant Major, and look at him now, *I'm trying to indiscriminately kill whoever or whatever is in front of me?* Harasin felt deep shame, an old combat soldier betraying his rules of engagement and slaughtering civilians.

"Cease fucking fire!" He screamed."Stop, stop shooting."

But as soon as the echoing gunfire ceased, Barcelona's men, hiding out until the shooting died down, rose and started firing at Harasin.

Two of Harasin's men went down. "Start firing!" Harasin screamed. "Kill those fuckers!"

Jim Imahuffin, with bullets zinging right and left around him, scuttled on all fours to the South slope and threw himself over, rolling over and over one hundred yards to the base of Monk's Mound.

Price Wayne, bruised and battered, tended his various injuries cowering beneath a Humvee, bullets bouncing off the thick metal just inches from his head, was furious at himself for his failure at self-protection: A fistfight degenerates into a firefight; bruises to bullets.

"Nice job, asshole, your survival skills suck!" He scolded himself.
****

"Let go, Yaz, we have to help Pawnee." Bessie May Chowder climbed out of the Humvee to help Pawnee when a volley of bullets struck, thunking loudly on the metal skin, scarring the thick windows. Bessie May was caught unawares; she couldn't climb back in because Yaz blocked the way, waiting to get out. Suddenly she felt very exposed and in danger.

In a moment, Yaz was right there, leaping up onto Bessie May to protect her from the bullets. They fell to the ground, and Bessie May grabbed Yaz hauling him behind the Humvee for protection. "Good boy, good boy," she told him.

Yaz felt mysteriously pleased by her words.

At that moment, Bessie May Chowder heard a sound that ripped her soul.

Like a watermelon exploding, Pawnee Painters' head was impacted by a 7.62mm round, killing him instantly, and he dropped bonelessly to the ground without a sound.

The horror of it before her eyes paralyzed her.

More bullets struck the vehicle. Glass from a shattered window covered her, and metal fragments cut her skin as more bullets struck. But she felt nothing and did not flinch.

"Oh, my god, no!" Bessie May said, her heartbroken. "No, Pawnee, no!" Quickly she scrambled to him, but there was nothing she could do. Pawnee was gone: Death had claimed him.

Barcelona, free from the brutal beating Pawnee was inflicting upon him, leaped to his feet and disappeared in the dark and rain toward his mercenaries.

"Ma'am, ma'am," Yaz, growling urgently, was pulling at her coat. "Ma'am, we have to get the Einstein Stone. Now!" He told her.

But Bessie May Chowder was stunned with grief, tears flowing; she could barely comprehend what Yaz was saying. "What?" The magnitude of the loss was unimaginable. *Pawnee was so alive, so vital, he couldn't be dead; he just couldn't.*

More bullets whisked past.

"We have to get the Einstein Stone! Didn't he have it?" Yaz pointed at Pawnee's backpack.

"Pawnee...Pawnee," Bessie May said slowly, agonizingly. The death was so sudden, so intense she felt as if moving in molten amber. Bessie May reached down and opened his pack. Taking out the round gem and a shard of bone, the Relic of St. Catherine, she looked up at Yaz.

More rounds were fired, this time by Barcelona's guards, and in the next moment, a full-fledged firefight was exploding all around them. Crossfire between Harasin on one side and the four Barcelona guards on this site erupted suddenly.

"What do I do now?" But nothing seemed important to her. She looked down at her friend, Pawnee, and nothing seemed to matter other than his death. She looked at the little green beagle and could only stare. Bessie May was so stunned by the loss of Pawnee Painter even her fabled survival instincts were numb. She realized she was overwhelmed, all the losses, the tragedies, the massive changes in her life and world, and now the loss of a man she deeply admired and respected.

"That's it! That's what was missing!" Yaz shouted with joy. "I knew there was something else I was supposed to have; it was that damn bone! Wow! It all worked out."

But Bessie May Chowder could only stand still, stunned with grief.

Pawnee is dead.

****

Charley was the first to arrive at the Humvee and found Bessie May bent over the still form of Pawnee Painter. He knew immediately Pawnee was gone. Blood and brains and bones fragments soaked the ground. Bessie May, tears streaming, gave Charley the most helpless expression he had ever seen.

They hugged.

Jade and Doc came running up, stopping suddenly when they saw what had happened.

Jade immediately thought of Clay, lying wounded back down in the meadow. She had no idea how she was going to tell him. She thought about the cruelty of life, the despair, the agony of loss, and not for the first time wondered why grief was such an integral part of this existence.

But it was too late. Pawnee was dead.

For a few moments, all stood over the body of Pawnee Painter; no one had any words, no one knew what to say as a fierce firefight continued between Harasin and Barcelona.

A sudden burst of bullets from Barcelona and his henchmen caused them to duck behind the Humvee's.

"It is like a light went out of the world," Doc said softly, hiding with Jade.

"I know this is crazy," Charley said sorrowfully, his voice hushed, filled with disbelief. "But I didn't think he could die."
****

Peter Paul God-Kock stopped his meandering across the muddy field and blinked several times. The voices calling him had stopped. Silence blossomed in his brain, and he was stunned by the change.

Suddenly the world became understandable again. God-Kock scratched his head; where had he been? He had little memory of the past few hours. Turning a full circle, he surveyed his location. The constant drumbeat of rain in the dark of night made this problematic. As far as he could tell, he was in the middle of a nicely tended park; there were trees, a bullet-torn school bus, and a sizeable indistinct hill in front of him.

Red, green, and white, flashes of light streaked across the very top of the hill told him a firefight was underway. The loud reports of rifle fire and men screaming drifted down to him.

To his right, about thirty feet away, was an abandoned Humvee, the doors open, engine running, and several bodies lying around. God-Kock knew divine intervention when he saw it.

Getting in, he noticed a canvass bag of grenades just lying on the passenger seat, like an invitation. "Yes!" God-Kock was elated that God had chosen to bless him again and again and again. Tears came to his eyes in gratitude for God's Love.

Slamming the Humvee into gear, P.P. God-Kock didn't know much, but what he did know was without doubt. He was destined to slaughter hated Liberals who refused to accept their proper place in society. God-Kock knew his mission. To restore God to the land by killing Liberals. Liberals who refused to follow the Oligarchs plans. Liberals who insist on equality. Equality? *The poor are not equal to the rich. This cannot be allowed to poison our people any further!* A patriotic zeal arose in his chest.

Just as he was gathering his energy for this final endeavor, Peter Paul God-Kock was startled by an urgent rapping on his window.

Jim Imahuffin stood outside the vehicle, so covered in mud only the whites of his eyes showed. "Let me in! Now!" He said between gritted teeth. Pulling the driver's door open he yanked God-Kock out, throwing him on the muddy ground. "You want to come along? You ride shotgun; I'm driving!"

God-Kock felt the insult against his divine self, but he knew mercy was a sought-after character trait by the common man, so he decided to behead Imahuffin later.

Imahuffin, muddy crucifixes flapping against his chest pumped the accelerator, revving up the engine until the pistons rattled, knew that vengeance awaited him at the top, let off the brake and broke into a song of praise as he began the ascent of Monks Mound: "Bringing in the sheaves, we will come rejoicing bringing in the sheaves..."

This time, Jesus was going to win.
****

"All right hold it right there!" Barcelona led his men out of the dark and surrounded the two Humvee's where Pawnee laid dead.

So overwhelmed with grief, all of them, Bessie May, Charley, Doc, Jade and the green beagle were held at gunpoint before they could react.
***

"Where's the traitor?" Muh demanded leaping from Harasin's Humvee. The sooner he got the Einstein Stone back the faster they could get to Indiana.

"Yeah, where is the orphan? We have questions for you buddy?" Jee was still incensed that he was the innocent one, being punished.
***

"Okay," snarled Barcelona, "We've got these fools, go kill them!" He pointed to Harasin's Humvee sitting seventy yards away on the North side. Barcelona noticed there were two green dogs over by that Humvee. He wondered where all the green dogs were coming from.

A firefight erupted between the two sets of Barcelona's mercenaries.

Just then, another Humvee, lights glaring in the misty rain, reached the summit and crashed down onto the fourth level

After the vehicle slid to stop, both Imahuffin and God-Kock jumped from the vehicle and ran to the front of the vehicle. Imahuffin didn't know who he would shoot and didn't care, he was here to slaughter, and so everyone was fair game. There were now so many crucifixes around his neck he had a bullet proof vest; several rounds pinged off a Twisted Jesus Crucifix and a ceramic Mexican Jesus.

Still woozy from the LSD, God-Kock strapped the bag of hand grenades around his neck and readied himself for martyrdom.

"If Jesus can do it, so can I!" God-Kock muttered. He wasn't sure about waiting three days to resurrect, though. That seemed like a long time to just lay around in a coffin. God-Kock figured an hour or two, and he would rise from the dead. That should be enough to get his point across. He adjusted the bag of grenades ready for war.

Imahuffin and God-Koch stood side by side, frozen; one totally unsure who to smite first, the other rethinking mortality plans.

***

The firefight had paused at the sudden intrusion, but then picked up in full force. All at once, tracers were flashing through the air, as another of Harasin's men went down under the onslaught. Harasin returned fire, but all he saw were flashes of light to shoot at. Quickly, he saw brief images of Barcelona in the dim, flickering light, so he threw several rounds, hoping to kill him.

A scream told him someone was hit.

Gunfire dwindled down to a single gun coming from Barcelona's position. Harasin was reasonable sure there was only one active gunman left. Good odds. He wanted to send his men in to wipe out the insurgent vehicle, but he looked around and no one left, except the two green dogs hiding behind the vehicle.

Both Imahuffin and his companion, God-Kock, now formed the third leg of the combat triangle. But neither had moved. They both stood silently, brazenly exposed in the glaring light of their head-lights, two fat targets.

Harasin knew his duty. *Never mind those idiots.* The last man standing was tasked with completing the mission, and Barcelona must die. Grimly he flopped to the ground; lowing crawling vigorously toward Barcelona's previous position, hoping it was Barcelona himself still alive.

He reached the two Humvee's and came upon a dead man being held by a small, elderly Black woman. Tears were streaming down her face. "Get your hands up!" Harasin snarled.

Bessie May Chowder wiped some of the tears out of her eyes to see the intruder better. "Put your fucking gun away," Bessie May said firmly, resolutely. "Enough is enough, this has to stop! What are we doing by killing each other? What are we accomplishing? An eye for an eye makes the whole world blind."
****

Captain Harasin lowered his rifle and considered the situation. Barcelona and his men were not here. What now? A few moments ago, he had realized how different his life was. After a highly successful twenty-six-year career in the US Army, he was now just a bloody mercenary hunting this little old black women and aliens.

Harasin stared at the old black woman, the green beagle beside her panted heavily, his pink tongue hanging out the side of his jaw.

"Fuck this!" Harasin decided.

Rising, he unchambered his round and replaced the bullet in the magazine. He walked over to the nearest Humvee. "Well, I'm done. I'm taking this fucking Humvee, and no one is going to stop me." Harasin didn't know where he was going, but he was gone from here.

Price Wayne saw his opportunity and didn't want to be run over by it. Quickly emerging from under the Humvee he shouted, "Hey! Let me come with you! Please, please!" Wayne put on his most pitiful and desperate facial expression. "I'll... I'll die here...mister... can't you help me? Please?" He blinked his eyes helplessly to elicit some sympathy, exuding innocence like a choir boy from Topeka, Kansas.

"You again?" Harasin looked at the whitest white man he'd ever seen. *Now twice.* Harasin wrinkled his nose and rubbed the rich black skin with his fingers.

Price Wayne nodded piteously. "Help...me."

"Sure, sure, get in, and shut up." Harasin smiled for the first time in months; the image of himself, six feet four inch Black man, skin as dark as a moonless night, and a scrawny little cracker with alabaster skin riding along together. It just made him smile.

Eagerly, Price Wayne clambered into the vehicle and strapped himself in. He was going to make it. *Wayne was going to live!* He didn't know where or what he would do, but it didn't matter. He was going to survive.

"Drive on!" He said, giggling in delight at his rescue.

"I said, shut the fuck up, or I will shoot you!" Harasin growled with genuine menace, put the Humvee in gear, accelerating over the edge of the Mound, he headed for trees in the distant night, the sounds of the engine fading into the gathering gloom.

~ 67 ~

CHAPTER SIXTY-FOUR

They watched the Humvee disappear with almost identical reactions: "I wish that were me."

"We must go now!" Yaz demanded, his eyes darting around fearfully. He could feel the internal pressure building within him. Something was urging him, commanding him to move. Like knowledge had hobnail boots and was stomping around in his mental attic. "We must go to the Northwest Corner and dig a hole!" As the urgency built, an almost frenetic compulsion gripped Yaz. "We must go now!" He shrieked piteously, hopping feverously up and down.

"The hell is he screeching about?" Muh, followed by Jee, trotted in from the dark drizzling rain. As soon as they realized Harasin wasn't returning to the Humvee and the shooting had stopped, Muh needed to find the Einstein Stone and get moving. "Hey, orphan! Get hold of yourself, your embarrassing us," he complained.

"He's babbling mindlessly," Jee replied. "Just like you, giving orders."

"Do not!"

"Do so!"

Yaz barked at Bessie May Chowder, urging her to her feet. "We must go now. Please, please, please!" His face held a pleading look that startled Bessie May with its intensity.

Bessie May Chowder had no idea why he was so insistent. "What? What do you want?" Her mind could not leave the body of her friend. She looked down at Pawnee, and another well of sadness came.

"Bring the Einstein Stone and the bone of St. Catherine and follow me; time is urgent we must hurry. But, you must rub blood on the bone. There," Yaz pointed at Pawnee. "The blood of a hero will do. We must hurry, or the death of your friend might be in vain." Quickly, he turned and set off for the Northwest corner, disappearing in the dark and misty rain. Somewhere in the dark was the location he sought, the Northwest corner of what used to be the main temple atop the Mound; a sacred spot shown to him by Watchful Raven.

Chowder picked up the Einstein Stone and the shard of bone and leaned over to Pawnee; carefully, she knelt down and reverently touched the bone to him, where it absorbed some of his blood. She stood up and felt a wash of guilt that she had somehow desecrated her friend by this action.

Jade touched Bessie May's arm and said, "This is the right thing to do; we honor Pawnee by including him in this ceremony. Remember, we are spirits visiting in human form; we will see Pawnee again. It is okay, Bessie May." She hugged the more petite woman, both shedding tears.

"Hey!" Yaz's voice echoed across the dark, expansive level. "Are you fucking humans going to participate, or am I just wasting my time trying to save your arrogant butts!"

"You wouldn't think a savior would be so belligerent," Charley muttered. "Come on, Doc, let's get over there."

"Hold your horses, toots, we're coming!" Jee yelled back. "Come on Muh; let's see what the orphan has got to show us."

"No. I am the leader of this mission, I say what we do, and I say we don't do this." Muh knew his attempts to retain his leadership position were futile. Still, he had to try. "I will be waiting in that Humvee for you to bring me the Einstein Stone. Then you can drive me to Indianapolis, where we will give the Einstein Stone to the President of the United Christian States, and then all of us will go to the Middle East to complete our mission. There, I have spoken."

"That you have, but you have two problems," Jee replied. "One, this President and the United Christian States don't exist after this solar storm, so this whole mission is gone. Two, you are an egotistical idiot."

"I have pictures of you," Muh said quietly. "Pictures that, well let's just say are delicate, even embarrassing, in situations that would demolish your VIA credentials."

"What pictures?" Jee asked carefully.

"Blutoc IV, when we were on the Oberlee Mission?"

"Oh." Jee came over and stood by Muh, his eyes and ears down, tail drooping. "Lead the way, master."

****

No sooner did they emerge from behind the Humvee's they noticed Imahuffin and God-Kock standing in front of a Humvee.

Both glared back at them with blood thirsty eyes. Both had weapons in their hands.

"Oh, oh," Charley muttered. "Forgot about those dirt bags."

Imahuffin and God-Kock charged.

As God-Kock raced across the seventy yards, his bag of grenades flopped against his chest in rhythm with the clump of crucifixes on Imahuffin's.

Both Charley and Jade got off quick shots at the attacking men only to watch the bullets ricochet off the enormous bundles of crucifixes on Imahuffin's chest.

"Wait, man," Doc called out. "The other guy has a bag, grenades or something!"

"Fucking shoot the bag!"

At that moment both weapons dry fired.

"What the hell?"

"How many stray bullets do you think I could find?" Jade defended herself. "That's it! No more ammo."

"Jesus Saves! Repent you sinners," Shrieked God-Kock.

Imahuffin closed on the group with murder in his eyes.

They were out in the open and out of ammunition. Charley tried to put Jade behind him to protect her; Jade tried to put Charley behind her to protect him.

Suddenly, Barcelona appeared out of the night, gun held ready, "Don't move or I kill all of you!" As soon as his last man fell, Barcelona took advantage of a sudden cease fire and escaped the Humvee's down the east slope. But as soon as he saw Chowder take out the stone, he had to strike and win his Blue-Green Emerald, his treasure!

Imahuffin and God-Kock had paused in their onslaught, momentarily surprised by his appearance.

"Oh for Christ's sakes," Chowder exclaimed, "Doesn't this ridiculous madness ever end?"

"Pling" The sound of a pin being pulled from a hand grenade caught everyone's attention.

All eyes were suddenly on God-Kock.

God-Kock knew it. He could feel it. The power of it. He looked at them and every eye, everyone's attention was directly on him. For the first time in his entire life, God-Kock knew people were taking him seriously. Finally, people would listen to him. It felt superb! Holding the live grenades, he advanced. "I see that you have failed to honor and respect your superiors." God-Kock felt a tingle in his nether regions. *Finally, a chance to stand up and speak for God, just as God wishes!* "You!" He pointed a hand grenade at the group.

"Are sinners that only WE can save. Only WE have God's love to share with you. Only WE can save your soul!" God-Kock then pulled the pin and threw one of the grenades straight at the group. "For the Honor and Glory of Jesus! Death to Liberals!"

Both Charley and Jade threw each other to the ground simultaneously.

Yaz went to the bottom of his hole, Muh and Jee ducked behind Barcelona. At the same time, Doc grabbed Chowder and threw her over the edge of the landing to safety. Then like an all-star short-stop, he reached out, caught the grenade in midair with his left hand, transferred it to his right, and pitched it straight back at Peter Paul God-Kock, an explosive knuckleball pitch, straight down the middle.

The last thing P.P. God-Kock expected was to see his hand grenade coming straight back at him. God-Kock screamed, "No!" and ducked. Unfortunately, the giant bag of hand grenades proved to be clumsy, and he fell onto Imahuffin just as millions of tiny pieces of sharp, jagged steel exploded two feet over their heads.

'Sympathetic detonation': Charley and Doc, as combat veterans, were familiar with the term describing a chain reaction of explosions as each hand grenade set off the next.

"Blam, blam, blam, blam, blam!"

Peter Paul God-Kock and Jumping James Imahuffin became a hole in the ground surrounded by a pink mist; white bone and shards of crucifixes circled them both.

$$\sim 68 \sim$$

CHAPTER SIXTY-FIVE

Slowly, they picked themselves up from the multiple deadly explosions.

Barcelona, deafened and wounded by several dozen tiny bits of metal, was the first to come to. He looked around at everyone laying flat on the ground. Quickly, nervously, he patted his body to see how much blood leaked and was relieved to see only minor punctures. "I survived. Hooray for me!"

Charley Bones and Jade were lying tangled in arms and legs. Doc was flat on his back and Chowder was nowhere to be seen.

Barcelona got up and nearly stepped on the two green beagles behind him. "What the hell is with all these fucking green beagles?"

Barcelona moved away from the strange dogs, irritated they might have fleas.

He glanced over at the small hole dug by one of the beagles and there it was. *A Blue-Green Emerald. The Einstein Stone.* Just laying there beside the hole, waiting for him to pick it up.

Barcelona walked over and picked up the Einstein Stone, weighing it in his hands. "Mine, I win."

Just then another green beagle erupted from the hole and bit him sharply on the leg.

"Fucking hell!" Barcelona dropped the gem into the hole.

As soon as he saw the Einstein Stone enter the pit, Yaz let go of Barcelona's leg, grabbed the Sacred Relic of St. Catherine now covered in the blood of a hero, and leaped in. He jammed the bone into the earth. "Cha Oka! Cha Oka! Cha Oka!" Feverously he chanted as he stabbed the soil with the bone.

Charley and Jade were up moving to intercept Barcelona and Doc was frantically searching for Bessie May Chowder, not sure just where he threw her when it went off.

The Einstein Stone.

A silent explosion of deep blue-green radiated from the pit so intensely all of them dropped to the ground, stunned by the power of the light.

"SNAP!"

Everyone went unconscious.

***

Charley looked up at the sky; the clouds seemed to be thicker, more fluffy today. The Sun caressed his face with cheerful warmth. It had been raining all night, but now it was day and beautiful. Charley wondered what happened to the rain; *the sky was intensely blue!* A flock of pigeons flew over, which amazed him. Charley hadn't seen flocks of pigeons in many years. Birds. Many birds singing songs he didn't recognize but somehow sounded as if they belonged. He stretched, his muscles felt good for a change.

"Something is different; something doesn't feel the same..." Charley ran his hands down his body, "I feel different. Are you okay?" He asked Jade.

"Ow, my head," she complained. "That hurt." But when she opened her eyes and looked around, the world was slightly changed. Jade shook her head, feeling as if it was stuffed with cotton. She blinked, and then rubbed her eyes. Somehow everything seemed brighter. Blue sky, the deep blue-green of the surrounding ever-greens, everything was luminous. The most colorful butterflies she had ever seen skipped by on a warm breeze.

Jade felt intensely alive. This surprised her. Jade Bi'ch Hai Bones wondered what had happened; she had been battered and beaten by a life on the road, which takes a physical toll, but now...she felt great! She looked at Charley Brown Bones, and it was as if seeing him all over again. Charley was the only man, beyond her adopted father, she had ever loved, and she knew deep in her heart that she must never let him go. Charley was one of only three human beings she could trust with her life.

Charley looked at Jade; she studied him in return. He couldn't say what was different, but she was changed. Her face softened, peaceful, untroubled by memories or fears. But even more curious, he wanted to tell her things about himself, things he had never spoken of to her or any living soul. Something within him was telling him: "It is okay, you are safe, and we are safe."

***

Doc, lying face up, staring at the columns of majestic clouds sweeping by thought about the arduous journey here, the loss of life, and the loss of civilization. *The Solar Flare ruined much and saved much. The Einstein Stone, the shin bone of St. Catherine, all of it may mean everything or nothing at all.* That was Doc's greatest fear: Not what it would do, but what it would not do.

***

Yaz found himself overcome by memories as if a blanket had been thrown over him, closing off the surrounding world. Yaz had the startling realization reality had shifted.

***

"You know, I'm new here, really, really new, I don't know a whole lot..." He jabbered to the tall, dark man, Watchful Raven,

"So what now?" Yaz asked. "I have been sent here by my Superiors and told to do as I was told." He shrugged. "Here I am." It was hot; Yaz wore a colorful one-piece shirt that came to his knees, his feet were covered in soft deerskin, and a nervous sweat coated his brow. Being small and alien to this planet was the loneliest feeling in the galaxy. Yaz thought.

"Why am I here?"

The old man in the group's center looked at the visitor and smiled. He didn't see many visitors these days, and he didn't see many visitors at all. Even blind, he knew this one was different.

"You have been chosen." The elder said simply.

Yaz was suddenly terrified he had missed something important, and now they would blame him for screwing everything up. "Did I...did I do something wrong?"

The old men smiled and looked at each other; they had seen this before, beings unexposed to the mystical stone.

"No, my friend, you are fine. Your uncertainty of behavior is a mark of your uncertainty of self. We know that many civilizations on this Earth are mired in superstition, fear, and ignorance. There are whole nations of people who live in anger and vengeance, who conduct a war for money and keep their civilization intact. Without war and bloodshed, they could not control their citizens."

"Yes, I know these people!" Yaz spoke up. "My brothers and I were here over a thousand years ago, and everybody was like that."

The old man nodded. "The three desert religions, indeed almost all of man's attempt at Religion, have locked humanity into a spiral of death and vengeance and war." He gestured around him. "We are not those people. This mystical stone has helped us mature, grow as human beings, learn that violence is unnecessary, that war is an utter failure of civilization, and that all beings are important. Everyone is important, from those who live underground to those who fly in the sky."

Another man, sporting a bright blue Macaw feathers and smoking a long wooden pipe with a stone bowl shaped like a bird. "We humans belong, but we do not own. No man can own land; that is impossible. The Earth does not belong to humanity; it is shared by all. Whatever we do, we must do with the understanding and acceptance of those beings. We cannot destroy a forest as there are beings that live there. We may take a single tree for our use, but we cannot take the forest. This would be an insult to our Creator."

Yaz nodded; as he listened, he realized that in their drunken exuberance, he and his brothers had inadvertently aided in the destruction of this planet by contributing to the creation of a civilization that cannot succeed and is doomed to failure. Their assistance to the three desert religions may have made them far more influential than they would have been without ET interference.

"The idea that humans are born as sinners is a ludicrous notion." The blind old man spoke softly but clearly. "Babies are innocent; only adults are given the choices for good or evil. The notion there can be one path to God is wrong. Remember, what is considered wrong or sinful changes from one civilization to another. In one place, human sacrifice is acceptable and honorable. In another, it is anathema. Yet both peoples would say their way of life is to honor God. This implies there must be many Gods and many ideas of acceptable. So what is God? God can only be Love. It is Love that brings us together. Love that unites. Love that binds and combines and creates. Anger and rage do nothing but push us apart. Which kind of universe would you rather live in?"

"Yeah, but there are a lot of really angry humans out there that just like to fuck things up." Yaz couldn't help but use a vulgar term but felt embarrassed to do so.

"Civilized people raise their children in a certain way that allows the child to feel accepted, nourished, and understood." A woman in a soft yellow robe with a beaver collar poured tea. "Others raise their children by beating them when they make a mistake, punishing them for being human, treating their children as if they were property, possessions to be owned and forced to grow only in prescribed ways. Because of these foolish, immature behaviors, Earth civilizations are often brutal and violent. We are not. What people you see before you were created by fairness, justice, honesty, equality. Not war. Not conquest, not murder."

An elder woman, dressed in clothing dyed a deep blue, spoke, "The idea that one must grovel before another human to speak to God is foolish. All of life is interconnected, and many have lost this understanding." Her eyes, sharp as hawk talons, held Yaz. "The idea that we live one life; a straight line from birth to death to afterlife, is mistaken. Nothing in nature is a straight line. Nothing. Nature is a circle, the cosmos is a circle, and the universe is a circle, always. Beings are born, live their lives, gain experiences, and then pass to the next world, where they may or may not return to earthly existence."

A small man shriveled with age and injuries was watching Yaz. The man's face was clear and bright. He pointed a painted and decorated dance stick at Yaz. "Everything is energy," his voice was cracked and withered; "there is nothing solid except our perception of things. All life exists on a plane, but not all on the same plane, and there are many planes."

The woman in blue spoke up. "Energy is immortal, and it cannot be either created or destroyed. You are energy; I am energy; all living beings exist in physical and energy selves. The mortal self perishes, and the energy packet that is the self continues to the next plane or realm."

"But why am I here?"

The man with the bird pipe tapped out the ashes. "Patience, my friend. We will get to that."

"We live in a world of opposites." The woman in yellow said. "Good, bad, happy, sad. We cannot understand joy without knowing grief. There always must be structure. The task of humans is to grow compassion in the face of fear, empathy in times of rage, understanding amidst the chaos. We are here to learn how to be better human beings. This is very difficult; we live in a hard world."

"But for this education to work...." The man with the bird pipe spoke.

"...Humans must-have choice. This is where the great tragedies and amazing triumphs come from." the woman in blue added.

"There are times when humanity needs help." He pointed his dancing stick at Yaz. "Remember this, we are here to help each other because the task of maturation is difficult and filled with traps. So there are times that assistance is called for." The dance stick waved at Yaz. "Civilizations can be stuck in quicksand; they need something to break the hold of the sand." He petted a small, grey brown dog beside him. "Have you ever wondered why dogs, and cats for that matter, are here?"

"Dogs? I have no idea." But he had noticed that they seemed everywhere, playing, hauling, hunting, guardians at night and companions each day. Never leaving the side of chosen humans.

"Long ago, when the human species was very young," The old man squinted at Yaz. "It was decided humans must have helper species. Although Intelligent, we humans are stubborn and willful to the point of self-destruction. So to prevent premature extinction, a co-species was selected. Dogs and Cat. Canine and Feline. They exist to teach us unconditional love and loyalty; two areas that we humans struggle with constantly.

"Infants and puppies give unconditional love," The woman in blue spoke up. "Both must be taught to hate, and that is precisely what humanity has done for millennia. Human civilizations, one after the other, are all based on hate, violence, and conquest.

The blind man pulled a pouch from his side and set it in front of him. He opened the leather bag and withdrew a sizeable ovoid stone, a curious shade of black.

"But sometimes more help is needed to save a species from self-destruction. The Mystery Stone," the blind man said softly. "This Stone came to us 743 years ago, and it changed us. This unassuming Stone and the ceremony that goes with it acted as a guide, a structure for sentient beings to follow."

Yaz looked down at the unassuming, smoothly rounded Stone. "So the Mystery Stone is sort of like an emotional generator; it energizes love?"

"No, it takes away the reasons NOT to love. Children love unabashedly, openly, enthusiastically if they feel safe, protected, and heard. Adult Humans refuse to love because of fear. This stone awakens courage and optimism and hope."

"The Mystery Stone can only belong to one group of people for so long before it must be passed along." Pipe man leaned forward to make his words clear to Yaz. "You are to return the Stone to your world. In time, you may be asked to bring it to another civilization, either on this world or another. Yaz, you ask why you; you and your brothers created a real nightmare for the human race. Because your influence gave these three desert religions power, they blossomed but in a distorted way, so this Blue-Green Emerald was gifted to straighten us out. Now you must be responsible for returning it."

"You, Yaz were chosen because you are the one who has gained influence from the Stone. Your brothers are oblivious, and the Stone does not affect all beings the same way."

What do you mean?

"DNA."

The gathered elders explained to Yaz human genetics and their influence over behavior. He never knew human reactions and beliefs were expressions of human DNA combinations. The Einstein Stone revealed that modern humans are an amalgamation of their pre-human ancestors. Homo Sapiens had many forebears; old strains of hominids didn't just disappear; they were absorbed. Each successive wave of hominids brought forward the DNA of more senior, extinct ones; Homo Neanderthalensis, Homo Heidelbergensis, Homo Rudolfensis, Homo Habilis, Homo Erectus, and more.

"All of these have contributed to the DNA of modern humans," The woman in blue explained. "The percentage of these various DNA streams determines how a person behaves. Those with heavy Neanderthal, with a heavy presence of Homo Habilis, and a complete absence of Home Rudolfensis tended to be very conservative, fearful, superstitious, aggressive people completely unable to understand beliefs separate from their own."

"Then those with just a touch of Neanderthal and no Habilis or Erectus tend to be very open and challenging and energetic. So you see, the DNA genetic combination strains create humans with very different capabilities, some of which do not mix well at all. In large part this accounts for so much fear of strangers, people outside the proper DNA percentages."

The old man handed a cup of liquid over to Yaz and said, "Please drink this; it will assist you in your task. This potion will hide these memories until you need them. When the Mystery Stone is in play again, these memories will return to you but will be hidden until then. The knowledge of the Stone and its actions must be held secret until the proper time.

Yaz drained the cup of the foul-tasting, chalky substance, and everything disappeared.

When he opened his eyes, Muh and Jee were studying him as if he were exotic road kill.

$$\sim 69 \sim$$

CHAPTER SIXTY-SIX

A bluish-green glow emanating from the soaked mud pit Yaz had dug. The Einstein Stone still displayed a shiny bright, cheerful color.

Jade looked at Charley, "I feel wonderful."

"Ah don't know what has been done to us," Doc got up and stretched, "but I think I am feeling better, my arthritis...is better! Rain always made it worse. But not now," he wondered why.

Barcelona, lying flat on his back, had no idea what happened. *One minute standing there, checking out the Einstein Stone, and suddenly the lights went on and then out.* Climbing awkwardly to his feet, he took in the scene: Charley Bones and Jade were just getting to their feet. Doc was sitting up but clearly woozy.

Barcelona went over to the hole and looked in. Yaz looked back.

Barcelona reached in, plucked the Einstein Stone, and said, "I'll take this."

"Wait a minute, hold it!"

"Since it seems your little Einstein Stone bauble is pretty worthless as a world-changer, I'll take my prize souvenir and return to Indianapolis, where I will reestablish American civilization. I, of course, as the President for Life. I will be the new George Washington, only I will rule for forever...and longer. I, Barcelona, will reestablish America as it was meant to be: A nation of Capitalism for

Capitalists! Only instead of America being controlled by multiple Oligarchs I will control. Just me!"

"You are a fucking thief, like all Billionaires; all super-wealthy humans are just assholes!"

Barcelona bowed a mocking gesture.

"Civilization is all that stands between man and animal!" Barcelona stated firmly. "Humans need structure, they need orders, and they need to be led. That is human nature."

"But look at the mess we are in? Look at what Capitalism and a Patriarchal belief system have given us?" Jade couldn't let this slide, and she had to speak up. "Look, Barcelona, we are destroying this world, killing its animals, plants, insects; we are changing the very fucking weather on this planet into something NO human has ever seen. And this is okay with you?"

"You fools!" Barcelona stormed. "First off, you Goddamned liberals are always whining for Communism to save you. Communism, Socialism, anything for a free ride on the backs of the working man."

"That is utter bullshit," Charley had enough. Barcelona, you do not believe that for a second!" Socialism is not Communism! That is the propaganda crap you feed ignorant Americans and people too stupid to read a book. Socialism is the enemy of Capitalism because Socialism is for the people. Capitalism is to create Capital or wealth for the few. Capitalists hate Socialism because it takes away their power.

Barcelona laughed. "Like I said, humans are sheep, they need to be lead."

"May be, but not by wolves." Doc added.

"You believe whatever nonsense about an Einstein Stone and peace and love you want, But the reality is that men of courage and destiny make their way. We take what we want. Humanity must be driven forward, or it will lapse into self-indulgent poverty. This is my duty; I, like all great men, Emperors, Kings, Presidents, leaders of humanity, have been chosen by God to lead humanity to greatness! Rich men are masters of the Earth, says so right in the Holy Bible, King James Version of course."

"You do not understand this at all, do you?" Sadly Jade shook her head.

"I understand that men of power and intelligence take what we want," Barcelona snarled at her. "I understand this 'love' shit you talk about is unprofitable. Love costs money, robs from profit. That is unacceptable!" Barcelona was gripped with a need to explain himself, something he rarely did. "We are the builders, the creators, the men who civilize humanity. The purpose of our existence is to praise Jesus and make money. Not necessarily in that order, you understand."

Oh, dear, you seem to completely misunderstand God. Yaz thought sadly. Suddenly the words of the Cha Oka Elders came back to him. He remembered their exact words: *"Two of the great religious books on this planet, the Holy Bible and Holy Koran, are clear that God is within us, not without. God isn't out there in space. God isn't in some other realm of existence. God is in you...God is you. We are all, all living beings, part of the Godhood."*

"Barcelona, it our relationships that define us. It our relationships with each other that matters, not gold or silver," Jade tried again to reach him.

"Well, aren't we full of ourselves? You little people need it, I guess. You need each other to comfort and protect. What a bunch of children!" Barcelona, waving his handgun, keeping a tight grip on the stone. "I am God as far as you peasants are concerned. Now, I will take my leave, and my Einstein Stone to add to my collection." He turned for his Humvee.

"So gold and silver are the ultimate in human achievement?"

"Oh no, power is the main thing," Barcelona stopped, turned back to look at them, and said almost wistfully. "The ability to make other people do what you want is the most priceless thing on this planet. So priceless it takes billions to achieve."

"Hey! Hey! Take us with you." Muh and Jee came running up to Barcelona. "We are VIA's, very important Aliens."

Barcelona stared in awe. "Talking green beagles. Amazing."

Muh and Jee grinned and wagged their tails.

"We all right, sure hope in, not every billionaire can say they have a pack of talking green beagles." Barcelona was certain this was one of the best days of his life. *Sweet victory!*

***

As they watched the Humvee disappear, Chowder felt a momentary pang of disappointment but refused to give in to it. Now was not the time for pessimism.

"Something profound has just happened, but I am not at sure what it is."

Jade nodded her head.

They heard Doc holler and ran over to the edge and looked down. Doc had found Bessie May. She had rolled all the way to the ground level after Doc saved her from the grenade. Shaken up, she was still grateful of Doc's quick thinking.

Jade and Charley, led an exhausted Yaz down Monk's Mound to join them.

"Well," Charley said heavily. "We have to get Pawnee buried."

"Shit!" Jade exclaimed. "Has anyone told Clay yet?"

~ 70 ~

AFTERMATH

The important thing is not to stop questioning. Curiosity has its own reason for existing. One cannot help but be in awe when he contemplates the mysteries of eternity, of life, of the marvelous structure of reality. It is enough if one tries merely to comprehend a little of this mystery every day. Never lose a holy curiosity.

Albert Einstein

Yaz stood before the gathering of humans and looked out over the attendees. He felt unusually calm, confident. Particularly since he was allowed to assume whatever shape he chose now that the 'Beagle' disguise was no longer needed. He gracefully stretched is long tentacles, them smoothed back the feathers around his head.

Yaz looked to the sky, the return shuttle was due any moment and he was sad about the pending departure. He had grown to like most humans.

"Welcome, Brothers." Yaz said to Muh and Jee as they joined him, waiting for the spaceship.

"Yeah, sure," Jee snarled, his neck feathers stuck straight out in outrage.

"Why am I here?" Muh crossed tentacles, nervously chewed on peanut.

"You and Jee have really messed this up for yourselves," Yaz scolded. "Joining up with that idiot Barcelona! Fools!"

"All right, all right," feathers glistening with pomade oil. Jee's replied irritably. He had no idea what fate awaited him upon their return. The Galactic Council was enigmatic and merciless at times.

"If you hadn't returned the Einstein Stone to us, things could be far worse for you."

Jee shuddered. Stealing back the Einstein Stone from Barcelona involved behavior he preferred to forget about.

Yaz sighed looking at his brothers. They had not changed. It had been a long metamorphosis for him. He realized it was true; only one in three of the Triplets usually made it to his new level of understanding. After this long and very curious journey, the Galactic Council had just announced Yaz elevation to 'Planetary Stewardship' and will be given his own arm of the Galaxy to supervise.

Yaz sighed, none of the triplet sets ever knew they were on a trial journey, testing them, challenging them, allowing them the opportunity to mature or not, he was just happy he made it.

He looked at his brothers, not sad they were to be imprisoned. The long lives of his species could be both boon and bane. But change only happens to one of the set; the others only grow more resolute in their insanity.

"You know," Yaz looked at his twin brothers. "You didn't have to take the road you chose."

"I had no choice!" Muh declared. "I am the oldest; by tradition, the oldest is always the leader. But you have ignored tradition, abandoned all principles of civilization, and have usurped my position. Therefore because my Leadership was stolen from me...I am not responsible."

"Neither am I," Jee added. "Because I was just following him." He pointed at Muh. "My leader."

Yaz had noticed that the more fanatic a being is, the more confident they are of their convictions, the greater their difficulty with reality.

****

A huge yellow dot was growing larger in the sky. The return shuttle was finally here.

Yaz looked at the gathered humans and was proud of their accomplishments. It had only been a few short years, and already there were clear signs of a human renaissance. He, and his brothers, was leaving now, having been summoned home by the Galactic Council.

"You Humans may join the Galactic Society when a state of maturity exists." He had told them. "Love is the natural condition of existence. Compassion, understanding, tolerance, and equality are strengths far greater than anger and hate. This is why they have again sent you the Einstein Stone."

He looked over at Bessie May. The remarkable woman had formed a flourishing coalition of groups into a patchwork quilt of a community. People from around the former state of Washington had been invited to partake in these meetings to reorganize society. Their outreach was growing.

"The Einstein Stone isn't anything by itself," Yaz explained to her. "It is a precious mineral, with a distinctive bluish-green hue, but it isn't its composite that matters; it is what it generates: Compassion. The Einstein Stone," he continued, "is a conduit stone, opening a new way of being in the world. Like the air after a heavy thunderstorm, the world becomes clearer, brighter, things become more understandable in this new light."

"Humanity will have at least 800 years, then the Einstein Stone moves on, and you either sink or swim," Yaz concluded. "Your task as a human being is quite simple. You are to learn how to love; you have one last chance to unlearn hate and violence. Otherwise, you are well and truly over. Human extinction is quite likely. So the Einstein Stone is your last chance. Use it wisely."

~ 71 ~

EPILOGUE

"The most important decision we make is whether
we believe we live in a friendly or hostile universe."
Albert Einstein

The venerable rig, "Pawnee" handled the building seas boldly
and well; the big man had just returned from another inspection of
the boat, battening down the hatches in front of this coming storm.
It had many years since his wounds had healed, but the use of his
right shoulder was still restrictive.

The sailor knew he would have little trouble for now, so he
opened a beer, Dead Man's Ale, his very favorite, and took a deep
drink.

*The past four years had been a time of high excitement and expansion
of human knowledge beyond anything in our history,* he mused. Remarkable to him was the differences in human beings. The Einstein
Stone's powerful change was not the same for all: For some people,
it was a revelation, an epiphany at every level of their lives; to
others, it was an acknowledgment of what they knew all along. Still,
others, like Barcelona, were unaffected to any noticeable degree.
Fortunately, they appeared to be in the vast minority.

Clay looked at his two crewmen, Greg Prichard and Newell, both
now seasoned sailors, good friends, loyal to the cause of humanity.
Their mutual decision to focus on healing their world rather than

bringing in more violence seemed to be working as people like Barcelona became more and more isolated.

He took another drink of beer and resettled himself in the cockpit; the seas were a bottle green, deep and gathering, swirled with streaks of foam; he could feel the wind pick up in intensity. Checking his gauges, they might just skirt the worst of it.

Clay shook his head; the past three years had been a non-stop tutorial in human existence, complicated by the presences of Intergalactic ET's.

The last he'd heard, Barcelona had indeed established his empire, but the Einstein Stone was swiped by Muh and Jee. Barcelona turned much of the old US Midwest into an armed camp of slavery and cruelty he named 'The Republic of Barcelona,' a growing hotbed of threat to all the rest of the surrounding communities. Tellingly, The Republic of Barcelona established a solid and virulent combat force to defend its borders; but they faced inward, not outward. From what he had learned, Barcelona was the exception, not the rule; everywhere, whole communities committed themselves to compassion and honesty, mutual support and interdependence, not conflict and rage.

Clay knew that Barcelona needed killing, but that was not his job. His job wasn't to destroy but to build.

A world vision, an upwelling of consciousness devoted to compassion and understanding had swept the planet. Peace seemed to settle over humanity like a warm, soft blanket.

His friends Charley and Jade had retired to Charley's farm; Jade is no longer a warrior, and Charley has his dogs and his small forest. Charley and his wife appeared to be very happy.

Bessie May Chowder, a natural-born leader, was busy organizing communes, where egalitarian values predominate. Clay was curious that she remained single and unattached, just a tiny Black dynamo changing the world one community at a time.

Doc Betters, last he heard, was on his way to Ashland, Oregon, where he was going to reestablish his clinic based on respect, honor, love, and excellent marijuana. Doc has given up emergency response medical care and is working on a training program for First Responders. Clay laughed. The last time Clay saw Doc, he was dressed in white; hat, cane, shoes, and a monocle. *An old fashion Southern Plantation Owner wearing a fucking monocle!* Clay shook his head.

He took another drink of beer, considering the changes in this world. Without computers and much of modern technology, humanity had to relearn what the indigenous cultures already knew: survival, indeed the future itself, is about cooperation, not about subjugation. Humans began to revere life, all life, not just theirs. Money became a curiosity because fair trade and barter created relationships between people; equality, not power.

A heavy gust of wind from the Northeast shook the boat. The sailor tightened his sails and picked out another beer; Dead Man's Ale, out of Ashland, Oregon. He drank it thirstily in one long swallow, then, putting the empty bottle down, tears streaming from his eyes, he looked up at the fast-moving gray clouds, a seagull, wings held stiffly, swept by quickly, and he thought of his papa.

Clay Park Painter, twenty-two nautical miles off the shores of Kauai, on his way to find his wife and his young son, joined his good friends in a salute to the sky with Dead Man's Ale:

"Here's to you Pawnee, I love you with all my heart, my papa!"

~ 72 ~

THE END

John Whitten is a retired Clinical Social Worker, artist, musician, writer, living quietly in a small forest with his wife, Golden Retriever, and a semi-feral cat named Sophie. He is a two tour combat veteran of Vietnam and an enrolled member, Potawatomi Nation, Shawnee Oklahoma.

www.ingramcontent.com/pod-product-compliance
Lightning Source LLC
Chambersburg PA
CBHW060900140726
47996CB00001B/57